Pursuit of Excellence in a Networked Society

Marca V. C. Wolfensberger,
Lyndsay Drayer, Judith J. M. Volker (eds.)

# Pursuit of Excellence
# in a Networked Society

Theoretical and Practical Approaches
Coming from the Conference
Evoking Excellence in Higher Education
and Beyond

Waxmann 2014
Münster • New York

Talent Development in
Higher Education and Society

**Bibliographic information published by die Deutsche Nationalbibliothek**
Die Deutsche Nationalbibliothek lists this publication in the
Deutsche Nationalbibliografie; detailed bibliographic data
are available in the internet at http://dnb.d-nb.de.

Print-ISBN     978-3-8309-3158-4
E-Book-ISBN 978-3-8309-8158-9

© Waxmann Verlag GmbH, 2014
Steinfurter Straße 555, 48159 Münster, Germany
Waxmann Publishing Co.
P. O. Box 1318, New York, NY 10028, U. S. A.

www.waxmann.com
info@waxmann.com

Cover Design: Inna Ponomareva, Münster
Cover Picture: © Visions-AD – Fotolia.com
Setting: Sven Solterbeck, Münster

Printed on age-resistant paper, acid-free as per ISO 9706

Printed in Germany

# Table of Contents

## 4. Professional Excellence

## 5. Ethics and Intercultural Perspectives

# Share your Talent – Move the World

*Marca Wolfensberger, Lyndsay Drayer and Judith Volker*

The walk of fame forms the main entrance of Hanze University of Applied Science Groningen in the Netherlands. The Dutch say that you cannot go further north than Groningen – so there is also nothing beyond this beautiful laid-back city with its canals, universities and good bread. The walk of fame lists the names of students, supporting staff, as well as faculty, and their accomplishments. Standing there for the first time, the skies were striking blue and the wind chilly. Under my feet, in orange letters, 'share your talent – move the world.' Students from all over the world passed by, talking about enginering, business, sports and chilling out together. I heard a tall brunette in front of me giggling to her blondish friend: "just imagine that your name is engraved here on this walk of fame!" The friend held back for a moment and then said: "Yes, just imagine, that would be quite something – wouldn't it?" This pride in the pursuit of excellence is a new mindset in the Netherlands and in many other countries. The papers in this book chart this shift towards a *culture of excellence* that may be transformative for Higher Education and beyond.

Hanze UAS' research centre for Talent Development in Higher Education and Society (hanze.nl/excellentie) wants to celebrate teaching and learning that fosters excellence. This is the reason why, in 2012, we organised the international conference "Evoking Excellence in Higher Education and Beyond". Around 400 scholars, practitioners, politicans, professionals and students from 13 different countries from around the world came to Groningen to share their newest insights on the theme.

This book offers a selection of the work of those presenting at the conference. 61 authors share here their knowledge and insights. Across six chapters, the following topics are discussed:

- teaching strategies,
- culture of excellence,
- students' perspectives,
- professional excellence,
- ethics and intercultural perspectives, and
- giftedness across educational sectors.

These 6 topics relate to the Integrative Model of Excellence Performances (see figure 1). This so-called IEPER-model was created by Wolfensberger to visualise and relate important aspects that are needed in the pursuit of excellence within education and professional life. The model underlines how we are interdependent of one another in our networked society and, at the same time, how we may grow in virtue of the dignity of difference.

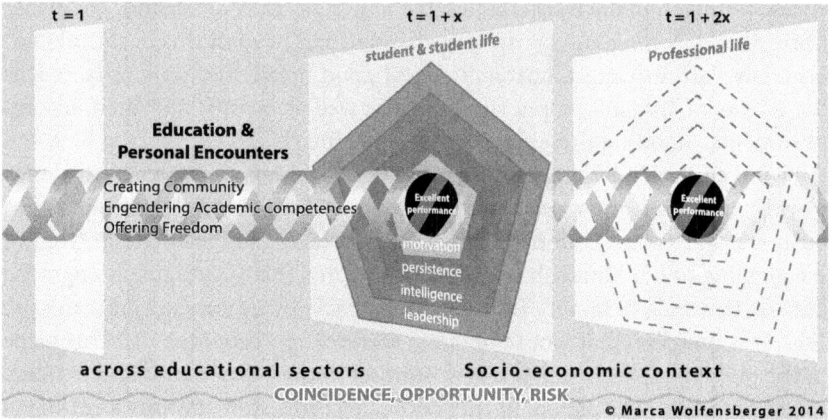

*Figure 1:     The Integrative Model of Excellent Performances (IEPER-model)*

Close encounters of all kinds spiral together in the IEPER-model as the spinal nerve/column needed for outstanding performance. The IEPER-model lays emphasis on those close encounters and the harmonised combination of creating committed community, enhancing academic competence and offering bounded freedom. All three dimensions are needed equally in order to create a teaching and learning environment fostering excellence. The papers in the sections 'teaching strategies' and 'students' perspectives' eleborate on these dimensions and add new perspectives.

The dimension of time is indicated in the IEPER-model with 't = 1', and 't = 1 + x'. Time indicates the importance of *talent development across educational sectors* as is also emphasised by the papers in the respective section of this book. As Renzulli and Little argue, "this more global view of providing high-quality, rigorous learning across levels allows us to consider excellence as an ongoing quest. It also encourages us to build partnerships and conversations between secondary and tertiary education in order to support continuous growth and opportunities for challenge for our advanced learners".

Time is also needed to build trust for reflection and personal growth. Time is necessary for deliberate practice so as to become an excellent professional and for the endeavour to reach out for wisdom. Hence, honours programmes specially designed for motivated and talented students aim to contribute to the successful professional and personnally fulfilling lives of its students. The papers in the section 'professional excellence' eleborate on the relationship between education and professional lives.

We want to acknowledge the board of the National Collegiate Honors Council from the USA (nchchonors.org), the organisation of Sirius (siriusprogramma.nl) and the Netherlands Educational Research Association (vorsite.nl) who assisted in linking people from all over the world during the conference 'Evoking Excellence in Higher Education and Beyond'. The international gathering strengthened the conversations about intercultural perspectives and ethical issues at stake in honours education. As Wolfensberger argues in this book, "The purpose of education must be to enhance, not compromise, human difference and dignity" in a democratic society whose mission should be to "provide all students with opportunities to develop their talents, taking into account all of the differences between them."

Colleges and universities are places for teaching. As Biesta (2013) points out – if one wishes, one can learn anywhere – but what makes the school a school is the fact that it is a designated place for teaching. This distinguishes a school from other institutions: a reason why we were delighted to locate the conference 'Evoking Excellence in Higher Education and Beyond' on the beautiful campus of Hanze UAS in the Netherlands. During the conference, we spoke about teachers' wisdom in evoking excellence. This concerns teachers who do not shy away from critical questions but who are willing to give and to work on questions about what makes a life well-lived and what it is that should have authority in our lives. The answers have everything to do with moral principles and values that give dignity to life. The answers may create slogans like 'Share your talent – move the world'. We are proud, here, to present the work of scholars and practitioners who are sharing their talents, committed to the pursuit of excellence in our networked society.

## References

Biesta, G. J. J. (2013). *The beautiful risk of education.* London: Paradigm Publishers.

# Foreword: The Pursuit of Excellence

*Joseph Renzulli and Catherine Little*

What is excellence? For educators focused on providing special learning opportunities for high-achieving and high-potential students, this timeless question was an appropriate theme for the 2012 International Conference on Evoking Excellence in Higher Education and Beyond and for the papers included in this book. Although there may be a wide range of opinions about the meaning of the term, we view excellence in formal educational settings as the outcomes that result from applying received and analyzed knowledge to the intensive investigation of issues and topics that are personally meaningful to students. It further implies that there is a creative element in the problem-finding and -focusing process, that a problem is pursued through the use of authentic investigative methodology, and that the results of the work are intended to reach and influence one or more targeted audiences beyond the teacher or professor. These criteria for excellence reflect the *modus operandi* of people who have made significant contributions to their respective fields of endeavour and have, in some cases, changed the world. We believe that these criteria are exactly the kinds of guidance that should be given to high potential students of all ages if we aspire to increase the world's reservoir of creative and productive individuals.

The conference on Evoking Excellence in Higher Education and Beyond brought together scholars and educators from around the world to share their work in promoting high-level learning experiences. Presenters discussed their research and practical efforts in honours programmes, gifted programmes, and other contexts aimed at promoting advanced learning for advanced learners. At the centre of the discussion was the somewhat elusive concept of *excellence*, emphasized as a central value and goal of advanced and honours programmes. Participants were invited to share their metaphorical representations of excellence and to define the specific and practical ways they seek it in their work.

The papers collected in this text reflect key questions about what excellence means and how we as educators may encourage its pursuit among students and faculty, as well as how we may study and understand it. The authors have examined learning contexts for promoting excellence, the types of instructional and learning experiences that support excellence, and the characteristics and expectations of students engaged in these learning experiences. These emphases reflect much of the work that frames the field of gifted and talented education, including several fundamental questions that are both highly practical and reflective of more large-scale conceptual perspectives. Each of the papers in this text wrestles in some way with one or more of these five basic – and fundamental – questions:

- Who are the students among whom we are promoting a culture of excellence, and what are their needs and perspectives?
- What are the content and structure of the learning experiences that we might use for promoting excellence?
- How does classroom learning fit within a larger overall experience of striving for excellence?
- How do we know what is working?
- How can we continue to develop and improve our efforts?

There is extensive literature that wrestles with the question of which students should be engaged in gifted or advanced programming, and the methods and procedures for identifying talent and potential continue to drive research and debate in the field. Yet the focus on striving for excellence allows us to examine the *who* question more from a direction of outcomes than from identification. Several of the papers in this text examine the *who* question by focusing on the characteristics of students who were successful in completing and showing high achievement in honours programmes, and then working to identify programme characteristics that may have supported those students. Such explorations of programme characteristics include broad-based studies of student outcome variables as well as studies of student perspectives on their own behaviour and experience. In either case, the papers explore how those programme characteristics may be modeled, replicated, and strengthened. Other papers examine the *who* question by focusing on specific groups of students who have not traditionally been well represented in honours programming. These papers describe programmes designed to provide access and promote excellence within underrepresented or unexamined groups based on the students' individual strengths, interests, learning styles, and preferred modes of expression. Across these papers exploring *who* the students are in advanced programmes, the central emphasis remains on creating optimal contexts for achieving excellence and providing access for students who have the potential for such achievement – so the focus is on the experience and the outcomes, not on who is or is not "gifted."

Schools and universities and other educational institutions are organized around the pursuit and the communication of knowledge and understanding. The goal of excellence, and specifically of promoting excellence among advanced learners, requires that the knowledge explored must be at a high level of depth and complexity, that the learning experience must be challenging and focused on high-quality outcomes, and that the questions and applications must reflect attention to the rigour of the disciplines. Many of the papers in this text reflect the struggle to differentiate a learning experience that is designed to promote excellence among advanced learners from a more general learning experience that focuses on merely acquiring and storing advanced information. In constructing such learning experiences to promote excellence, educators strive to raise levels of expectations to support high engagement, and to provide safe opportunities for risk-taking and experiences of struggle – or even failure – while also keeping students focused on the potential and the drive for success. A firm foundation for promoting excellence through learning experiences may be found in a focus on engaging students with multiple types and levels of knowledge – excellence is not achieved when students only receive knowledge, or even when they analyze received knowledge in great depth. Rather, excellence emerges through a combination of these types of knowledge with application and problem-solving opportunities that engage their creativity and critical thinking thus resulting in new questions, new directions, and created knowledge. This knowledge may not be original "for all mankind," but learning the process provides young people with the skills and the mindset necessary for a positive attitude toward continued inquiry and the joy of finding out new things. Thus, many of the papers in this text address learning experiences that require students to do much more than acquire knowledge, but rather to use it toward advancing new knowledge and new questions that will help us understand our world and its complexities more deeply.

Learning experiences and the pursuit of excellence go far beyond the context of specific classrooms, projects, and terms. Many of the scholars whose papers appear in this publication are involved in honours education not only at the course level but also at the programmatic level, and their work focuses on students' overall learning and growth experiences. Scholars in honours education have highlighted that effective honours programming involves not only high-level courses but also opportunities for students to build communities with their peers, to develop the noncognitive characteristics that will support the pursuit of excellence, and to have access to mentors and guides beyond the classroom setting. Thus, several of the papers address the broader development of students, examining characteristics that link to their academic learning but are not fundamentally about academics. In addition, a central focus of the conference and the papers incorporated here was on how learning experiences are strengthened and articulated across secondary and higher education to promote excellence and high engagement throughout students' educational careers. This more global view of providing high-quality, rigorous learning across levels allows us to consider excellence as an ongoing quest. It also encourages us to build partnerships and conversations between secondary and tertiary education to support continuous growth and opportunities for challenge for our advanced learners.

The final two questions that underlie many of these papers are interrelated and focus strongly on the work of the professionals who are involved in honours programming and the varied efforts to promote and evoke excellence. Authors of many of the papers in this text explore questions of how to measure the desired outcomes of efforts to promote excellence. Many of the students likely to engage in advanced courses and programmes are already high achievers with "excellent" grades and, therefore, some types of outcome variables may be too limiting, from a research and evaluation perspective, in terms of how much range and variance in achievement they allow. At the same time, the criteria for "excellence" at the societal level may be far above what is a reasonable goal for secondary or tertiary courses or programmes. Thus, the definitions of excellence and its tangible representations in student outcomes are a point of discussion and debate. Several of the papers address evaluation efforts centered on key aspects of programming, including both outcomes for students as just discussed but also other kinds of indicators of success or areas for growth.

Connected to these efforts to define success and areas for growth, the final question underlying the papers is one of describing and exploring efforts toward continuous improvement in programming to promote excellence. A central focus of these efforts is professional development of faculty who work with students in honours and advanced programming. Several of the papers describe faculty development efforts and experiences, including a focus on how faculty themselves are engaged in the pursuit of excellence from the perspective of defining excellent teaching.

Across the papers in the conference and in this publication, educators have shared their own visions of excellence and how they have sought to evoke it in students' work and to pursue it in their own. By exploring questions of *who, what, how,* and *how well* around honours and advanced programming, these authors have shared their efforts toward a common quest, striving to construct experiences and contexts that promote high quality and high engagement in the learning endeavour. Aristotle once wrote of the high intention, sincere effort, and intelligent execution that underlie the pursuit of excellence; the papers in this book reflect these elements in the quest for excellence in higher education and beyond.

Joseph S. Renzulli and Catherine A. Little

# The Interdisciplinary First-Year Seminar

## Serving a Multi-disciplinary Student Population at Barrett, The Honors College at Arizona State University

*Karen Bruhn*

A first-year seminar can serve as an important tool for evoking excellence in talented and motivated students. What follows are reflections on "best practices" regarding the shaping and teaching of such a seminar. I base these reflections on the evolution and expansion of the first-year seminar required of all students admitted to Barrett, The Honors College at Arizona State University.

Explicitly, I want to identify the assumptions, the questions and the policies that have contributed to a very successful first-year seminar at Barrett institution that serves a large student population with majors in over 250 areas. Implicitly, I want to establish the value of such a seminar. Evoking excellence means that we must do more than train our students for a particular career; we must also help our students recognize both the privileges and the responsibilities that come with being smart. At Barrett, we want students to understand that intellect is a gift to be cherished, nourished, and shared. Whether or not embracing and exercising one's intellectual abilities affects one's income, participating in the life of the mind makes a person's life better, and it makes the lives of those around him/her better.

Barrett faculty members strive to hold fast to this philosophy, despite rapid expansion. We have managed to maintain common standards for our interdisciplinary first-year seminar – entitled "The Human Event" – while still allowing individual faculty to draw on their own strengths when composing a reading list for the course. In recent years, we consciously have tried to offer an academically diverse student population a version of "interdisciplinarity" that goes beyond humanistic texts taught by people trained in the humanities.

Barrett is the largest honours college in the United States, and one of the best. We have approximately 4200 matriculated students; currently there are 1200 freshmen across four campuses (per a mandate from the top administration of Arizona State University, we have expanded our 2013 entry to class to 1500 students). Readers' Digest has named us the best honours college in the nation; within the last year, articles in the *LA Times*, *The Atlantic Monthly*, and *The Reader's Digest* have congratulated us for offering students a small liberal arts college experience within a larger, affordable university; and delivering "as fine an education as the Ivy League" (Crouch, 2011).

All first-year students must take The Human Event. We have twenty-seven faculty whose academic home is in Barrett – not in a disciplinary department – and whose primary obligation is to teach multiple sections of this seminar. (In the fall 2013 semester, seventy four sections will be offered over four campuses.) Each section must adhere to common standards, but we do not have a common reading list. The sections do not enroll by major; we consciously mix majors in each section. The texts are primary texts that have investigated the nature and purpose of human experience, represent world cultures, and draw from a variety of disciplines.

The course has been a core requirement since founding of the College in 1988. The Human Event was based on Columbia University and University of Chicago models, providing undergraduates with a common vocabulary and set of references on the basis of which they would be able to interact with one another regardless of discipline. As Barrett founding Dean Ted Humphrey has argued, critical reading, discussion of ideas and writing carefully crafted argumentative papers equip the students with the habits of mind necessary for pursuing an honours education (Humphrey, 2008). All sections of the course hold common objectives to:

- Broaden the student's historical and cultural awareness and understanding
- Improve the student's skill in analyzing written material.
- Improve the student's skill in expressing ideas, both orally and in writing.
- Instill intellectual breadth and academic discipline in preparation for more advanced honours courses.
- Encourage the student to think critically and seriously about the nature of human existence and to formulate his or her own views and insights regarding ethics, philosophy, religion, history, literature, etc.

Taken together, course contents of the two semesters must be chronologically presented from origins to recent times, and HON 171 must end with the Renaissance. Each course must include representative works of world culture. Each syllabus must clearly articulate that.

15–20 pages of text-based, argumentative writing are required for at least 50% of the final grade; and that participation in class discussion counts for no less than 20% of the final grade. We have established a writing centre specific to Barrett, and have established common objectives and criteria for the papers.

Since the course description states that the texts are drawn from a variety of disciplines, both faculty and students have long regarded The Human Event as interdisciplinary in nature. In 2005, motivated in part by the increasing numbers of natural science and social science majors, the leadership of new deans, and a mandate to grow enrollment, the faculty revisited the issue of interdisciplinarity. They discovered that A) with one exception, all faculty members but one were trained in the humanities (at that time there were eight faculty in total), and B) syllabi were not adequately reflecting texts in the natural sciences. Because the course seeks to instill intellectual breadth and academic discipline for more advanced honours courses, the faculty determined that these deficiencies should be addressed. The faculty identified three key strategies:

1.  Current faculty would commit to broadening their knowledge regarding the social and natural sciences, and incorporate this knowledge into their syllabi.
2.  As the college expanded, future faculty searches would concentrate on recruiting from the natural social sciences.
3.  While all sections of the first semester of The Human Event would retain a common course designation and number (HON 171), the second semester would offer three different course numbers that would reflect the focus of the instructor (HON 272 humanities, HON 273 natural sciences, and HON 274 social sciences).

Attention to faculty development helped us realize our first goal. Mark Jacobs, the current dean of Barrett, procured donor support that allowed faculty to take the time to stretch their areas of expertise. We also brought scholars in to conduct colloquia. We realized that we were "going against the grain" when we devoted resources to this kind of faculty development. One of the challenges of offering a course like this is finding faculty to teach it, and teach it well. Scholarly training is increasingly specialized, and young scholars often have neither the training nor the proclivity to be able to guide students through centuries of human thought. We all live in the age of specialization – and for good reason – but the danger is that we all become so specialized that we become narrow-minded. From the beginning, we want our students to experience – and try out –, a variety of perspectives and that means faculty must commit to this experience as well.

We were able to meet our second goal and diversify our faculty. As mentioned above, when we began this reexamination, we had eight faculty on the main campus; in the fall of 2013, Barrett will be home to twenty-seven faculty (spread over four campuses), all of whom have been hired to teach multiple sections of The Human Event. Since 2005, we have added seven faculty trained in the natural sciences, nine faculty trained in the social sciences, and three faculty trained in the humanities. In 2006, we implemented a faculty-mentoring programme designed to help new faculty stretch themselves across disciplinary boundaries. This includes classroom visits by both mentors and mentees. The mentoring committee has also featured faculty members giving "teaching talks" on their areas of expertise. Instead of presenting original research to one's peers, our faculty present on how one might effectively teach a text outside one's "comfort zone."

The faculty unquestionably have expanded their teaching proficiencies by interacting with colleagues from a variety of academic backgrounds. All faculty report benefitting from one another' expertise; a faculty member trained in Religious Studies, for example, feels much more comfortable teaching a text by Heisenberg when she can confer with the physicist in the office next door. We are also able to offer student mentoring in a wider variety of subjects.

Regarding our third goal – to obtain three different course numbers for the second semester of The Human Event that would reflect the disciplinary training of the faculty offering the particular section – we were successful in making that change. However, in 2012, the faculty voted to discontinue the three different course numbers, and return to a solitary course number. By 2008, all three of the HON 200 series had received university approval and had been approved for appropriate general studies credit. This initiative was the most labor intensive and, as is so often the case, yielded the least positive results. Many of the sections became "history of the science/social science," and new faculty were often unsure of what constituted a "social science" perspective as opposed to a "humanities" perspective, for example. We found that our commitment to interdisciplinarity was being undermined by an expansion that somehow also felt constrictive.

A spring 2011 survey demonstrated that over half of the students choose to stay with the professor who taught their first semester seminar, regardless of the disciplinary focus of the second semester. "Academic Focus of the Course" was the option chosen last by students when asked to identify why they had chosen their HON 200 section. As faculty have continued to analyze this enterprise, we concluded that the course remains essentially a humanistic enterprise; the interdisciplinarity is constituted by the texts themselves.

A task force examined various syllabi and found that the most frequently used texts in the first semester represented a fair sampling from different disciplines; and we have begun a digital library of early texts written by women to correct what we saw as an overabundance of male voices. A 2010 sampling of the assigned texts in the second semester showed that, out of the forty-eight authors represented on the nine humanities-focused syllabi, twenty-eight also were represented on a social science or natural science syllabi (seventeen of those twenty-eight were represented on all three). Consequently, the faculty voted to collapse the three courses back into one. While expanding the faculty to include scholars from a variety of disciplines, our "parsing" into "perspectives" had confused faculty and students alike.

We have concluded that a person – whether student or teacher – approaches interdicsiciplinarity from a particular perspective; however, best conversations are not bound by any one perspective. Being "interdisciplinary" requires that we approach a text from a variety of perspectives, and also explore how that text affects and is affected by other texts and other discourses. Our advising staff are trained to steer a student toward a particular faculty member when the former deem it appropriate, usually because they see a potential mentoring partnership.

Since 2012 Barrett received another mandate from the university president: to grow to 6000 by 2014. Obviously, this presents a number of challenges, but we remain committed to the interdisciplinary first-year seminar that adheres to common standards, but also allows the faculty to choose the texts and ask the questions that each feels will be most effective. Our efforts so far have achieved gratifying results. As a faculty, we have expanded our individual scholarly horizons, and have re-examined the boundaries between disciplines. This makes us better teachers, and demonstrates to our students that a culture of excellence can and should continue throughout one's life. For bright and motivated people, a culture of excellence must include the life of the mind, a love of knowledge for its own sake, and the ability and willingness to take on and examine a variety of perspectives.

## References

Crouch, M. (2011). 10 Reasons to Skip the Expensive Colleges. *Reader's Digest*, September, 2011. http://www.rd.com/advice/saving-money/10-things-every-parent-should-know-about-college/.

Humphrey, T. (2008). The Genesis of an Idea. In Peter C. Sederberg (Ed.). NCHC Monograph Series *The Honors College Phenomenon* (pp. 11–22). Lincoln, NE: University of Nebraska.

# When Worlds Collide

## Analysis of and Recommendations for Successful Interdisciplinary Team-Teaching

*Linda Frost and Barbara Hussey*

Interdisciplinary instruction is a mainstay of honours pedagogy in the United States. Utilizing teams of faculty members to represent varying disciplines is commonly understood to be among the "best practices" for innovative classroom instruction. While the list of 'Basic Characteristics of a Fully Developed Honors Programme', published and endorsed by the National Collegiate Honors Council (NCHC), includes no specific reference to interdisciplinary team instruction, the NCHC's web resources on "Honours Course Design" include the directive to honours instructors that honours students should be "carefully exposed to and guided through the methods of many disciplines," indicating also that "honours courses should try to explore with students the questions and methods common to all intellectual endeavors and those that differentiate the disciplines" (nchchonors.org/faculty-directors/honors-course-design/). Surely, few pedagogical practices can more fully – and obviously – realize these results than interdisciplinary team-teaching.

Regardless of its apparent preferentiality among U.S. honours educators, interdisciplinary team-teaching is difficult to initiate and sustain for institutional, disciplinary, and personal reasons. In fact, scholars writing about the practice will at times argue actively *against* it, even as they work to describe its overall pedagogical impacts and the desirability of its possible outcomes. In 1996, James R. Rowland spoke about the team-taught interdisciplinary sophomore mathematics course in which he was involved at the University of Kansas, noting that his "preference as a faculty member for 30 years and as an accreditation programme evaluator for 10 years" was that only one department, maths, should provide the teaching faculty for that course (p. 2).

Donald Richards (1996) has argued that his "own evolving conviction is that team teaching is a poor vehicle for interdisciplinary undergraduate education" (p. 127). He arrives at this conclusion by asserting that

> "what separates a good interdisciplinary undergraduate course offering from a mere multidisciplinary one has a lot to do with how well the course is crafted to highlight what I have referred to earlier as interdisciplinary connections.

*The amount of prior preparation and effort on the part of the instructor(s) of such courses is not to be underestimated. Team-taught courses that lay a claim to interdisciplinarity often fail to achieve their objectives precisely because the individual members of the instructional team themselves never really begin to understand their common concerns in a fashion that may properly be called interdisciplinary. This failure is often all too apparent to their students." (p. 127)*

Richards' point is well made: although multidisciplinarity may be achieved utilizing multiple faculty members from different disciplines, a truly interdisciplinary experience requires an integration of perspective that many teams do not actively or fully accomplish.

While the benefits of interdisciplinary work for faculty members are great (Lattuca, 2001), less research seems immediately available as to its benefits for students. But, evaluating interdisciplinary instruction overall is no easy task. Class format differs tremendously from course to course and large-scale quantitative assessment tools such as those created by the Individual Development and Educational Assessment Center (IDEA) are, by IDEA's own admission, poor evaluators for course success in multi-faculty-led courses.

Despite what appears to be a lack of clear evidence to support the benefits of teaching in teams, major universities in the U.S., as well as the honours community at large, have upheld it as the preferred method of delivering interdisciplinary instruction. For over twenty years, the Honours Programme at Eastern Kentucky University (EKU) has in fact put interdisciplinary instruction at the heart of its offerings. Because of EKU honours' historic and future commitment to interdisciplinary instruction delivered in teams, we wanted to explore its impact on our students. Using ten years of additional "comment" portions of student evaluations from one long-standing interdisciplinary, team-taught honours course, Honours Rhetoric, we analyzed these unscripted narratives to see what they could tell us.

Honours Rhetoric (HON 102) has been a core component of the Honours Programme at EKU since the programme was founded in 1988. Originally designed as a first-semester, 5-day-a-week, six-credit-hour course that satisfies the general education requirement of two semesters of English composition, HON 102 develops students' skills in written and oral communication while drawing on content from philosophy, history and literature. Rhetoric students read copiously and, we hope, carefully and critically. They write daily and give formal presentations in addition to participating regularly in informal class and group discussions. The teaching teams have ranged from as few as two to as many as five members.

Even before EKU identified the development of higher order critical thinking skills as a primary instructional goal for the entire campus, the goals for HON 102 were aligned with Bloom's (revised) taxonomy (Anderson et al., 2000), a classification of levels of intellectual behaviour that gives primary importance to activities such as analyzing, evaluating, and, above all, creating new knowledge. The philosophy guiding HON 102 was that the challenge of working across disciplines and integrating information from different fields, would actively engage students and help them recognize the interconnectedness of knowledge. We implemented team-teaching as an interactive approach best suited to an interdisciplinary course.

Criticism of interdisciplinary team-teaching is often directed at the failure of the teaching cohort to come together, of, as Richards expressed it, not "understanding their common concerns." The challenge facing the HON 102 teaching teams was not small: we needed to stitch together a course that included Plato, Nietzsche, Schopenhauer, newspaper articles and Congressional speeches from the American Civil War, slave narratives, Civil War art, cartoons and sometimes music, a silent film, a novel by William Faulkner and a memoir by Mark Twain – among other things. As most researchers agree, any interdisciplinary course requires careful and coordinated advance planning and preparation, and ours was no different. Grading standards, work expectations and course policies were agreed upon in advance. Most important though, and especially in a freshman class, was our ability to anticipate and articulate the disciplinary connections that could be made between such disparate texts and genres rather than relying on the students to furnish those connections as they go along. We were able to do this by stepping outside our own disciplines; by becoming familiar with each other's texts, connecting ideas outside of class, and teaching material from disciplines different from our own. We also attended all of our partners' classes and entered into the discussion as we learned alongside our students. Most of these practices are among those recommended for interdisciplinary team-teaching by proponents such as Stanford University's Center for Teaching and Learning, so the course design for HON 102 was not atypical.

To support our instructional methods and goals, we designed a range of assignments that would guide students in applying information from one subject area to another and encourage them to consider the construction of knowledge in different disciplines. In all formal papers for the course, students were required to connect two of the course disciplines in a meaningful, non-trivial way. A student might compare a literary representation of a Civil War battle to an historical account with reference to Aristotle's assertion that poetry is superior to history. Students might invent dialogues between authors of the daily reading assignments, such as a debate between Plato and a contemporary feminist philosopher who challenges his ideas about women in war. A culminating class event called Meeting of Minds required student groups to invent and perform conversations between select philosophers, authors, historical figures, and literary characters. The invention of such dialogues would occupy the highest level in Bloom's taxonomy – creativity or the construction of new knowledge. This assignment also underscores the belief that learning should be a recursive process whereby prior knowledge is continually applied to new subject matter, a process to which interdisciplinary coursework lends itself. The final course activity involved a panel presentation of individual research projects. Again, students were required to bring together information from their various research projects and highlight interconnections.

While criticism of interdisciplinary team-teaching often focuses on the potential for conflict between individual faculty members, the time-consuming preparation involved, and the possibility that the centre will not hold, we have found that, when we followed commonly recommended practices, we have been able to seamlessly rotate ten different instructors into the course. Moreover, we strongly believe that well-implemented interdisciplinary team teaching has the potential to raise the level of all instruction to a uniformly high standard and set a higher standard for student performance.

In order to examine the success of the interdisciplinary team-teaching utilized in HON 102, we undertook a qualitative data analysis of the student evaluations completed for 31 sections of HON 102. These 31 course sections spanned the years 2000–2010 and included the involvement of 10 faculty members overall (with no less than 2, no more than 5, and typically 2 or 3 instructors teaching in a single section). We had a total number of 558 evaluations, each with narrative portions that we individually coded. A sample evaluation is provided in Appendix A; this particular form was used for the entire span of evaluations in our study. Note that nowhere does the evaluation ask the student to specifically comment on the interdisciplinary, team-teaching aspect of the course.

We first examined a sample of the course evaluations to see what trends in them were of interest to us. Given our desire to record whatever impression interdisciplinary team-teaching might have had on these students, we decided to create the following categories for our evaluative codes. *Specific faculty mention* indicated a comment that clearly identified, by name or other characterizing element, any individual faculty member; we then coded these as either *positive*, *negative*, or *mixed* in their evaluative responses. *Non-specific faculty mention* referred to any comment on the course instructors as a group, with no individual characterization of them at all; we also coded these either *positive, negative,* or *mixed. Overall response* referred to the evaluation of the course as a whole, coded either *positive, negative,* or *mixed.* We also recorded a recurring syntactical construction in the evaluations that we started to notice when we were initially coding the texts; we will come back to this momentarily.

A sample response we coded *non-specific, positive faculty mention* looked like this: "All of the professors showed passion and interest in what they taught about and always presented a unique perspective on the information presented" (2006; 11897). The comment, "The instructors were knowledgeable about course material and seemed to put lots of time and effort into the course. Sometimes they failed to mention important events," was also *non-specific faculty mention* in that it did not refer to any individual faculty member, but we coded it *mixed* because of its more ambiguous evaluative tone (2006; 11898). Positive, mixed, and negative responses for individual faculty members can be left to the imagination. If a single response included both very positive and very negative individual comments on specific faculty members from the same team, we coded these as *specific, mixed faculty mention.*

While a *positive overall response* to the course might be, "I have learned so much because of this course" (2006; 11899), a *mixed overall response* might say, "Overall I found this to be an intriguing course however some areas were confusing and seemed rushed" (2006; 11899). A *negative overall response* to the course was likely to focus on workload – "I personally think that this course serves no purpose. All it did this semester was take away time I could have spent on my other classes" (2008; 10958).

Overall, the course evaluations were very positive; less than 3% of the evaluations we coded were negative in their overall response to both the course and its instructors. Since the students were not asked specifically to comment on the course's instructional design – i.e., interdisciplinary team-teaching – few intentionally did. Nevertheless, the students' tendencies to comment specifically on their instructors – or not – did correspond to their tendency to rate the course more or less positively.

Of the 491 students who spoke of the faculty only as a group, with no specific mention of any one of them, 274 or roughly 56% were positive in their response to both the class and the instructors. Another 18% of this 491 who also only commented on the faculty as a group – the next largest group of responses in that collection – still responded positively to the instructors even as they granted the course an overall mixed response. Only 11% of this same group of 491 students who spoke about the faculty as a group gave both the course and the faculty members teaching it a mixed response.

Of the 143 students who commented on at least one faculty member specifically, only 17% responded positively to both the instructors on which they commented and the course overall. The majority of this group – 40 of the total 143 or 28% – spoke positively about the course, but had mixed responses to the faculty member on whom they commented. While only 10% of the 491 evaluations speaking of the faculty as a group gave both the course and its teaching team a mixed review, 27% of the 143 evaluations that gave mixed responses to specific faculty members also gave the course a mixed review. While 18% of the 491 evaluations that gave the course a mixed evaluation still gave the teaching team a positive response, only 8% of the 143 evaluations that gave the course a mixed evaluation gave the individual instructors identified a positive response.

In other words, students who responded positively to the class overall were less likely to comment on specific faculty members; students more likely to talk about specific faculty members were also more likely to have a mixed, rather than a strictly positive response to the class. What is interesting to us about these results is that – at least in this sample – the teaching teams appeared to be more successful if the faculty in the teams did not stand out as individuals worthy of mention, either *positively or negatively*. We noticed an increase in mention of specific faculty members in particular sections where teams were obviously not working; faculty members discussed in glowing terms were often juxtaposed with criticized team members, highlighting their supposed deficiencies. Our research suggests, then, that for an interdisciplinary teaching team to be successful, it has to function as a unit with no clear standout members.

As we were analyzing the ten years of evaluations, we were also struck by the prevalence of a particular kind of phrase marked by the use of what in logic is called a *discounting term,* a connective such as "but" or "although." These terms allow the speaker to deal with mutually exclusive rhetorically points and hold them together in argumentative solution. Comments utilizing this construction were common in the evaluations: statements such as: "The course is an English class, but it makes you think about things going on outside of the literary world" and "I really loved coming to class although I'm really burnt out."

We decided to chart the occurrence of the statement itself, whether negative or positive, and found that a full 40% of students offered an unsolicited comment typical of this type of construction. We found ourselves wondering if a student's decision to frame their course experience as a synthesis of two contradictory thoughts might also evidence dialectical thought, one of the most advanced forms of cognition. We are very curious as to whether we would see equal incidences of this construction in other honours courses that either used interdisciplinary team-teaching or didn't.

While we have another 12 years of HON 102 evaluations with which to work, we also have over 20 years of evaluations from other team-taught interdisciplinary honours courses as well as evaluations from courses that, while taught in teams, were not interdisciplinary. We imagine that comparing the varying impacts of these differently configured teaching teams as traced through their evaluations may tell us something more definitive about their effectiveness in teaching critical thinking. Specifically, we wonder if considering more carefully the ongoing presence – or absence – in them of the contradictory, discounting statements we found in the evaluations with which we worked here might indeed be evidence of the higher order dialectical thinking we hope students will learn to successfully negotiate on their own as independent critical thinkers. Moreover, we hope to bring forward continuing evidence that can either justify or undo our faith in the interdisciplinary team-teaching model that is a signature pedagogy for honours instruction in the United States.

## References

Anderson, L. W., Krathwohl, D. R., Airasian, P. W., Cruikshank, K. A., Mayer, R. E., Pintrich, P. R., Raths, J., & Wittrock, M. C. (2000). *A Taxonomy for Learning, Teaching, and Assessing: A revision of Bloom's Taxonomy of Educational Objectives*. New York: Pearson, Allyn & Bacon.

HON 102, "Honours Rhetoric," student evaluations from 2000–2010, including the following sections: 38436, 38447, 38472, 12863, 12875, 13829, 13823, 13833, 11861, 11852, 11810, 11809, 11811, 11556, 11897, 11898, 11899, 11071, 11073, 10958, 10959, 10960, 14828, 10898, 10899, 10900, 14071, 15522, 10894, 10895, 10896.

Lattuca, L. (2001). *Creating Interdisciplinarity: Interdisciplinary Research and Teaching among College and University Faculty*. Nashville: University of Vanderbilt Press.

National Collegiate Honors Council. "Basic Characteristics of a Fully Developed Honors Program." http://nchchonors.org/faculty-directors/basic-characteristics-of-a-fully-developed-honors-program/ Accessed 3 January 2014.

National Collegiate Honors Council. "Honors Course Design." http://nchchonors. org/faculty-directors/honors-course-design/. Accessed 3 January 2014.

Richards, D. (1996). "The Meaning and Relevance of 'Synthesis' in Interdisciplinary Studies." *The Journal of General Education*. 45. 2 (1996): 114–128.

Rowland, J. R. (1996). "Interdisciplinary Team Teaching." Annual Frontiers in Education Conference. University of Kansas.

# Matching – Reflection on Personal Strengths to Evoke Excellence

*Bouke van Gorp, Brenda Vos and Marca Wolfensberger*

## Abstract

Matching – within selection and admission procedures – is equally important for honours programs as for regular degree programmes. As such, matching should not be restricted only to the intake of students entering an honours programme. At the end of each academic year, students of Honours College Geosciences (HCG) of Utrecht University (The Netherlands) therefore submit their reflective portfolio. The content of this reflective portfolio demonstrates how they have performed and also allows the students to reflect on their progress, their ambitions and to re-evaluate their participation in HCG. An intervention was implemented in an attempt to improve the skills necessary to write such a reflective piece. This intervention consisted of reflective workshops inspired by Gallup's approach of focusing on personal strengths in order to evoke outstanding performances. Students thus learned to reflect on their talents and strengths and were stimulated to consider the consequences this might have on their personal development towards becoming professionals. The workshops provided an eye-opener for the students and increased their 'enthusiasm' for reflection.

## Matching

'Matching' is a new buzz word in Dutch higher education and at Utrecht University specifically. Matching is related to selection and admission. Matching, in its current application at Utrecht University, focuses on whether the prospective student's wishes, ambitions, interests, and motivation match with the objectives and ways of teaching in a degree programme (Utrecht University, 2012). It is, however, seen to be part of the larger trajectory of tutoring. This is especially important in the Netherlands as most students enter directly into specialized degree programme. If students conclude, after a few months, that the topics dealt with in their chosen field of study deviate from their interests and expectations, they will most likely be faced with delays that usually accompany the process of switching disciplines. With (financial) pressure[1] on the students to finish their degree in a limited amount of time, and pressure on the institutions to raise efficacy, it is becoming more and more important for all parties involved that students, from the start of their academic career, choose the programme that suits them. Honours programs are no exception to this, even though they have stricter requirements that students need to meet. Matching thus requires of students that they know who they are, what their talents, motivations and ambitions are, or that they develop the reflective skills to figure out the answers to such questions.

Honours College Geosciences (HCG) admits students based on their above average grades and their professed motivation. Although students are admitted with the expectation that they will finish the whole honours programme, we do not want this to be 'automatic'. Matching, selection and admission need to mirror the honours vision. As HCG focuses on leadership and talent development (along with geo-content, multidisciplinarity and research skills), a possible match cannot be seen as static. Thus, each year students need to reconsider whether the programme is offering them the challenges they need and if they are willing and able to confront these challenges. A reflective or learning honours portfolio is the means to achieving this. Based on this portfolio and the project work completed, student and honours coordinator discuss if student and programme still match.

## Excellence Requires Autonomy

If an honours student and an honours programme are 'a match', the programme will be meaningful to the student and the student will very likely be intrinsically motivated. Research has shown that intrinsic motivation is related to autonomy, mastery and purpose (Ryan & Deci, 2000; Pink, 2009). Autonomy is the urge to be self-directed. Mastery means the urge to become better at something that matters. Mastery demands engagement: it begins with 'flow', the optimal experience when challenges match our abilities (Csikszentmihalyi, 1990). Mastery requires direction, a goal or a 'why' that provides short-term actions with long-term meaning: purpose. Purpose is the fulfillment one gets when doing something more enduring than oneself. Current activities derive meaning from the idea of possible future states, ambitions and ideas (Baumeister, 1991, p. 36). It requires good reflective skills from students to

---

1    State allowance requires students to finish a Bachelors degree in four years or else they will be fined.

figure out what their purpose is and to use the honours programme as one of the means of fulfilling this.

An honours programme may accommodate a student's need for intrinsic motivation by creating effective degrees of freedom, both in the curriculum and in projects. The earliest honours programmes, at Swarthmore colleges, recognized this need for freedom and ever since many programs have created different degrees and kinds of bounded freedom (Van Gorp, Wolfensberger & De Jong, 2012; Wolfensberger 2012). HCG was designed around three different kinds of freedom: passion, learning strategies and involvement & responsibility (Van Gorp et al., 2012). The match between students and the programme arises when students discover their passions and ambitions and design their honours projects around them. Freedom also entails that students learn to discover and apply the learning strategies that best suit them. Bounded freedom, moreover, means that students are held responsible for their own planning and progress.

Thus, students need to figure out who they are, what they want, who they want to be, and how they could use the freedom offered in HCG in pursuit of these ambitions. The reflective portfolio[2] serves the two separate but strongly related processes of matching and learning to deal with the freedom that HCG offers. Working on this reflective portfolio is not an easy task for it requires good reflective skills. Over the years, we have learned that gifted students need not automatically also be gifted reflective thinkers. Reflection, like any other skill, requires training. To train these skills, a number of workshops were incorporated in the programme offered by HCG. This paper presents more details on the workshops and then moves to the outcomes of this intervention.


## Reflective Workshops

Since spring 2011, HCG has offered reflective workshops (three per academic year) challenging and teaching students to reflect on their strengths in relation to their ambitions (purpose), their actions (mastery) and the choices they make (autonomy). These workshops, it was hoped, would not only contribute to enlarging the skills students need when writing their portfolio, but would also increase the effectiveness of their actions and interventions and promote excellence. The workshops were inspired by the ideas of Gallup International

---

2   The use of learning or reflective portfolios in honours programmes is very common. See, for example, Zubizarreta (2009). *The learning portfolio, reflective practice for improving student learning.* Wiley and Sons.

Research & Education Centre. This organisation states that most education is built upon two, what they believe to be flawed, assumptions: the first being that each person can learn to be competent in almost everything, the second being that each person's greatest room for growth is in their area of greatest weakness (Buckingham & Clifton, 2001, p. 5). Research by the Gallup organisation has shown that excellence can only be attained through awareness of one's natural strengths and that people should have autonomy when choosing which competences they want to focus on. A person's talents are enduring and unique. It is therefore in the areas of their strengths where the greatest room for growth lies (Buckingham & Clifton, 2001, p. 6). Encouraging students to excel might thus not be attained by having students solely reflect on or invest in their weaknesses or failures. The workshops therefore focused on having students discover their strengths and on having students think about how they match who they are with how they (re)act (mastery), how they look upon themselves, what really matters to them (purpose), and the choices they make as a result of this (autonomy). These leadership skills are important beyond the matching and reapplication procedures of HCG: students might need these skills in their transition from student to employee or entrepreneur, as well as during their future careers.

## Outcomes

This paper will now give the first results of this intervention from the perspective of both students and staff. Evaluations of the workshops, interviews with students and staff, together with text analyses of portfolios, demonstrate how focusing on strengths and connecting these to ambitions and aims can assist in matching the honours programme with its aims and students.

Overall, students seem to have appreciated the workshops. In the year 2011–2012, evaluation of the HCG workshops were the highest ranked activity (with an average score of 8,4 on a 10 point scale) and the majority of the students found the workshops (very) useful (Schippers, 2011). Students not only appreciated the workshops but also the focus on strengths and talents. For many of them, this offered a new perspective on reflection and personal growth: from weakness and failure to success and to facing challenges relying on ones strengths and talents. "*I did not know that one could see it from this perspective*", "*Usually I focus on what I can not accomplish*", or "*I did not know that one can use one's talents to acquire new skills or to gather new knowledge*" is what students reported in their portfolios. Students told teachers after the workshops that they enjoyed the focus on strengths, instead of focusing on what needs improvement.

Judging from the portfolios, a number of students have really incorporated the new perspective on reflection. *"If I were to sketch my future, then I would like to see myself as an all-round academic who has contributed to a more sustainable and natural world. (..) If I want to combine my strengths (achiever) with my positive attitude towards learning, then – as a researcher – I should not focus on one topic for the rest of my life. I have to come up with smaller research projects, and switch topics. I can practise this in the research master[3] by experimenting with smaller projects and see how that works for me."*

Although we must allow for differences in mastery of these skills, a number of students demonstrate that they have not just gained a new perspective on reflection but can master a number of important skills such as setting tangible and practical goals that relate to who they are and which therefore matter to them. *"As an honours student I have learned to expand my horizon and follow my ambition. I no longer sit back and wait but let my eagerness to learn guide me. I translate my dreams into (research) projects. By being decisive and by taking initiative, I grow as a person and can add value to my environment. I want to create an ambitious setting where enthusiasm grows and where cooperation and mutual appreciation flourish."*

The teachers who evaluated the portfolios and reapplications noticed these newly acquired skills in two different ways. Firstly, some students explicitly refer to the experiences and outcomes of the workshops. Secondly – and perhaps more importantly – their reflective skills seem to have improved. As one teacher stated: *"Students can point out their strengths and say what they want to achieve. They do that in a very convincing way I do not usually come across".* Another teacher stressed that, overall, she got the impression that students had started to recognize reflection as an important skill, and learned to see it as a skill that can be trained and thus improved. This does not mean that all students now enjoy reflection or working on their reflective portfolio, but they do see the need for it and understand how it can help them get the most out of their education.

Although the teachers recognize the new skills in the reflective portfolios, not all students seem to be convinced that they have mastered these skills sufficiently to be able to change their behaviour. As one student said: *"I am still in doubt".* The workshop did change their perspective on reflection, however.

---

3    The student refers to a specific two-year master programme Human Geography and Planning.

Still, the workshops were never intended to present students with the answer to all the choices they have to make.

## Discussion and Conclusion

Overall the intervention seems to have been successful. Students seem to have acquired new skills that could make them more effective in reflecting on their participation in HCG. They can make a better decision in regard to whether they match with the programme. Moreover, these reflecting skills also allow students to take full advantage of the freedom that the honors programme has to offer. This is where matching and freedom meet: it stimulates students to make choices that are relevant to them. This leads to involvement and leadership. Students also learn to take responsibility for their choices, to make durable choices, and to become truly involved in HCG itself by organizing events, creating content and so on.

In the course of the two years that these workshops have taken place, we have discovered that workshops on such personal topics as reflection and strengths require a certain degree of community and confidence of the students to succeed. Because of the small size of groups and the effort by the trainer to create an open mind, she was able to use peer feedback to the fullest. The workshops themselves became important tools in creating community. Students discovered that their fellow students see their talents in action. For more than one reason, it is thus important to start early on in the programme with a workshop on the basic tools needed for reflecting on strengths. It helps students at an early stage to see possibilities in the freedom that the programme offers. It also bonds students.

This paper stresses the need to see matching as a continuous process of reflection and to see reflection as a skill that requires training. Their personal development throughout the year asks of students that they rethink their current position and their ambitions, plans and also, therefore, their participation in the honours programme. A student's motivation and ambitions might match with the programme at the beginning of year one, but this does not mean they will still match by the end of the year. This does not necessarily mean that the student will quit. A high degree of freedom allows students to consider how they can mould (parts of) the programme in such a way that it still matters to them.

## Acknowledgements

The authors would like to thank Franca Geerdes, Harro van Lente, and Nelleke de Jong for their valuable input.

## References

Baumeister, R. (1991). *Meanings of life*. Guilford Press.

Buckingham, M. & Clifton, D.O. (2001). *Now, Discover you Strengths – How to develop your talents and those of the people you manage.* The Gallup Organisation.

Csikszentmihalyi, M. (1990). *Flow. The Psychology of Optimal Experience.* HarperCollins Publisher.

Gorp, B. van, Wolfensberger, M., & De Jong, N. (2012). Setting them free: students as co-producers of honors education. *Journal of National Collegiate Honors Council 13*(2), p. 183–195.

Pink, D. (2009). *Drive – the surprising truth that motivates us.* Riverhead Books.

Ryan, R.M. & Deci, E.L. (2000). Self-Determination Theory and the Facilitation of Intrinsic Motivation, Social Development and Well-Being. *American Psychologist, 55*, p. 68–78.

Schippers, V. (2011). *Analyse Jaarevaluatie Honours College Geowetenschappen 2011–2012.* Honours Opleidings Commissie & Honours College Geowetenschappen Universiteit Utrecht.

Utrecht University (2012). *Utrecht University: curiosity driven, relevant to society. Strategisch Plan Universiteit Utrecht 2012–2016.* Retrieved from http://www.uu.nl/university/utrecht/NL/Profielenmissie/Documents/Strategisch_Plan_2012-2016.pdf. Matching, pas jij wel bij deze opleiding? DUB 20 December 2011, http://www.dub.uu.nl/artikel/matching-pas-jij-wel-deze-opleiding.html

Wolfensberger, M.V.C. (2012). *Teaching for Excellence. Honors Pedagogies Revealed.* Waxmann: Münster.

Zubizarreta, J. (2009). *The learning portfolio. Reflective practice for improving student learning.* Wiley and Sons.

# Teaching Talented Students at a Research-Intensive University

## Towards Professional Development for Honours Faculty

*Marieke van Haaren and Roeland van der Rijst*

The main goal of this study is to gain insight into the strategies lecturers use to engage and inspire talented students in honours programmes at Leiden University. This small-scale qualitative exploratory study focuses on faculty's conceptions about the qualities of lecturers in honours programmes at a research-intensive university. Eight faculty members were individually interviewed about their conceptions of the qualities of honours lecturers. Three qualitatively different categories of lecturer qualities were identified: (1) charismatic content expert, (2) emphasis on cognitive self-directed development of the students, and (3) evoking students' critical thinking abilities. The outcomes emphasise that honours faculty value the cognitive development of individual students and work on strengthening students' critical thinking abilities. This paper will give some suggestions for lecturers to improve their teaching in honours programmes.

## Introduction

The main goal of this small-scale exploratory study is to gain insight into the teaching strategies of lecturers in order to engage and inspire talented students in honours programmes. Faculty members at Leiden University were interviewed about their experiences in the various honours programmes. The findings will help us to foster specific lecturer qualities for honours programmes. Based on the results in this study, we plan to develop professional development activities aimed at lecturers in honours programmes.

### Professional Development for Faculty Members in Honours Programmes

In their discussion of the literature about the benefits of honours education, Reis and Renzulli (2010) argue that the training of lecturers is essential for maintaining a high quality of any form of honours education. A lack at lecturer professional development activities will eventually lead to less differentiated teaching strategies, more underachievement, higher drop-out rates, and diminished academic performance of excellent and talented students. Investment in professional development activities for lecturers in honours programmes will contribute to the quality of honours programmes. Although the majority of studies Reis and Renzulli (2010) present concern gifted education for secondary education students, the similarity with the higher education context seems evident. Lecturers who are able to differentiate their instruction of the subject matter for each individual student are more capable of stimulating excellent and talented students to perform at their cognitive ability and even to outperform. In order to facilitate lecturers in honours programmes to improve the quality of their instruction for the specific group of high-ability students, time for their professional development and support is necessary.

Van Eijl, Renique and Reimer (2011) discuss the importance of lecturers' attitudes towards educational innovation for the quality of honours programmes and honours teaching. Both innovative initiatives within the programme and initiatives of excellent students themselves need to be stimulated by the lecturers in order to foster students' creative thinking. Van Eijl et al. (2011) also suggest that peer-to-peer interactions among equal-ability students are stimulating for students. Furthermore, students highly value lecturers who show interest in students and who invest time in them. Lecturers in honours programmes are designers of education and transmitters of knowledge but, even more, they are role-models for the students.

Several studies address the specific competencies for lecturers in honours programmes. Based on these studies, VanTassel-Baska and Johnsen (2007) gave an overview of these competencies, in which they distinguish between knowledge and skills necessary for teaching excellent and talented students. These lecturers, for example, need knowledge about the characteristics of excellent students and need a repertoire of instructional strategies specifically related to these student characteristics. Furthermore, these lecturers need to be able to engage excellent and talented students in their subject.

The literature about teaching gifted and talented students shows that various themes are related to the quality of instruction in honours programmes. The central research question in this study is: What are honours faculty members' conceptions of the qualities of lecturers in honours programmes at a research-intensive university? The practical relevance of this study is related to the improvement of teaching and learning of talented students at research-intensive universities and to promote lecturers' professional development in programmes for high ability students in higher education.

## Leiden University Honours College

The Leiden University Honours College provides bachelor-level students with specific extra-curricular disciplinary programmes for talented and motivated undergraduate students who seek more challenges alongside their regular undergraduate programme. First-year students can apply for the programme, or can be invited to take part in orientating activities. Students are selected based on their previous academic achievements and motivation. Furthermore, they have to be on schedule in their regular undergraduate programme. In every honours track, second or third year students are supposed to take part in an interdisciplinary honours class. Students who fulfil all requirements receive an honours certificate in addition to their diploma. Students have the opportunity to select an honours track related to their regular programme, or they can choose an unrelated track. Some of the honours tracks require specific pre-knowledge and are therefore only open to students from a specific regular programme, Law and Medicine for example. Other tracks, such as Philosophy and Art & Literature, are open to all students.

## Research Design

This small-scale qualitative exploratory study focuses on honours faculty conceptions of the qualities of lecturers in honours programmes at Leiden University, a research-intensive university. Eight faculty members were individually interviewed about their conceptions of lecturer qualities in honours programmes. Various faculty members' background characteristics such as age, gender, and teaching experience were extracted using a short survey. The participants came from different honours tracks within Leiden University. The open-ended interview questions were designed to be flexible, offering participants opportunities to raise matters they considered to be important. The interviews were audio-taped, transcribed verbatim and analyzed using a grounded theory approach in which emerging categories were constantly compared.

### Faculty Interviews

The interviews with the participating faculty members lasted between 35–55 minutes and were held in faculty members' work environments. The semi-structured interview protocol provided opportunities for the faculty to address their views about the special programmes for talented undergraduate students at the university. During the interviews specific attention was given to faculty's own experiences with honours education and to the lecturer qualities necessary for teaching talented and motivated students in honours tracks. Faculty members' views about lecturer qualities were identified inductively and categorized. First, the audio-tapes were re-listened to and all transcripts were read to acquire a global picture of the broad variety of the views expressed. Second, the transcripts were re-read and all fragments in which the faculty expressed their conception about lecturer qualities were identified and labelled using words from the fragments. Third, all selected fragments were re-read and fragments with similar labels were clustered into more generic categories. Finally, these categories were discussed among higher education experts (Dialogical reliability; Sandbergh, 1997).

## Results

Honours education in the programmes in which the participants worked could be characterized as small-scale and active participation for students. The teaching focused primarily on the cognitive development of the students and not so much on the reproduction of facts or knowledge. During the analysis of the interview transcripts, characteristic lecturer qualities in honours programmes emerged. Three qualitatively different categories of lecturer qualities were identified as follows: (1) charismatic content expert, (2) emphasis on cognitive self-directed development of the students, and (3) evoking students' critical thinking abilities.

### Charismatic Content Expert

The participating honours faculty most often emphasised that lecturers in honours programmes need to be enthusiastic, motivated and, above all, charismatic in their teaching. Lecturers with these qualities can engage and inspire students to outperform. Lecturers need to motivate talented students to engage in detailed study of the course content. The following fragment from the transcripts depicts that being a content expert is necessary, and that presenting the course content in a charismatic way is highly valued.

> *"What we need to expect of good honours lecturers is first of all that they have much content knowledge and second that they show a whole lot of enthusiasm.*

*And this enthusiasm should be focused on the content as well as on student learning."* (Social Sciences)

Nearly all participating faculty members indicated that content expertise is an important lecturer quality in honours programmes. This content expertise is not only related to a single theme or topic of study, but even more related to an overall perspective on the domain of study. Lecturers in honours programmes are expected to explain to students the position of the topic in the domain.

*"Good honours lecturers are lecturers who are above the specific topics on which they have published one or two articles; they are scholars with a helicopter-view and a vision on the discipline."* (Archaeology)

## Emphasis on Cognitive Self-Directed Development

The participating faculty members emphasize that excellent lecturers on honours programmes focus on the cognitive development of individual students. An important precondition for 'good' honours education is that the teacher has affinity with the group of students, keeps his focus on individual development, and tries to meet the individual interest of students. In short, these qualities boil down to developing a good interpersonal relationship between teacher and students. Teachers who have good relationships with students have the opportunity to focus more on the cognitive development of the individual student by engaging in intellectual discussions on the topics, or by giving students more responsibility for the design of the sessions, for example. In the next interview fragment, one of the participants formulates this.

*"Talented students have more individual recognizable interests. Thus the question is: What characterizes that students' talent in particular and in what way can I as a teacher contribute to developing that talent?"* (Philosophy)

Participating faculty describe a strong personal approach directed to the individual student's needs as an important characteristic of their honours programme. The personal approach, on the one hand, provides the possibility to adapt teaching strategies and assignments to the pre-knowledge and personal interests of the students. On the other hand, the personal approach has the advantage of creating a safe learning environment in which talented students can improve their academic performance. Furthermore, taking responsibility over their own learning is highly motivating for talented students. In the interview fragment below, one of the participating faculty members explains how she explores ways of improving the self-directed teaching and learning of her students.

> *"Once in a while we take the students to the pub on the corner of the street after a seminar and will eat and drink. Then we always discuss how to go further. In this way we try to involve the students when planning the next sessions, for example what are the themes of interest."* (History)

*Evoking Critical Thinking*

One of the objectives of honours programmes mentioned is to stimulate students' critical thinking skills. Critical thinking is not only focused on critiquing work of peers, but also on getting a better understanding of your own abilities through the lens of self-reflection. Pedagogical strategies which lecturers in honours programmes can use to stimulate students' critical thinking abilities and which were mentioned during the interviews are: (1) discussing topics at a high academic level, (2) using undergraduate research, (3) making learning objectives clear for the students, and (4) stimulating students' self-reflection. Classroom discussion formats are a powerful pedagogical tool which is used by many of the participants. These discussions can be stimulated, for example, by inviting speakers who are an authority in their discipline or by discussing students' research projects. Some participants emphasize that a safe learning environment is crucial for effective classroom discussions.

## Discussion and Implications for Faculty Professional Development

The outcomes of this exploratory study show that honours faculty value the cognitive development of individual students and the emphasis on students' critical thinking abilities. Furthermore, faculty on honours programmes value teaching strategies in which students' critical thinking abilities are stimulated. The central themes relating to the qualities of lecturers in honours programmes at research-intensive universities can be used during the design and re-design of honours programmes, and are also relevant for the development of regular bachelor programmes. Although this study is an exploration into specific qualities for lecturers in honours programmes and should be refined with more empirical data, the themes are remarkably similar to the principles and conditions of 'good teaching' (Chickering & Gamson, 1987; Tinto, 2012).

In her literature review relating to honours education, Rogers (2007) gives five recommendations for the design of high quality teaching for excellent students the need to (1) challenge excellent and talented students in their specific talents; (2) challenge excellent and talented students to work independently towards the development of their specific talents; (3) offer students different acceleration possibilities; (4) offer possibilities for excellent students to work and learn with 'like-ability peers'; (5) offer each different subject in a differentiated way in terms of speed, quantity, and organization. These five recommendations can be used during professional development activities for teachers in honours programmes in order to support them during the design and improve of their instruction.

A theme which is not always mentioned in analyses of 'good teaching' (e.g. Chickering & Gamson, 1987), but which is valued in honours education, is to provide students with authentic research experiences. This theme is specifically directed towards stimulating an inquisitive attitude among students. This is strongly related to fostering students' critical thinking dispositions. Critical thinking is perceived as an essential part of a student's research disposition (Beishuizen, Spelten, & Van der Rijst, 2012; Van der Rijst, Visser-Wijnveen, Verloop, & Van Driel, 2013). Based on their meta-analysis, Furtak, Seidel, Iverson and Biggs (2012) argue that inquiry-based teaching has several benefits for student learning. Supporting students with authentic research experiences guided by an experienced faculty member, as well as providing students with autonomy in their research project, are especially effective. There are many other ways of teaching honours courses which might aim to achieve other goals and objectives that teachers in honours education might have (Van Eijl, Pilot, & Wolfensberger, 2010), but the inquiry-based approach is a potentially fruitful teaching approach in research-intensive university programmes (cf. Manathunga, Kiley, Boud, & Cantwell, 2012).

The themes presented above can be used as reference points for both honours and regular bachelor programmes. Furthermore, these themes provide potential input for teacher professional development trajectories for beginning lecturers in honours programmes. The underlying advice to lecturers in honours programmes is to focus on students' conceptual change and to foster a strong interpersonal relationship with them. Furthermore, we advise lecturers in honours programmes at research-intensive universities to use a variety of instructional techniques with a clear structure and in which students are engaged in relevant and authentic disciplinary research practice.

## References

Beishuizen, Y., Spelten, E., & Rijst, R. M. van der (2012). Professionaliteit van docenten: academische houding in het hbo. *Tijdschrift voor Hoger Onderwijs, 30*, 245–258.

Chickering, A. W., & Gamson, Z. F. (1987). Seven principles for good practice in undergraduate education. *American Association of Higher Education Bulletin, 39*(7), 3–7.

Eijl, P. van, Pilot, A., & Wolfensberger, M. (2010). *Talent voor morgen: ontwikkelingen van talent in het hoger onderwijs.* Groningen: Noordhoff Uitgevers.

Eijl, P. van, Renique, C., & Reimer, P. (2011).Werken aan excellentie: van experiment naar cultuuromslag. *Tijdschrift voor Hoger Onderwijs en Management, 4*, 10–15.

Furtak, E. M., Seidel, T., Iverson, H., & Biggs, D. C. (2012). Experimental and quasi-experimental studies of inquiry-based science teaching: A meta-analysis. *Review of Educational Research, 82*, 300–329.

Manathunga, C., Kiley, M., Boud, D., & Cantwell, R. (2012). From knowledge acquisition to knowledge production: Issues with Australian honours curricula. *Teaching in Higher Education, 17*, 139–151.

Reis, S. R., & Renzulli, J. S. (2010). Is there still a need for gifted education? An examination of current research. *Learning and Individual Differences, 20*, 308–317.

Rijst, R. M. van der, Visser-Wijnveen, G. J., Verloop, N., & Driel, J. H. van (2013). Undergraduate science coursework: Teachers' goal statements and how students experience research. *Innovations in Education and Teaching International, 50*, 178–190.

Rogers, K. B. (2007). Lessons learned about educating the gifted and talented: A synthesis of the research on educational practice. *Gifted Child Quarterly, 51*, 382–396.

Sandbergh, J. (1997). Are phenomenographic results reliable? *Higher Education Research and Development, 16*, 203–212.

Tinto, V. (2012). *Completing college: Rethinking institutional action.* Chicago: University of Chicago Press.

VanTassel-Baska, J., & Johnsen, S. K. (2007). Teacher education standards for the field of gifted education: A vision of coherence for personnel preparation in the 21st century. *Gifted Child Quarterly, 51*, 182–205.

# Talent-Index

## The Motivating Potential of a Strength-Based Learning Approach

*Djoerd Hiemstra*

How to create a stimulating learning context that motivates students to excel? At NHL University, we developed and tested a new method for mentoring and coaching students, based on a strength-based development approach: *Talent-Index* (www.talentenwijzer.com). The basic principle of this method is that students assess their talents and set learning goals that aim at further developing their talents during their education. In this contribution, we briefly introduce this method and report our main experiences.

### Developing Strengths Versus Diminishing Deficiencies

In higher professional and vocational education, competency-based learning is a common practice. Typically, a competency-based learning approach entails that (a) the standards that students have to meet are laid out in a competency profile, (b) students' actual level of competency is reviewed relative to these standards, and (c) learning activities are being aimed at diminishing the discrepancy between students' present level of competency and the required level of competency (e.g. Arguelles & Gonczi, 2000; Harris, Snell, Talbot, & Harden, 2010).

However, although diminishing deficiencies is clearly indispensable for mastering a profession, from a motivational point of view, this way of setting learning goals may have a drawback. Specifically, because a competency-based approach frames students' present level of mastery as a shortcoming (relative to the required level), it emphasizes students' *incompetency*. As articulated by influential motivation theories, such as *self-determination theory* (Ryan & Deci, 2000) and *effectance motivation theory* (Harter, 1992), self-perceived competency is an important prerequisite for intrinsic motivation. Therefore, a competency-based approach may not be the best way to strengthen students' intrinsic motivation and to motivate them to excel.

To address this issue, several scholars (Clifton & Anderson, 2002; Kluger & Nir, 2011; Linley, Nielsen, Gillett & Biswas-Diener, 2010) have recently proposed an alternative, that is, a strength-based development approach. This approach entails that individuals assess their strengths and strive to further develop their strengths, rather than assess their shortcomings and aim at diminishing their shortcomings. Because, this approach emphasizes students' individual qualities, it may be a more effective way to bolster their intrinsic motivation, and to promote excellence.

Although more research is required, indeed, some studies indicate that focusing on strengths enhances students' motivation. For example, Linley and colleagues (2010) found that using strengths was associated with goal progress. Louis (2008) found that developing strengths enhanced students' academic control, and Rechter (2010; in Kluger & Nir, 2009) found that strength-based reviewing enhanced participants' self-efficacy and effort. Therefore we reasoned that a strength-based development approach might make a valuable complement to our common competency-based learning approach.

## Talent-Index: A Strength-Based Development Method

To gain experience with a strength-based development approach in the context of higher professional education in The Netherlands, we developed, tested, and implemented the *Talent-Index* programme, a talent development programme which includes a self-assessment instrument, a workbook with exercises for students, and a coaching manual for teachers. The *Talent-Index* programme comprises 5 sequential steps: (1) identifying your individual qualities, (2) exploring your individual qualities (3) using your individual qualities (4) setting learning goals that aim at developing your individual qualities, and (5) selecting, planning and performing learning activities to develop your individual qualities.

We tested this programme in several pilot projects, and conducted two randomized experimental studies to examine the effects of *developing strengths,* as opposed to *diminishing deficiencies,* on students' motivation. Evaluations of the pilot projects showed that both students and teachers highly appreciated the programme. Specifically, the average student satisfaction score of the *Talent-Index* course that was part of our excellence programme was 7.8 on a 10-point scale, and the overall teacher satisfaction score of the *Talent-Index* programme was 7.0 on a 10-point scale. Moreover, the results of the two randomized experimental studies showed that, relative to students who pursued deficiency-based learning goals, students who pursued strength-based learning goals were higher in perceived competency, intrinsic motivation and effort intentions (Hiemstra & Van Yperen, 2012).

## Conclusion

Based on these experiences, we concluded that a strength-based development approach provides a valuable complement to our educational practice. Therefore, we decided to incorporate the Talent-Index method into our mentoring programme. Although more research is needed, our findings suggest that a strength-based approach may bolster students' perceived competency, intrinsic motivation, and willingness to put effort into their learning. Therefore, this approach may contribute to a stimulating learning context that motivates students to excel.

## References

Arguelles, A., & Gonczi, A. E. (2000). *Competency-based education and training: A world perspective.* Mexico City: Grupo Noriega Editores.

Clifton, D. O., & Anderson, E. (2002). *Strengths Quest: Discover and develop your strengths in academics, career, and beyond.* Washington, DC: Gallup Organization.

Guay, F., Ratelle, C. F., & Chanal, J. (2008). Optimal learning in optimal contexts: The role of self-determination in education. *Canadian Psychology, 49,* 233–240.

Harris, P., Snell, L., Talbot, M., & Harden, R. M. (2010). Competency-based medical education: Implications for undergraduate programs. *Medical Teacher, 32,* 646–650.

Harter, S. (1992). The relationship between perceived competence, affect, and motivational orientation within the classroom: Processes and patterns of change. In A. K. Boggiano, T. S. Pittman (Eds.), *Achievement and motivation: A social-developmental perspective* (pp. 77–114). New York, NY: Cambridge University Press.

Hiemstra, D., & Van Yperen, N. W. (2012). *How to motivate professionals to put effort into self-directed learning activities: The motivating potential of strength-based learning goals.* Paper presented at the WAOP Conference 2012, Groningen.

Kluger, A. N., & Nir, D. (2009). The feedforward interview. *Human Resource Management Review, 20,* 235–246.

Linley, P., Nielsen, K. M., Gillett, R., & Biswas-Diener, R. (2010). Using signature strengths in pursuit of goals: Effects on goal progress, need satisfaction, and well-being, and implications for coaching psychologists. *International Coaching Psychology Review, 5,* 6–15.

Louis, M. C. (2008). A comparative analysis of the effectiveness of strengths-based curricula in promoting first-year college student success. *Dissertation Abstracts International: Section A, 69.*

Rechter, E. (2010). *Emotional and cognitive reaction to feedforward intervention.* Paper presented at the 11th Annual Meeting of the Society for Personality and Social Psychology, Las Vegas, NV.

Ryan, R. M., & Deci, E. L. (2000). Self-determination theory and the facilitation of intrinsic motivation, social development, and well-being. *American Psychologist, 55,* 68–78. doi:10.1037/0003–066X.55.1.68

Stipek, D. (2002). *Motivation to learn* (4th ed.). Boston: Allyn & Bacon.

# The College of Pharmaceutical Sciences

## An Inquiry-Based Undergraduate Honours Programme for the Training of Pharmaceutical Scientists

*Irma Meijerman, Berend Olivier and Andries Koster*

### Objective

In addition to a bachelor-master trajectory for the education of practising pharmacists, Utrecht University offers a research master-level programme, Drug Innovation (Koster, Meijerman, Blom, & Schalekamp, 2009). Recently, it was decided to design an additional undergraduate honours programme aimed at attracting talented students from an international context and who are interested in a research career within the pharmaceutical field. This initiative is in accordance with the University's policy of sustaining its position as a research institution of high international quality and providing research focus areas with an interdisciplinary approach. The programme started in September 2010.

### Design Principles

The College of Pharmaceutical Sciences (CPS) was designed according to the principles of inquiry-based learning (Lee, 2004). Several reasons prompted this educational approach. First, the selected students are expected to be highly motivated, gifted and talented. Several characteristics of these students demand an adaptation of the educational environment; their learning skills call for more speed, less repetition and more challenge. Furthermore, they profit from a less structured environment, leaving room for personal initiative and space for experimentation (Scager, 2008; Scager, Akkerman, Pilot, & Wubbels, 2012; Wolfensberger, 2012). Second, these students will be trained for the discovery and development of drugs in a research environment. Being a research scientist is more than just having theoretical knowledge and being a skilled practitioner in the laboratory. Research scientists must have higher order thinking skills and a critical attitude to be able to understand the research process, define a research question and develop an experimental design. They must be able to critically analyse primary literature, interpret data, and present and discuss their results in a professional, scientific way (Coil, Wenderoth, Cunningham, & Dirks, 2010; Feldman, Divoll, & Rogan-Klyve, 2009). Teaching undergraduates research-skills has been shown to improve their understanding of science content, science process skills like critical thinking, motivation, learning and collaborative skills. Finally, students must be trained to be able to deal with the fast development of knowledge and they need to be prepared for the complex and challenging world will they will face as professionals (Brew, 2006; Barnett, 2000).

Inquiry-based learning (IBL) is a student-centred pedagogy that stimulates a deep learning approach, analytical abilities, process skills and critical thinking, and strengthens the connection between research and teaching (Spronken-Smith & Walker, 2010; Justice, Rice, & Warry, 2009; Healey, 2005). IBL consists of those approaches to learning that are driven by a process of inquiry. Student-centred approaches encourage students to actively explore and seek new evidence. The role of teachers is to support and facilitate students in developing their own personal understanding of scientific concepts (Garcia-Cepero, 2008). In this way, the students are stimulated to take more responsibility for their own learning process. IBL is usually organized as collaborative work in small groups, thereby having the additional advantage of improving the team-working and project-management skills of students. Educational approaches that can be used within IBL include all instructional practices that are student-led and designed to promote higher order intellectual and academic skills (Justice, Rice, Warry, Inglis, Miller, & Sammon, 2007). They can include fieldwork, case studies, individual and group projects, and research activities.

One single course is not sufficient for students to learn complex research skills and higher order thinking skills; IBL should be embedded throughout the whole bachelor programme (Fraser, Crook, & Park, 2007, Justice et al., 2009). Students will also benefit more from IBL when it is integrated into the whole curriculum (Spronken-Smith & Walker, 2010, Spronken-Smith, Bullard, Ray, Roberts, & Keiffer, 2008). For the College of Pharmaceutical Sciences, therefore, it was decided to implement an inquiry- and research-based programme throughout the whole undergraduate programme.

## Curriculum

The "drug development pipeline" functions as the organizing principle for the first year of the curriculum; from drug discovery to drug development. Most pharmaceutical and pharmacy undergraduate programmes start with courses about basic chemical knowledge of drug molecules. Many students experience this subject matter as difficult and often fail to see why this knowledge is important to them in the light of their future profession, leading to student demotivation and lack of interest. Therefore, in order to connect to the incoming students' world as well as possible and to follow a natural course of interest-driven study at progressively more detailed physiological, cellular, biochemical and molecular levels, later in the year CPS students follow the drug pipeline in reverse order; from therapeutic application to molecular design. At the same time, this sequence repeats the historical development of the relevant science areas. The first year consists of four 10-week courses: Drug Use (epidemiology, therapeutics), Drug Delivery (pharmaceutics, pharmacokinetics), Drug Action (physiology, cell biology, pharmacology) and Drug Target (medicinal chemistry). In their second year, students follow two mandatory courses in Neuroimmuno-pharmacology and Analytical Techniques, followed by a wide choice of electives offered in the chemical, biomedical and pharmaceutical field (6 courses, spread over 30 weeks; 2 courses in parallel). In year 3, students follow a mandatory course, Drug Discovery and Development, as a preparation for their individual undergraduate research project, which is carried out in their final half year. Besides their regular courses, the students have to work on a portfolio and are stimulated to expand additional activities on top of their regular curriculum (*e.g.* organize symposia, extra research activities, social activities).

## Teaching-Learning Environment

Students should become familiar with a research environment as soon as possible. Therefore, all courses are constructed around a set of authentic problems: examples are writing a disease file or drug file, designing a clinical trial, designing and carrying out an epidemiological study, biochemical experiment or chemical synthesis. Most of the time, students are free to choose the subject or research question they want to work on. Practical work by the students is carried out in the research laboratories of the department, rather than in designated teaching facilities, and direct interaction with principal investigators, PhD-students and/or technicians is organized throughout the curriculum. The student project teams are small and consist of 2–5 students. The inquiry-based environment, supported by contact with researchers, provides a research-based environment in which the students are stimulated to learn and work as a researcher (Healey & Jenkins, 2009). The English language is used exclusively for all courses and the tutoring of students.

## Teachers

Not all teachers are willing or able to play the role that the programme requires. Participating teachers were selected on the basis of their teaching experience (Pilot, 2007) and/or their active involvement in the research programme of the department and they are subsequently trained in the following areas: use of new media, collaborative learning, group dynamics and teaching in English. Professor Mick Healey (HE consultant, University of Gloucestershire, UK) offered a workshop on inquiry-based learning.

## Selection of Students

After application, students are selected on the basis of their motivation, research interests, scientific orientation and language capability. The selection procedure involves submission of a motivation letter and letters of reference, writing a (timed) essay about a biomedical or pharmaceutical subject, and a personal interview. A maximum of 50 students is selected annually. Since 2010, students have been selected from the following countries: The Netherlands (28), India (1), Denmark (1), France (2), Nigeria (1), Sweden (1), United Kingdom (1), Jordan (1), Germany (1) and Egypt (1). Four of the international students lived in the Netherlands and had an International Baccalaureate. The number of students that started in the three consecutive years was 8 in 2010, 20 in 2011 and 16 in 2012.

## Student Experience

Although formal and quantitative curriculum evaluations are limited at the time of writing, the first results show that most students appreciate the learning environment. The average of the student evaluations of three consecutive years (2010–2013) of the first six compulsory courses in year 1 and 2 show that the students find the courses intellectual challenging (4.0 ± 0.5 on a 5-point scale), that the courses encouraged independent thinking (3.8 ± 0.3) and that they stimulated students' creativity (3.7 ± 0.3) and motivation to learn (3.7 ± 0.4). Working on different projects (4.0 ± 0.1), on research projects of their own choice (4.0 ± 0.2) and determining their own research methods (3.9 ± 0.1) stimulated them to do their best work. These results are confirmed by the following quotations cited from students' course evaluation questionnaires:

- *"Good teamwork is the key to success. Designing a trial makes you look at the tiniest details. You don't need lectures to learn"*
- *"I like to find out stuff for myself. I don't like that teachers say how to do it. And I like to discuss that in a group what we should do with the info we got from teachers"*
- *"This course, by letting us find the research question and performing an experiment, makes you feel like a real scientist"*
- *"Learning about research strategies makes me aware of pitfalls and challenging points in research"*
- *"The research in this course, even though a lot needed to be collaborated, really pushed me into learning"*
- *"The student-driven approach did work for me by challenging my level of reasoning and views on scientific subjects"*

## Conclusion

A novel international, selective, research-based undergraduate honours programme, aimed at the training of research scientists in the pharmaceutical field, was developed by CPS (CPS, 2013). The first evaluations indicate that students feel highly challenged by the programme and are stimulated to be creative and independent learners.

## References

Barnett, R. (2000). University knowledge in an age of supercomplexity. *Higher Education 40*, 409–422.

Brew, A. (2006). Imperatives and challenges in integrating teaching and research. *Higher Education Research and Development 29*, 139–150.

Coil, D., Wenderoth, M. P., Cunningham, M., & Dirks, C. (2010). Teaching the process of science: Faculty perceptions and an effective methodology. *CBE Life Sciences Education 9*, 524–535.

College of Pharmaceutical Sciences (CPS) (2013). Information for prospective students. Retrieved from: www.uu.nl/honours/cps

Feldman, A., Divoll, K., & Rogan-Klyve, A. (2009). Research education of new scientists: implications for science teacher education. *Journal of Research in Science Teaching 4*, 442–459.

Fraser, G., Crook, A., & Park, J. (2007). A tool for mapping research skills in undergraduate curricula. *Bioscience Education 9*, 1–12.

Garcia-Cepero, M. C. (2008). The enrichment triad model: nurturing crea-tive-productivity among college students. *Innovations in Education & Teaching International 45*, 295–302.

Healey, M. (2005). Linking Research and teaching to benefit student learning. *Journal of Geography in Higher Education 29*, 183–201.

Healey, M., & Jenkins, A. (2009). *Linking discipline-based research and teaching through mainstreaming undergraduate research and inquiry.* Retrieved from: http://insight-dev.glos.ac.uk/tli/resources/toolkit/resources/Documents/ Linking%20discipline-based%20research%20with%20teaching%20to%20 benefit%20student%20learning.pdf. Accessed 3 May 2013.

Justice, C., Rice, J., & Warry, W. (2009). Academic skill development – Inquiry seminars can make a difference: evidence from a quasi-experimental study. *International Journal for the Scholarship of Teaching and Learning 3*, 1–23.

Justice, C., Rice, J., Warry, W., Inglis, S., Miller, S., & Sammon, S. (2007). Inquiry in higher education: Reflections and directions on course design and teaching methods. *Innovative Higher Education 31*, 201–214.

Koster, A. S., Meijerman, I., Blom, A. T. G., & Schalekamp, T. (2009). Pharmacy education at Utrecht University: an educational continuum. *Dosis 25*, 85–93.

Lee, V.S. (2004). *Teaching and learning through inquiry.* Sterling, USA: Stylus Publishing.

Pilot, A. (2007). *The teacher as crucial factor in curriculum innovation, the case of Utrecht University.* Paper presented at the conference "Teaching and learning according and after Bologna", Swiss federal institute of technology (ETH), Zurich, Switzerland.

Scager, K. (2008). Vragen talentvolle studenten ander onderwijs? *Onderzoek van Onderwijs 37*, 66–69.

Scager, K., Akkerman, S.F., Pilot, A., & Wubbels, T. (2012). Challenging high-ability students. *Studies in Higher Education*, First Article, 1–21.

Spronken-Smith, R., Bullard, J., Ray, W., Roberts, C., & Keiffer, A. (2008). Where might sand dunes be on Mars? Engaging students through inquiry-based learning in geography. *Journal of Geography in Higher Education 32*, 71–88.

Spronken-Smith, R., & Walker, R. (2010). Can inquiry-based learning strengthen the links between teaching and disciplinary research? *Studies in Higher Education 35*, 723–740.

Wolfensberger, M. (2012). *Teaching for Excellence – Honors pedagogies revealed.* Münster: Waxmann.

# The Contribution of Passion and Commitment to the Explanation of Motivation and Persistence in Deliberate Practice

## Reviewing Theoretical Conceptualization and Empirical Evidence

*Julia Moeller*

> "I have no particular talent, but am just passionately inquisitive"
> (Albert Einstein, 1952, as cited in Weinzierl, 1982, p. 135).

## Introduction

This article discusses the potential contribution of passion to the explanation of motivation and persistence in deliberate practice. A review of the literature about the motivation underlying deliberate practice shows that it is still unknown why those (people) becoming experts persist in deliberate practice despite the fact that it is a frustrating and aversive experience (Ericsson, Krampe, & Tesch-Römer, 1993). Empirical findings on the links between passion, motivation, deliberate practice and performance are summarized. It is then pointed out that there are other constructs that could explain the same phenomenon, particularly the construct of commitment, which is very similar to passion and also promises to explain persistence in deliberate practice. The article ends with the suggestion that the integration of the constructs passion and commitment promises to contribute to the explanation of motivation and persistence in deliberate practice.

## The Motivation Underlying Deliberate Practice

Deliberate practice is a form of training with the explicit aim of improving skills. It is a highly structured, instructor-led and goal-directed practice and the practising individual has to concentrate hard on the tasks (Ericsson et al., 1993; Ericsson, Roring, & Nandagopal, 2007; Gembris, 2006). Before they eventually become experts in their fields, individuals have to endure about 10.000 hours and 10 years of deliberate practice, which demands the investment of personal and often monetary resources, endurance of dry spells and the sacrifice of conflicting goals and interests. Persistence in the face of such demands requires particularly strong motivation. The motivation underlying deliberate practice and the long-term persistence in this form of training is not well investigated (Bonneville-Roussy, Lavigne, & Vallerand, 2011; Ericsson & Charness, 1994; Gembris, 2006). Theoretical assumptions and research findings regarding this motivation are inconsistent: Ericsson and colleagues (1993; 2007) claimed that deliberate practice was incompatible with intrinsic experiences because of the implied frustration, struggle, and absence of flow, and stated that extrinsic rewards were also rare in that context.

However, several studies have shown the compatibility of deliberate practice with intrinsically-motivated forms of practice (Côté, Baker, & Abernethy, 2003; Helsen, Starkes, & Hodges, 1998; Moraes, Rabelo, & Salmela, 2004; Salmela & Moraes, 2003; Scanlan, Carpenter, Schmidt, Simons, & Keeler, 1993; Soberlak & Côté, 2003; Starkes, 2000). For example, Starkes et al. (1996) found that excellent athletes experience their sporting activity as more enjoyable than less performing athletes. Côté et al. (2003) describe a form of engagement that is at the same time enjoyable and compatible with deliberate practice, namely the construct 'deliberate play', a purposeful structured form of play aiming at the greatest possible experience of joy. Deliberate play is characterized by strong task-focus, involvement, and pleasure. In general, play has been described as a form of learning and skill performance (Oerter, 1999) and, in particular, deliberate play is related to the acquisition of outstanding skills: Soberlak and Côté (2003) showed that elite hockey players spend more time in deliberate play than in deliberate practice until the age of twenty (see also Ford, Ward, Hodges, & Williams, 2009). In contrast to the assumptions of Bloom (1985) and Ericsson et al. (1993), playful learning is not substituted by deliberate practice at a certain age or performance level, but continues as a frequent activity during breaks or leisure time of professional athletes (Moraes et al., 2004; Salmela & Moraes, 2003). Deliberate practice and deliberate play do not only alternate, but they also both share common structural characteristics which are compatible with intrinsic experiences. According to Ericsson and colleagues (1993), deliberate practice improves skills if tasks are clearly defined, are challenging but not too difficult, if feedback is provided and if the practicing individual strongly concentrates on the task. These are the typical conditions in which individuals experience flow (Csikszentmihalyi 1996), a state of intrinsic experience which has often been found in playful activities (see Oerter, 1999), but which is thought to be absent during deliberate practice (Ericsson et al., 1993). Play generally serves the exercise of skills (Oerter, 1999) and is consequently a form of learning. According to Oerter (1999), one of the two main motives in play is 'existence enhancement', the experience of over-coming previous limitations and mastering tasks which previously exceeded the individuals' capacities. Such enhancement is experienced intrinsically and it coincides with the basic purpose of deliberate practice: the enhancement of skills. The repetition of behavioural sequences is also typical of both play (Oerter, 1999) and deliberate practice (Ericsson et al., 1993). Deliberate play and deliberate practice basically differ in their purpose: deliberate practice aims at skill improvement, whereas play aims at pleasure maximization.

In conclusion, despite the description of deliberate practice as a frustrating, effortful and aversive experience, there are arguments and empirical evidence to suggest that deliberate practice might be reconcilable with intrinsic forms of learning, and that individuals who engage both in deliberate practice and joyful, playful forms of learning might learn more persistently. A theoretical integration of deliberate practice and playful learning might contribute to the explanation of persistence and performance. Moreover, it would be interesting to find out whether the practical integration of these forms of learning in training interventions leads to better adjustment and more robust persistence among the trainees than forms of training that unilaterally rely either on deliberate practice or playful activities. Future research and theoretical models are needed to explain how exactly intrinsic learning and deliberate practice might affect persistence and performance.

## The Contribution of Passion to the Explanation of Motivation in Deliberate Practice

Despite the demands of intense training, many individuals who are intensively engaged in deliberate practice report a passionate motivation (Bonneville-Roussy et al., 2011; Fredricks, Alfeld, & Eccles, 2010). This observation has inspired many researchers to discuss the potential effect of passion on motivation in practice and learning (Bonneville-Roussy et al., 2011; Fredricks et al., 2010; Moraes et al., 2004; Vallerand et al., 2007; von Károlyi & Winner, 2005). The most investigated psychological concept of passion defines passion as "a strong inclination toward an activity that people like, that they find important, and in which they invest time and energy" (Vallerand et al., 2003, p. 756). Several slightly different psychological definitions of passion (for a review see Moeller and Grassinger, 2014a), which agree with Vallerands' concept in their emphasis on intense, mostly positive emotions, approach motivation and long-term commitment as characteristics of passion (Cardon, Wincent, Singh, & Drnovsek, 2009; Fredricks et al., 2010; Moeller &

Grassinger, 2014a; Renzulli, Koehler, & Fogarty, 2006; Vallerand et al., 2003). Vallerand and colleagues distinguish between two types of passion: the adaptive harmonious passion and the maladaptive obsessive passion. A number of studies have investigated the assumed affect of harmonious and obsessive passion on deliberate practice and performance. For instance, Vallerand et al. (2007) found that harmonious passion directly predicted deliberate practice, and that this effect was mediated by the pursuit of mastery goals. In contrast, obsessive passion predicted directly both deliberate practice and mastery goals, but also performance approach and avoidance goals, of which the latter were negatively related to performance. The findings were replicated in several studies by Vallerand et al. (2008) and Bonneville-Roussy et al. (2011). Comparable findings were reported by Duckworth, Kirby, Tsukayama, Berstein, & Ericsson (2011, p. 174), who found that the combination of passion and dispositional persistence predicted performance, and that this effect was mediated by deliberate practice. However, Duckworth and colleagues (2007) conceptualize passion as the consistency and long-term pursuit of particular interests, which differs from the above described dual model of passion from Vallerand and colleagues (2003). Future research is needed in order to find out to what extent these definitions of passion and measures overlap and how they can be integrated in a model to explain why individuals are motivated to engage and persist in deliberate practice.

## Alternative Explanations for Motivation in Deliberate Practice

Beyond passion, further constructs can be expected to explain persistence in partially aversive courses of action. Another construct explaining how "attracting powers overwhelm repelling forces" is commitment (Le & Agnew, 2003, p. 37). The investment model of commitment (Rusbult, Martz, & Agnew, 1998) and the related sport commitment model (Scanlan et al., 1993; Scanlan, Russell, Magyar, & Scanlan 2009) define commitment as a psychological state that predicts persistence in sport activities and in relation to other persons or to sport teams (Rusbult & Buunk, 1993). The sport commitment model in particular has been linked to the explanation of persistence in highly performing sport teams (Scanlan et al., 2009). Other constructs which are put forward to explain the persistence in learning contexts are, for example, 'school engagement' (e.g. Salmela-Aro & Upadhyay, 2012; Shernoff, Csikszentmihaly, Schneider, & Shernoff, 2003), and 'grit', which describes the stable disposition to be strongly interested and to persist in particular activities (Duckworth et al., 2007, see above).The personality trait of conscientiousness, particularly its facets that generally predict persistence despite aversive experiences, has also been discussed (see McCann, Duckworth, & Roberts, 2009; Roberts et al., 2005). It would be desirable in future research to disentangle the particular contribution of all these constructs to the explanation of motivation and persistence in deliberate practice.

## Synthesis: Defining Passion as Coincidence of Commitment and Desire

Passion and commitment are often mentioned synonymously or as closely related constructs (Bélanger, Lafrenière, Vallerand, & Kruglanski, 2012; Bierly III, Kessler, & Christensen, 2000; Bonneville-Roussy et al., 2011; Bullis, Clark, & Sline, 1993; Crosswell & Elliott, 2004; Fredricks et al., 2010; Hopfl, 2000; Kottler, 2000; Renzulli et al., 2006; Sternberg, 1986; Vallerand, 2008). Passion and commitment overlap in many aspects (see Moeller and Grassinger (2014a)): both constructs share the central components a) intention, b) long-term goals, and c) identification; they include affect intensity and approach motivation as aspects of passion; they integrate intrinsic and extrinsic motives in a joint model, and this is an important desideratum in the research on deliberate practice (see above). Passion and commitment have also been shown to predict persistence in a course of action, even despite aversive experiences such as frustration, obstacles and dissatisfaction. Both constructs are described as stable, and to have long-term effects on motivation. Furthermore, both are conceptualized as double-edged swords with positive and negative outcomes: they both include irrational and risky persistence with negative consequences and are related to symptoms of psychic dependence. Because of these similarities, Moeller and Grassinger (2014a) have suggested an integration of the research on commitment and passion within the 'passion and commitment model' (short: com.pass model). In this model, passion is defined as the coincidence of desire and commitment. Desire describes an intense approach motivation accompanied by high affective arousal, and commitment describes the motivation to persist, according to the investment model of commitment (Rusbult et al., 1998) and the related sport commitment model (Scanlan et al., 2009). In line with these concepts, Moeller and Grassinger (2014a; 2014b) distinguish between three subcomponents of commitment: 1) 'continuous intent to engage and persist', 2) 'long-term goals', and 3) 'identification with the activity'. Several studies support the assumed similarity of passion and commitment (Moeller and Grassinger, 2014b). This integration of specific components of passion and commitment within one framework, and the emphasis on general degree rather than types of passion, are the central differences between the com.pass model and the d dual model of passion from Vallerand et al. (2003) described above. Moeller and Grassinger assume that the coincidence of commitment and desire towards an activity might explain why some individuals persist in learning processes that are frustrating, demanding and at least temporarily aversive, and why these individuals nevertheless claim that they are passionate about what they do. This could be one part of the puzzle in research on motivation and persistence of deliberate practice. Future research is needed in order to determine the extent to which specific intrinsic and extrinsic experiences motivate individuals to engage and persist in deliberate practice, and how long-term persistence can be predicted.

## References

Bélanger, J.J., Lafrenière, M.-A. K., Vallerand, R. J., & Kruglanski, A. W. (2012). When Passion Makes the Heart Grow Colder: The Role of Passion in Alternative Goal Suppression. *Journal of Personality and Social Psychology, 104(1),* 126–147. doi:10.1037/a0029679

Bierly III, P. E., Kessler, E. H., & Christensen, E. W. (2000). Organizational learning, knowledge and wisdom. *Journal of Organizational Change Management, 13(6),* 595–618. doi: 10.1108/09534810010378605

Bloom, B. S. (1985). *Developing Talent in Young People.* New York: Ballantine Books.

Bonneville-Roussy, A., Lavigne, G. L., & Vallerand, R. J. (2011). When passion leads to excellence: The case of musicians. *Psychology of Music, 39(1),* 123–138. doi:10.1177/0305735609352441

Bullis, C., Clark, C., & Sline, R. (1993). From passion to commitment: Turning points in romantic relationships. In P.J. Kalbfleisch (Ed.), *Interpersonal communication: Evolving interpersonal relationships* (pp. 113–136). Hillsdale, New Jersey: Lawrence Erlbaum Associates.

Cardon, M. S., Wincent, J., Singh, J., & Drnovsek, M. (2009). The nature and experience of entrepreneurial passion. *Academy of Management Review, 34(3),* 511–532. doi: 10.5465/AMR.2009.40633190

Côté, J., Baker, J., & Abernethy, B. (2003). Practice: A developmental framework for the acquisition of expertise in team sports. In: J. Starkes, K. A. Ericsson (Eds.), *Recent advances in research on sport expertise.* Champaign, IL: Human Kinetics (pp. 89–110).

Crosswell, L., & Elliott, R. G. (2004). Committed teachers, passionate teachers: the dimension of passion associated with teacher commitment and engagement. *AARE 2004 Conference, 28th November – 2nd December,* (pp. 1–12). Melbourne, Australia.

Csikszentmihalyi, M. (1996). *Creativity and the psychology of discovery and invention.* New York: HarperCollins.

Duckworth, A. L., Kirby, T. A., Tsukayama, E., Berstein, H., & Ericsson, K. A. (2011). Deliberate Practice Spells Success: Why Grittier Competitors Triumph at the National Spelling Bee. Social Psychological and Personality Science, 2(2), 174–181. doi:10.1177/1948550610385872

Duckworth, A. L., Peterson, C., Matthews, M. D., & Kelly, D. R. (2007). Grit: Perseverance and Passion for Long-Term Goals. *Journal of Personality and Social Psychology, 92(6),* 1087–1101. doi:10.1037/0022-3514.92.6.1087

Ericsson, K. A., & Charness, N. (1994). Expert performance: Its structure and acquisition. *American Psychologist, 49,* 71–76. doi:10.1037/0003-066X.49.8.725

Ericsson, K., Krampe, R. T., & Tesch-Römer, C. (1993). The role of deliberate practice in the acquisition of expert performance. *Psychological Review, 100,* 363–406. doi:10.1037/0033-295X.100.3.363

Ericsson, K., Roring, R., & Nandagopal, K. (2007). Giftedness and evidence for reproducibly superior performance: An account based on the expert performance framework. *High* Ability Studies, 18(1), 3–56. doi:10.1080/13598130701350593

Ford, P. R., Ward, P., Hodges, N. J., & Williams, A. M. (2009). The role of deliberate practice and play in career progression in sport: the early engagement hypothesis. *High Ability Studies, 20,* 65–75. doi:10.1080/13598130902860721

Fredricks, J. A., Alfeld, C., & Eccles, J. S. (2010). Developing and fostering passions in academic and nonacademic domains. *Gifted Child Quarterly, 54(1),* 18–30. doi:10.1177/0016986209352683

Gembris, H. (2006). The Development of Musical Abilities. In: R. Colwell (Ed.), *MENC Handbook of Musical Cognition and Development.* New York: Oxford University Press (pp. 124–164).

Helsen, W. F., Starkes, J. L., & Hodges, N.J. (1998). Team sports and the theory of deliberate practice. *Journal of Sport & Exercise Psychology, 20,* 12–34.

Hopfl, H. M. (2000). Ordered passions: commitment and hierarchy in the organizational ideas of the Jesuit founders. *Management Learning, 31(3),* 313–329. doi:10.1177/1350507600313003

Károlyi, C. von, & Winner, E. (2005). Extreme giftedness. In R. J. Sternberg, & J. E. Davidson (Eds.), *Conceptions of Giftedness (2nd Ed.)* (pp. 377–394). New York: Cambridge University Press.

Kottler, J. A. (2000). *Doing good: Passion and commitment for helping others.* Philadelphia: Brunner-Routledge.

Le, B., & Agnew, C. R. (2003). Commitment and its theorized determinants: A meta-analysis of the investment model. *Personal Relationships, 10,* 37–57. doi:10.1111/1475-6811.00035

McCann, C., Duckworth, A. L., Roberts, R. D. (2009). Empirical identification of the major facets of Conscientiousness. *Learning and Individual Differences 19*, 451–458. doi:10.1016/j.lindif.2009.03.007

Moeller, J. & Grassinger, R. (2014a). A review of passion concepts and their overlaps with commitment: Opening a can of worms. In: J. Moeller. *Passion as a psychological construct. Conceptualization, assessment, inter-individual variability and long-term stability* (Doctoral dissertation; University of Erfurt, Germany). Retrieved from http://www.db-thueringen.de/servlets/DerivateServlet/Derivate-29036/DissJuliaMoeller.pdf

Moeller, J. & Grassinger, R. (2014b): Measuring passion and commitment with one joint scale: psychometric properties and validity of the com.pass scale. In: J. Moeller. *Passion as a psychological construct. Conceptualization, assessment, inter-individual variability and long-term stability* (Doctoral dissertation; University of Erfurt, Germany). Retrieved from http://www.db-thueringen.de/servlets/DerivateServlet/Derivate-29036/DissJuliaMoeller.pdf

Moraes, L. C., Rabelo, A. S., & Salmela, J. H. (2004). Papel dos Pais no Desenvolvimento de Jovens Futebolistas [The role of parents in the development of young soccer players]. *Psicologia: Reflexão e Crítica, 17(2)*, 211–222. doi:10.1590/S0102-79722004000200009

Oerter, R. (1999). *Psychologie des Spiels [The psychology of play]*. Weinheim und Basel: Beltz Taschenbuch.

Renzulli, J. S., Koehler, J. L., & Fogarty, E. A. (2006). Operation Houndstooth intervention theory: Social capital in today's schools. *Gifted Child Today, 29(1)*, 14–24.

Roberts, B. W., Chernyshenko, O. S., Stark, S., & Goldberg, L. S. (2005). The structure of conscientiousness: an empirical investigation based on seven major personality questionnaires. *Personnel Psychology, 58*, 103–139.

Rusbult, C. E., & Buunk, B. P. (1993). Commitment processes in close relationships: An interdependence analysis. *Journal of Social and Personal Relationships, 10*, 175–204. doi:10.1177/026540759301000202

Rusbult, C.E., Martz, J.M., & Agnew, C.R. (1998). The investment model scale: Measuring commitment level, satisfaction level, quality of alternatives, and investment size. *Personal Relationships, 5*, 357–391. doi:10.1111/j.1475–6811.1998.tb00177.x

Salmela J. H. & Moraes, L. C. (2003). Development of expertise: The role of coaching, families and cultural contexts. In: J. L. Starkes & K. A. Ericsson (Eds.), *Expert performance in sports: Advances in research on sport expertise*. Champaign, IL: Human Kinetics (pp. 275–293).

Salmela-Aro, K. & Upadhyay, D. K. (2012). The Schoolwork Engagement Inventory Energy, Dedication, and Absorption (EDA). *European Journal of Psychological Assessment, 28(1)*, 60–67. doi:10.1027/1015–5759/a000091

Scanlan, T. K., Carpenter, P. J., Schmidt, G. W., Simons, J. P., & Keeler, B. (1993). An Introduction to the Sport Commitment Model. *Journal of Sport and Exercise Psychology, 15(1)*, 1–15.

Scanlan, T. K., Russell, D. G., Magyar, T. M., & Scanlan, L. A. (2009). Project on elite athlete commitment (PEAK): III. An examination of the external validity across gender, and the expansion and clarification of the sport commitment model. *Journal of Sport & Exercise Psychology, 31*, 685–705.

Shernoff, D. J., Csikszentmihaly, M., Schneider, B., & Shernoff, E. S. (2003). Student engagement in high school classrooms from the perspective of flow theory. *School Psychology Quarterly, 18(2)*, 158–176.

Soberlak, P., & Côté, J. (2003). The developmental activities of professional ice hockey players. *Journal of Applied Sport Psychology, 15*, 41–49.

Starkes, J. L. (2000). The road to the expertise: Is practice the only determinant? *International Journal of Sport Psychology, 31 (4)*, 431–451.

Starkes, J. L., Deakin, J., Allard, F., Hodges, N. J., & Hayes, A. (1996). Deliberate practice in sports: What is it anyway? In K. A. Ericsson, *The Road to Excellence: The Acquisition of Expert Performance in the Arts and Sciences, Sports, and Games* (p. 81–106). Mahwah, NJ: Erlbaum Associates.

Sternberg, R. J. (1986). A triangular theory of love. *Psychological Review, 93(2)*, 119–135. doi:10.1037/0033-295X.93.2.119.

Vallerand, R. J. (2008). On the psychology of passion: In search of what makes people's lives most worth living. *Canadian Psychology, 49(1)*, 1–13. doi:10.1037/0708-5591.49.1.1.

Vallerand, R. J., Blanchard, C. M., Mageau, G. A., Koestner, R., Ratelle, C., Léonard, M., et al. (2003). Les passions de l'âme: On obsessive and harmonious passion. *Journal of Personality and Social Psychology, 85(4)*, 756–767. doi:10.1037/0022-3514.85.4.756

Vallerand, R. J., Mageau, G. A., Elliot, A. J., Dumais, A., Demers, M.-A., & Rousseau, F. (2008). Passion and performance attainment in sport. *Psychology of Sport and Exercise, 9(3)*, 373–392. doi:10.1016/j.psychsport.2007.05.003

Vallerand, R. J., Salvy, S.-J., Mageau, G. A., Elliot, A. J., Denis, P. L., Grouzet, F. M., et al. (2007). On the role of passion in performance. *Journal of Personality, 75(3)*, 505–534. doi:10.1111/j.1467-6494.2007.00447.x

Weinzierl, U. (1982). *Carl Seelig, Schriftsteller* [Carl Selig, Writer]. Wien, Löcker.

# Challenging Strong Students in Tertiary Education

## The Case of Karel de Grote University College

*Dries Vervecken and Geert Speltincx*

## Abstract

Higher education is faced with the task of providing high quality education to very heterogeneous student groups differing in their cognitive (e.g., language competence, mathematical competence), psycho-social (e.g., self-efficacy, motivation) as well as their studying and learning (e.g., deep learning style, unregulated learning style) characteristics. Whereas education generally focuses on the level of the "average" student and many efforts are usually made that aim at supporting "weaker" students, "stronger" students remain unchallenged all too often. This contribution illustrates how providers of tertiary education can tackle this challenge by portraying the personalized education programme of Karel de Grote University College in Antwerp, Belgium. More specifically, in this contribution we focus on our alternative tracks designed for so-called strong students.

## Introduction: The Double-Edged Sword of Tertiary Education Democratisation

Participating in and successfully finishing tertiary education is both beneficial for individuals as it is for an entire society and its economy (Barrow & Rouse, 2005; Kyllonen, 2012; OECD, 2011). For instance, statistics from the Organisation for Economic Co-operation and Development (OECD) clearly show that, in all member states, individuals with a tertiary level of education are less likely to be unemployed and generally earn more money compared to individuals without a tertiary level of education. Additional benefits for individuals related to having a tertiary level of education include, besides employment and earnings, greater job satisfaction, better sense of achievement, and working in higher status jobs (e.g., Oreopoulos & Salvanes, 2011). Benefits of tertiary education that exceed the individual level relate to various measures of social outcomes such as electoral participation, political interest, interpersonal trust, volunteering, good health, satisfaction with life and crime reduction (e.g., Coley & Sum, 2012; Grossman, 2006; Lochner & Moretti, 2004; OECD, 2011).

More and more research suggests that this relationship between education and social outcomes is causal (e.g., Card, 1999; Hanushek & Woessmann, 2007). Hence, education can be a relatively cost-effective means of improving health and reducing crime (e.g., Lochner & Moretti, 2004) and for economic growth (e.g., Hanushek & Wössmann, 2007). Also, tertiary education might help individuals develop skills, social status and access to networks that could lead to greater satisfaction with life (OECD, 2011).

Informed by such findings, several governmental efforts have been made to open up tertiary education to the wider public. These efforts are often categorized under the label "Democratisation of education" (Groenez, 2010). As a result, enrolment in tertiary education increased dramatically in past decades (Groenez, 2010; OECD, 2011). Along with the expansion of tertiary education comes an increased heterogeneous composition of student groups. Especially students from layers of society that lack a tradition in tertiary schooling (often students with a lower socioeconomic background) increasingly find their way into tertiary education (e.g., Elchardus, Huyge, Kavadias, Siongers, & Vangoidsenhoven, 2009; Groenez, 2010). This is even more so in Belgium which has a tertiary education system that lacks enrolment restriction (besides having a secondary school degree) or selection process. Hence, there are large differences between students starting tertiary education in variables relevant to academic achievement and retention such as intellect, motivation, self-efficacy, interest, study skills, study attitudes and previous knowledge (Donche & Van Petegem, 2011; Van den Berghe & Kirsch, 2010).

With an instructional praxis that traditionally focuses on the "average student" and programmes aimed at reinforcing the "weaker student", the "strong student" all too often remains unchallenged (Rinn, 2008; Spil & Snoek, 2008). When the demands of the educational environment are set too low and do not meet the student at her or his zone of proximal distance, learning is not optimally facilitated. For instance, the demand, control and support model (DCS-model, Karasek, 1979; Karasek & Theorell, 1990) proposes that high demands (in combination with high levels of control and social support) are crucial determinants for positive learning behaviour and competence development.

Hence, in an attempt to provide an adequate learning environment that puts high demands on "strong students", so-called honours education grew in popularity over the past decades (Sederberg, 2005). Honours education generally consists of some kind of exclusive study route for a select group of students "by which a college or university seeks to meet the educational needs of its ablest and most highly motivated students" (Austin, 1986).

In summarizing this introductory section, the democratisation of tertiary education is like a double-edged sword: on the one hand a growing number of young people (often with lower social backgrounds) gain access to tertiary education which increases the individual's professional and social chances and boosts democracy, public health as well as economy on a societal level; on the other hand, increasingly heterogeneous student groups make it difficult to organize tertiary education in such a way that "strong" students are maximally challenged as well. Unchallenging learning environments are detrimental for academic achievement (e.g., gain in competences) and retention. More and more providers of tertiary education organize some kind of honours education in order to meet the needs of so-called strong students.

## The Personalized Education Programme of Karel de Grote University College (KdG)

The personalized education programme is KdG's answer to the challenges contemporary tertiary education is faced with. Figure 1 visualizes the programme schematically. The general idea is that we make efforts to increase students' performance and retention rates on two levels (course and curriculum) and focus on three stages in the educational process (input, throughput and output). During the *input*-stage, we want to orientate our students (i.e., getting the right students in the right programme). Assessments that map their cognitive (e.g., language competence, mathematical competence, prior knowledge), psycho-social (e.g., self-efficacy, motivation) as well as their studying and learning (e.g., deep learning style, unregulated learning style) characteristics are crucial at this stage. Next, in the *throughput*-stage, we use the assessed information to provide a fitting environment in terms of demands placed on, and support given to, a student. By doing so, we strive to maximize the retention likelihood for as many students as possible. In the *output*-stage, efforts are made that aim at boosting students' development in basic, advanced and personally-chosen competence areas.

Applied to our "strong" students, the personalized education programme at KdG tries to identify so-called strong students very early on, surround them with an extra-challenging environment to keep them motivated and to facilitate an optimal growth in several competence domains.

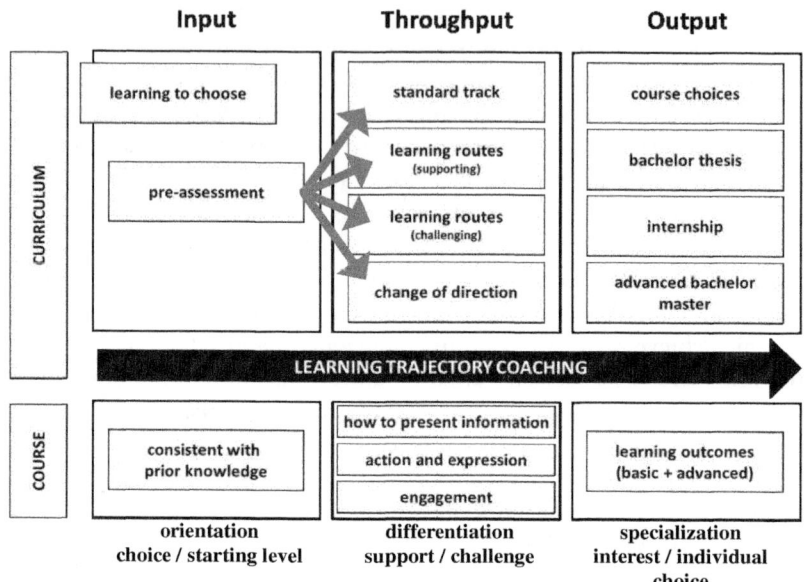

Figure 1:    *A schematic visualization of the personalized education programme at Karel De Grote University College*

## "Strong" Students

Talking about "weak", "average" and "strong" students is tricky as these words have an evaluative nature which depends, of course, on the norms used to define "weak-average-strong". These norms may vary quiet substantially depending, among other aspects, on time and culture. Traditionally, policy makers and researchers focussed on high school Grade Point Average (GPA) and standardized test scores. Meta-studies demonstrate that a combination of these two predictors account for about 25% of variance of first year GPA (see ACT, 1997; Kuncel, Crede, & Thomas, 2007; Robbins, Lauver, Le, Davis, Lagley, & Carlstrom, 2004, for reviews). Recently, other meta-studies have demonstrated that, besides traditional intellectual measures (e.g., GPA, scholastic assessment test), psycho-social factors (e.g., self-efficacy, motivation) (see Robbins et al., 2004) and study behaviour (e.g., skills, attitudes) (see, Crede, & Kunzel, 2008) are also significant predictors for academic achievement. Hence, a "strong" student (in terms of academic achievement and retention) possesses not only high intellectual capabilities but also high psycho-social levels and strong study behaviour.

## Projects to Challenge "Strong" Students

Research on our own students confirms the above-mentioned tendencies: (1) in KdG a substantial group of students feels unchallenged by the current curriculum (De Coninck, 2010) and (2) cognitive, psycho-social and study-behavioural factors are significant predictors of academic achievement for students at KdG University College (Kyndt, Donche, Mertens, & Gijbels, 2013). One way we strive to challenge our "strong" students is by providing special tracks of which we will now briefly highlight two.

### Tailor-Made Education for "Strong" Students at the Teacher Trainee Center

The first programme we wish to describe is called "tailor made education for strong students" which will be implemented in 2013–2014. This track has been designed for "strong" bachelors in education, the so-called teacher trainees (i.e., kindergarten, primary and secondary education) since we detected the need of a group of students who feel unchallenged by the current curriculum. To enable us to guide the right students into this track, we first ran an inferential statistical analysis with a large group of teacher trainees to identify predictors of successful students (i.e., retention and performance). On the basis of these results, we were able to identify a cluster of characteristics typical for "strong" students at our teacher-trainee center. In line with general findings on academic achievement (see Crede, & Kuncel, 2008; Kuncel et al., 2007; Robbins et al., 2004 for reviews), our "strong" students do indeed possess a cluster of cognitive (e.g., mathematical competence), psycho-social (e.g., self-efficacy) and studying and learning (e.g., lack of regulation) characteristics.

Although the track itself is integrated in the standard curriculum (i.e., same minimal learning outcomes have to be achieved), students are able to progress much faster through it. In order to achieve this goal, many courses do not have to be followed in class but are replaced by workplace and distance-learning tasks creating a very flexible learning environment. The track builds on three main principles: (1) accelerating courses, so that "strong" students are able to progress faster and have time to (2) deepen the basic contents by means of doing applied research and (3) broaden their knowledge and experiences by visiting courses of personal interest in different disciplines in different departments. This personalized track relies heavily on students' self-directedness, emphasizes workplace learning and applied research so that theory and practice are strongly intertwined.

*Differentiation in French Language Courses in the Car Technology Bachelor Study Programme*

The second programme we wish to describe is called "advanced French communication". The car technology sector in Belgium is highly concentrated in the Brussels area and has strong connections with French car brands (e.g. Citroën, Peugeot, Renault). Therefore, the sector is for a major part French-speaking, whereas our students in Antwerp (situated in the Flemish part of Belgium) speak Dutch. In KdG University College, we decided to challenge the "strong" students on their French-speaking skills as a preparation for their possible internship and later job opportunities in Brussels or France. In their second bachelor year, all students start with an assessment of French. The twenty five best students are engaged in an extracurricular programme that focuses on self-reliance in a French-speaking context. This programme substitutes for the standard French course. The extracurricular programme is organized by a Center for Adult Education (in close cooperation with our own French teacher). The lessons take place at our own campus but consist of twice as much contact hours. What motivates these "strong" students to follow the intensive course instead of the standard French course? First of all, they get prepared for a real need in their own field. Second, the "strong" students work on their skills and feel challenged, something that would hardly happen in the standard course. Third, these students are guaranteed to receive a credit just for actively taking part in the course for a whole year. In fact, they already proved that they commanded the minimal required competences on the assessment at the start of the course. In this way, "strong" students are confronted with real challenges, whereas the weaker students receive more intensive support in the standard course.

## Discussion: Effective and Efficient?

This brief contribution illustrates with two examples that KdG, like many other tertiary education institutions worldwide, organizes separate study tracks aiming at challenging "stronger students". Indeed, from a theoretical point of view, it seems legitimate to provide extra-challenging tracks in order to maximize growth in competence for "strong" students, as high demands (in combination with freedom to explore and with adequate support) are crucial for learning behaviour (DCS-model, Karasek, 1979; Karasek & Theorell, 1990). However, empirical support in favour of so-called honours education is scarce and rather unconvincing (see Slavin, Coladarci, & Pratt, 2008). Also, from an organisational point of view, providing extra-study tracks (i.e., honours education) can be expensive and time-consuming, hence not realistic for every institution.

Against this background, it seems important to start a more profound discussion of the how and why we wish to combine the task of democratising tertiary education with challenging every single student at her or his level of proximal distance, and where "strong students" fit into this picture. Honours education largely focuses on separating "strong" students from other students in order to maximize competence development, whereas other approaches aim at preserving the heterogeneous group composition. For instance, differentiated instruction focuses on providing adequate instruction that takes differences in students' readability, interest, ability and learning styles into account (see Chamberlin & Powers, 2010; Tomlinson, 2005).

At KdG, we are currently setting up some experiments to investigate whether differentiated instruction in tertiary education is a more effective means than traditional instruction and a more efficient means than honours education in fostering competence development in all students. The importance of testing innovative educational interventions on their effectiveness and efficiency in relation to the development of high quality education cannot be stressed enough. Only by working evidence based we can find out what really works in higher education and thereby create learning environments that truly evoke excellence.

## References

ACT (1997). *ACT assessment technical manual.* Iowa City, IA: Author. Ajzen, I., & Fishbein, M. (1977). Attitude–behavior relations: A theoretical analysis and review of empirical research. *Psychological Bulletin, 34,* 888–918.

Austin, C. G. (1986). Orientation to honors education. In P.G. Friedman & R.C. Jenkins Friedman (Eds.), *Fostering academic excellence through honors programs* (pp. 5–16). San Francisco CA: Jossey Bass.

Barrow, L., & Rouse, C. E. (2005). Does college still pay? *The Economists' Voice, 2,* 1–8.

Berghe, W. van den, & Kirsch, M. (2010). Werkdruk van de lectoren in de Vlaamse hogescholen. Syntheserapport. [Work pressure of lectors in Flemish university colleges]. Downloaded at 21 January 2011: http://regcom.hogent.be/dl/Werkdruk%20van%20de%20lectoren%20in%20de%20Vlaamse%20hogescholen_syntheserapport.pdf

Card, D. (1999). The causal effect of education on earnings. In O. Ashenfelter & D. Card (Eds.), *Handbook of Labor Economics* (pp. 1801–1863). Amsterdam, Netherlands: Elsevier Science.

Chamberlin, M. T., & Powers, R. A. (2010). The promise of differentiated instruction for enhancing the mathematical understandings of college students. *Teaching Mathematics and Its Applications, 29*, 113–139.

Coley, R., & Sum, A. (2012). *Fault lines in our democracy: Civic knowledge, voting behavior, and civic engagement in the United States.* Princeton, N.J.: Educational Testing Service, Center for Research on Human Capital and Education, Research and Development.

Crede, M., & Kuncel, N. R. (2008). Study Habits, Skills, and Attitudes: The Third Pillar Supporting Collegiate Academic Performance. *Perspectives on Psychological Science, 3*, 425–453.

De Coninck, L. (2010). Onderzoeksrapport: Een extra opleidingstraject voor sterke studenten. Bevraging van doelgroepstudenten. [Niet-gepubliceerd rapport Departement Lerarenopleiding, Karel de Grote-hogeschool]

Donche, V., & Van Petegem, P. (2011). The relationship between entry characteristics, learning style and academic achievement of college freshmen. In M. Poulson (Ed.), *Higher education: Teaching, internationalisation and student issues.* New York: Nova Science Publishers.

Elchardus, M., Huyge, E., Kavadias, D., Siongers, J., & Vangoidsenhoven, G. (2009). Leraars. Profiel van een beroepsgroep [Teachers. The profile of a professional group]. Tielt: Lannoo Campus.

Groenez, S. (2010). Onderwijsexpansie en -democratisering in Vlaanderen. [Expansion and democratisation in education] *Tijdschrift voor Sociologie, 31*, 199–238.

Grossman, M. (2006), Education and Nonmarket Outcomes. In E. A. Hanushek & F. Welsch (Eds.), *Handbook of the Economics of Education.* Amsterdam: Elsevier.

Hanushek, E. A., & Woessmann, L. (2007). The Role of Education Quality for Economic Growth. *World Bank Policy Research Working Paper No. 4122.* Available at SSRN: http://ssrn.com/abstract=960379.

Karasek, R. A. (1979). Job demands, job decision latitude, and mental strain: Implications for job redesign. *Administrative Science Quarterly, 24*, 285–308.

Karasek, R. A., & Theorell, T. (1990). Stress, productivity and reconstruction of working life. New York: Basic Books.

Kuncel, N.R., Crede, M., & Thomas, L.L. (2007). A comprehensive meta-analysis of the predictive validity of the Graduate Management Admission Test (GMAT) and undergraduate grade point average (UGPA). *Academy of Management Learning and Education, 6*, 51–68.

Kyllonen, P. C. (2012). The importance of higher education and the role of non-cognitive attributes in college success. *Pensamiento Educativo. Revista de Investigación Educacional Latinoamericana, 49*, 84–100.

Kyndt, E., Donche, V., Mertens, E., & Gijbels, D. (2013). Leer- en regulatiestrategieën van studenten die de lerarenopleiding aanvangen. [Learning- and regulation strategies]. Manuscript submitted for publication.

Lochner, L., & Moretti, E. (2004). The Effect of Education on Crime: Evidence from Prison Inmates, Arrests, and Self-Reports. *The American Economic Review, 94*, 155–189.

Oreopoulos, P., & Salvanes, K. G. (2011). Priceless: The nonpecuniary benefits of schooling. *Journal of Economic Perspectives, 25*, 159–184.

Organisation for Economic Co-operation and Development (2011). *Education at a Glance 2011: Highlights.* Paris, France: OECD Publishing.

Rinn, A. (2008). Pre-College Experiences and Characteristics of Gifted Students. In: L. Clark & J. Zubizarreta (Eds.), *Inspiring Exemplary Teaching and Learning: Perspectives on Teaching Academically Talented College Students*, (pp. 9–18). Birmingham, AL: National Collegiate Honors Council Publication.

Robbins, S.B., Lauver, K., Le, H., Davis, D., Langley, R., & Carlstrom, A. (2004). Do psychosocial and study skill factors predict college outcomes? A meta-analysis. *Psychological Bulletin, 130*, 261–288.

Sederberg, P. (2005). Characteristics of the contemporary honors college. A descriptive analysis of a survey of NCHC member colleges. *Journal of the National Collegiate Honors Council, 6*, 121–136.

Slavin, C., Coladarci, T., & Pratt, P.A. (2008). Is student participation in an honors program related to retention and graduation rates? *Journal of the National Collegiate Honors Council*, pp. 59–69.

Spil, S., & Snoek, M. (2008). Excellentie in Educatie. [Excellence in Education]. Amsterdam: Educatieve Hogeschool van Amsterdam. Downloaded at 16 December 2010: http://www.kenniscentrumonderwijsopvoeding.hva.nl/content/kenniscentrum/lereneninnoveren/documenten/eindverslag_sanne-spil.doc

Tomlinson, C. A. (2005). Grading and differentiation: Paradox or good practice? *Theory into Practice, 44*, 262–269.

# The Challenge of Writing a PhD Proposal in Honours (Undergraduate) Education

## A Group Project as Significant Learning Experience

*Fred Wiegant, Karin Scager, Anton Peeters and Johannes Boonstra*

### Introduction

Over the past 5 years, the Advanced Cell Biology course at the University College Utrecht has increasingly gained the reputation of being challenging but rewarding in terms of gains in knowledge as well as in the development of important academic skills, including cooperation and critical thinking. Recently, the different elements of this student-driven advanced undergraduate course were described (Wiegant, Scager & Boonstra, 2011), as well as the challenges this course entails (Scager, Akkerman, Pilot, & Wubbels, 2012a; Scager, Akkerman, Boonstra, Pilot, Wiegant, & Wubbels, 2012b). The aim of the current paper is to summarize how students experience motivation and learning gains in relation to (perceived) challenge and skills required to work on the complex assignments of this course. According to Csikszentmihalyi (1975), learning will be most efficient when students are motivated and when the challenge of assignments is in balance with the skills students have developed (Figure 1). In previous years, students reported that, during some phases of this course, the challenge was much higher than their actual skills thus preventing them from solving the presented problems. Nevertheless, in the end they were able to come up with high-quality projects that impressed a jury of experts. The relevant question is therefore whether an over-challenge of (honours) students affects their motivation and learning outcome. In the present paper, three questions are central:

1) How, throughout the course, do students experience the balance between levels of challenge and ability?
2) In cases when (honours) students experience an over-challenge, and thus an imbalance between perceived challenge and ability, how does this affect their motivation and perceived learning?
3) What factors constitute challenge in this course?

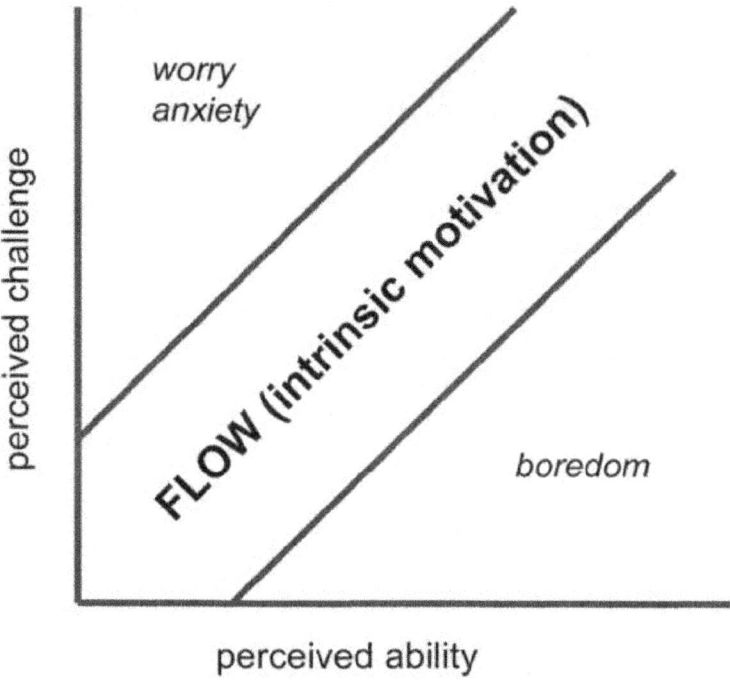

*Figure 1:    Flow model (adapted from Scager et al., 2012a).*

## Course Set-Up and Student Activities

In this course, three small teams of students (4–5 students each) cooperate intensively to formulate three PhD proposals within an overarching theme. Since this course is student-led, the students make all decisions, the instructors having a facilitating role, including asking critical questions and providing feedback. Most importantly, the instructors are not involved in making decisions concerning the various elements of the research proposals.

The following phases and aims are discerned in this course: (1) Orientation: Students will get familiar with reading, presenting and discussing primary papers in the field in which research proposals will be formulated; (2) Research question: In this phase, a gap in the knowledge needs to be identified so that relevant research questions can be formulated that are aimed at moving beyond what is currently known; (3) Research methods: in which a set of appropriate techniques in the field of molecular and cellular biology has to be identified in order to answer the research questions. This phase, in which experts are contacted and laboratories are visited in order to get a thorough understanding of advanced research technologies, is usually experienced as very challenging; (4) Writing and defending: To complete this course, the students present and defend their research programme and PhD proposals before a jury of experts.

During this fifteen week course, the groups of students cooperate intensively in order to achieve these goals. Throughout the course, there are many presentations and discussions on ideas and progress on the different elements of the research project and in the formulation of the research proposals. A programme leader, together with project leaders, is responsible for the coherence of the programme and to prevent overlap between projects. Critical readers provide peer feedback on each other's projects and a layout team is responsible for composing a report and printing the research programme. An important factor in achieving cooperative learning and team coherence is the requirement that all students are responsible for the content of the project and that all students need to be able to answer critical questions on their project asked throughout the course and by the jury members at the end of the course.

## Student Experience

All thirteen students were interviewed individually in the week after the course ended, in a 45-minute semi-structured interview that was audio-taped, using the so-called storyline method (Beijaard, Van Driel, & Verloop, 1999). Students were informed that their individual statements would not be discussed with their teachers, and that their experiences and direct quotations would be used anonymously in subsequent reports. All students gave their consent. Four themes were central to the interviews: students' learning, their motivation, their perceived ability, and perceived challenge. The perceived challenge was conceptualized as the level of difficulty experienced by students. An example of a 'storyline' graph from one of the students is presented in Figure 2. The mean scores of challenge, ability, motivation and learning of all students are shown in Figure 3.

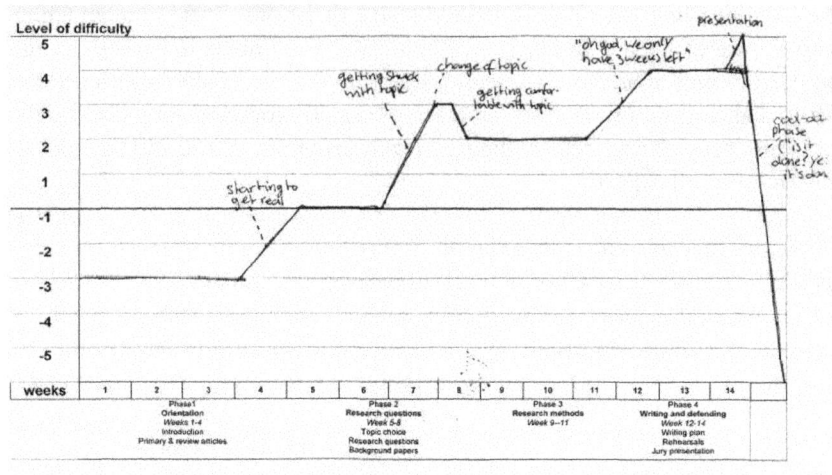

*Figure 2:*   *Example of a 'storyline' graph of one of the students.*

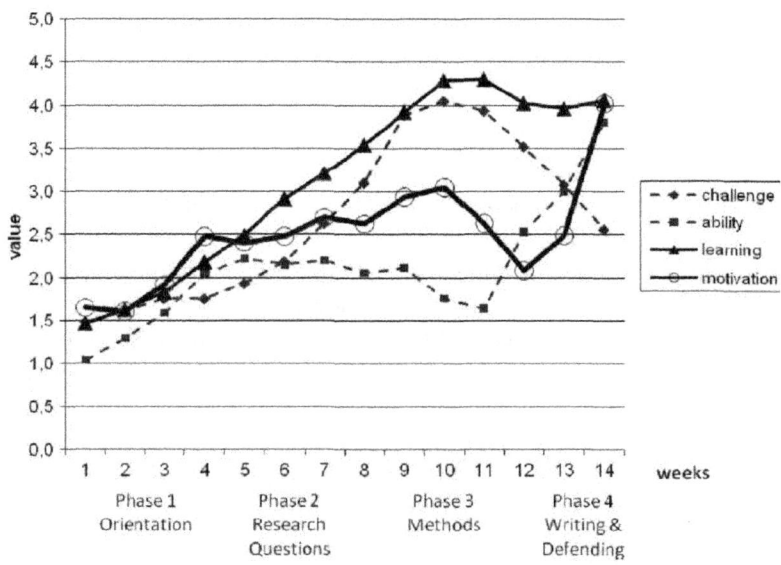

*Figure 3:*   *Means of the graphs for 'learning', 'motivation', 'challenge', and*
            *'ability' throughout the 14 weeks (adapted from Scager et al., 2012a).*

In the first two phases, students experienced a balance between challenge and ability. However, in the third phase, where they needed to identify appropriate techniques, the challenge was much higher than what they considered themselves as being able to cope with (Figure 3). In this period, frustration appeared to occur frequently and they indicated missing guidance by the instructors. Nevertheless, students continued to learn a great deal and finally came up with an excellent product. The level of quality the students were able to produce as well as the command of the subject matter expressed in the discussions during the defense before the jury impressed jury members without exception.

## Does Over-Challenge Affect Motivation and Perceived Learning?

Interestingly, students' perceived learning was at its peak in the period in which the challenge level most exceeded the ability level (Figure 3). According to Csikszentmihalyi (1975), if challenge exceeds perceived skills, people feel worried and anxious, which are negative emotions that decrease feelings of flow and intrinsic motivation. Especially in the third phase of this course, students reported a significant difference between their perceived ability level and the level of challenge. During this phase, many students experienced feelings of worry and frustration. Their motivation graphs fluctuated heavily during this period. A closer inspection of students' stories about their motivation, however, revealed that, although their enjoyment decreased during these periods of decline in motivation (as shown in their graphs), their drive did not weaken, and their efforts even increased. Students apparently interpreted the concept of motivation as a combination of drive, which they emphasized in their stories, and enjoyment, which guided their graphs. Students' learning graphs were at their peak during this period of fluctuating motivation. This finding is unexpected, given that negative emotions have been understood to impede intrinsic motivation (Csikszentmihalyi 1975; Meyer & Turner 2006). An explanation for students' increased efforts, despite a lack of enjoyment, could be found in the support that was received from their peer group. Firstly, students in their project groups cooperated in a face-to-face mode, reading, writing, emailing and discussing together. In the busiest phase of the course, students kept working most evenings, and all through the weekend. Face-to-face settings for group work have been found to support intrinsic motivation significantly better than virtual group work (Järvela, Järvenoja & Veermans, 2008). Secondly, the groups could have developed team coherence and a sense of collective efficacy. Collective efficacy – a group's shared belief in their collective power to produce desired results – affects group motivational efforts, and engenders persistence in the face of difficulties (Goncalo, Polman & Maslach, 2010). Thirdly, several students reported that the social support of their team members helped them during the moments of crisis they experienced during the difficult phases in the course. Accordingly, we assume that social support can prevent or overcome situations of over-challenge and the accompanying feelings of worry and frustration. This assumption is in agreement with the findings of Bakker and Demerouti (2006), who studied factors that cause or prevent burnout in work settings and found social support to be one of the most important factors that balance out high job demands.

In short, although the enjoyment associated with intrinsic motivation and flow was not there in the difficult phase of the course, drive and persistence were maintained due to the social support of the group. In this respect, group cohesion keeps teams together and creates shared responsibility for success during stressful periods.

## Challenging Factors

Three factors could be distilled from the aspects that students mentioned as challenging elements in this course: 1) The complexity of the task. A number of elements in this course are experienced as complex, such as the novelty of working with primary research articles, the specialized field of knowledge in cell biology, the dynamics of the process in which a large number of decisions needed to be made, and the conflicting demands of writing a research project that should be novel, relevant and feasible. In Csikszentmihalyi's model, complexity is related to challenge; 2) The lack of guidance by instructors was experienced as very challenging and, at times, frustrating, although, in the end, students realized that this was the best way to learn most during the process. Looking back at the course, in all students feelings of pride and satisfaction replaced earlier frustration. 3) The high expectations that teachers had, but also the willingness of students to achieve a higher quality than the groups of previous years, were experienced as additional challenging factors.

## Discussion and Conclusion

The combination of the complex task, the lack of teacher guidance, and the high expectations, increased students' worry and insecurity during the course. In hindsight, however, these factors made up the challenge, and increased students' efforts and perceived learning. The results of this study allow us to propose a different view of Csikszentmihalyi's (1975) flow-model, one that is specifically interesting in the context of teaching high-ability students. The processes students described led to the notion that the balance between challenge and ability was lacking during a period of several weeks during this course; students were over-challenged and experienced various emotions in the process. Positive emotions were experienced when students made progress, whereas maximum effort and (perceived) learning were experienced when the perceived challenge exceeded the level of ability the most, resulting in feelings of being worried and frustrated. These findings indicate that the balance between ability and challenge is vital for enjoyment, but not necessarily for effort, persistence, and learning. We recommend further research to analyze whether the three-factor model of challenge (complexity, lack of guidance and high expectations) also applies to challenging courses in which students have to work either individually or in groups with a larger number of students, and whether it applies to other challenging university courses in different disciplines.

Based on our analysis, it can be concluded that: 1) students appeared to learn most during the phases in which they were 'over'-challenged, 2) (temporary) frustration did not appear to be detrimental, and 3) less guidance by the instructor was beneficial for learning. Students indicated that intensive cooperation within the group allowed them to cope with all challenges. Together, they helped each other out of dips and achieved a product of which they were proud. Cooperative learning and team cohesion might therefore be the explanation for the fact that honours students performed amazingly well even in situations where challenge and skills are no longer in balance.

# References

Bakker, A. B., & Demerouti, E. (2006). The job demands-resources model: State of the art. *Journal of Managerial Psychology, 22,* 309–328.

Beijaard, D., Driel, J. van, & Verloop, N. (1999). Evaluation of story-line methodology in research on teachers' practical knowledge. *Studies in Educational Evaluation, 25,* 47–62.

Csikszentmihalyi, M. (1975). *Beyond boredom and anxiety: Experiencing flow in work and play.* San Francisco: Jossey-Bass.

Goncalo, J. A., Polman, E., & Maslach, C. (2010). Can confidence come too soon? Collective efficacy, conflict and group performance over time. *Organizational Behavior and Human Decision Processes, 113,* 13–24.

Järvela, S., Järvenoja, H., & Veermans, M. (2008). Understanding the dynamics of motivation in socially shared learning. *International Journal of Educational Research, 47,* 122–135.

Meyer, D. K., & Turner, J. C. (2006). Re-conceptualizing emotion and motivation to learn in classroom contexts. *Educational Psychological Review, 18,* 377–390.

Scager, K., Akkerman, S. F., Pilot, A., & Wubbels, T. (2012a). Challenging high ability students. *Studies in Higher Education* (iFirst), 1–21.

Scager, K., Akkerman, S., Boonstra, J., Pilot, A. Wiegant, F., & Wubbels, T. (2012b). Uitdagen van excellente studenten. *Onderzoek van Onderwijs, 41,* 16–21.

Wiegant, F. A. C., Scager, K., & Boonstra, J. (2011). An undergraduate course to bridge the gap between textbooks and scientific research. *CBE-Life Sciences Education, 10,* 83–94.

# Key Components when Teaching for Excellence[1]

*Marca Wolfensberger*

The overarching research question for the book *Teaching for Excellence* was formulated as follows: what are the key components of honours pedagogy and how do these translate into honours teaching practice? The reasons for asking this question were twofold. First, few empirical studies have been conducted on honours teaching within higher education with the aim to systematically uncover, analyze and describe honours pedagogies (see, for instance, Clark & Zubizarreta, 2008; Cosgrove, 2004; Rind, 2007; Shushok, 2002). To my knowledge, the present study is one of the first attempts to systematically investigate which teaching approaches are appropriate for honours education. That is why the research question has academic relevance. Secondly, the question serves a practical need. Honours education is a relatively new phenomenon in Europe (Wolfensberger, in press). This has created a need for empirical research on honours pedagogies, the outcomes of which may be used in faculty development, training and coaching of honours teachers.

Honours programmes are specially designed for gifted and motivated students who are willing and able to do more than they could in a regular programme. In the search for *key components of honours pedagogy*, the first step was to explore relevant bodies of literature: the practical and often case-based descriptive literature about teaching practices in American honours programmes; the empirical and theoretical literature about giftedness, with a specific focus on implications for teaching; and an important strand of theoretical and empirical work in motivational theory – self-determination theory – which can be linked to honours education because of the above-average motivation of honours students and the importance of understanding teaching and learning strategies that support and build upon such high motivation. By doing so, honours pedagogies have been analyzed through the lenses of three relevant fields of knowledge.

On the basis of this literature review, I hypothesized that at least three dimensions of honours education are important: *creating a sense of community* within honours programmes; enhancing *academic competence*; and offering *freedom* to honours students in their learning. After the completion of the literature review, which was reported in the book, I was able to specify the

---

1 The article is a slightly adapted version of the seventh chapter of Wolfensberger's book, *Teaching for Excellence – Honors Pedagogies Revealed*.

research question for the empirical part of the study in the following way: *to what extent do honours teachers approach their teaching differently – with regard to creating community, enhancing academic competence and offering freedom – with honours students compared to regular students?*

Data were collected from honours teachers from multiple institutions that work with different models for their honours programmes. This diversity allowed me to develop a rich empirical basis on which to describe honours pedagogies in terms of three approaches.

In the present study, the three approaches were studied from the perspectives of various informants. Using a mixed methodology, questionnaires were distributed among honours teachers in the United States of America (n=127) and honours teachers in the Netherlands (n=313), and interviews were conducted with honours teachers in the U.S.A. (n=30). The same questionnaire was used to survey both American and Dutch university honours teachers.

The survey research among American and Dutch honours teachers gave evidence that the three teaching approaches – creating community, enhancing academic competence and offering freedom – are indeed more relevant in honours settings than in regular higher education. The interviews with American honours teachers provided a wealth of additional information about the concrete teaching strategies and forms of behaviour that teachers say they apply in order to create the conditions of community, enhanced academic competence, and freedom.

The answers to the research questions are treated in the next section. In the discussion section, the findings of this study are presented, with special attention to questions for further research, and the practical implications and applicability of the outcomes.

## Key Components of Honours Pedagogy

My approach to the body of literature was a mix of deduction and induction. Having read the potentially relevant honours literature, it was evident that most of the teaching practices treated there could be classified under three headings: 'community', 'academic competence' and 'freedom'. These three concepts were then used for organizing the literature review.

First, I examined the American literature on honours in higher education. There is a substantial body of well-documented reports on good practice. While the number of empirically-grounded publications is growing, rarely do these empirical studies deal with teaching practices, however indeed, most honours studies are descriptive, based on experience and the examination of a single institution.

The next step was to analyze the literature on giftedness, a field with a solid theoretical basis and ample empirical output. Publications in this field contain not only definitions of concepts such as excellence but also extensive studies on instructional models. Furthermore, the giftedness literature queries whether it is legitimate to differentiate between teaching strategies for honours and regular students, mainly at the level of pre-university education. Studies reveal that gifted students, on the whole, have different characteristics than regular students in the same age range and need distinct learning opportunities. According to several state-of-the-art publications, relatively few studies have dealt with the teacher qualifications and teaching approaches for working with gifted students in higher education. Nevertheless, I was able to link outcomes of giftedness research to the teaching approaches I had identified in the literature and subsequently adopted as the three dimensions of honours teaching: creating community, enhancing academic competence, and offering freedom.

Teachers of the gifted should have knowledge about gifted students that engenders effective teacher-student relationships. This corresponds to the dimension of creating community. To be successful with gifted learners, teachers must be scholars, offer enrichment, have a passion for their discipline and be able to support complex learning by offering escalating opportunities. Altogether, this profile resembles the dimension of enhancing academic competence. Gifted learners bloom through independent projects. Accordingly, teachers of the academically gifted need to adopt flexible approaches in providing content and encouraging learning. This requirement echoes the dimension of offering freedom.

Thirdly, I turned to motivational theory, specifically self-determination theory, for further theoretical underpinning of the three teaching approaches of honours teaching. Self-determination theory has proven useful in explaining the variation in students' learning strategies, performance and persistence, even though self-determination theory was not specifically developed with (university) education or honours teaching in mind. The theory indicates that the extent to which teachers support students' motivation is positively associated with strong student performance. According to self-determination theory, three basic psychological needs should be supported: relatedness, competence and autonomy. If a student's need for all three is not satisfied, one's self-motivation, self-determination and wellbeing will be jeopardized. The need for relatedness, or feeling connected with significant others, resonates with the notion of a sense of community. The need for competence refers to the desire for increasing mastery and for a sense of satisfaction in exercising and extending one's capabilities. As such, it resembles our dimension of enhancing academic competence. Feelings of competence, however, will not increase one's intrinsic motivation unless a student perceives the educational context as being supportive of autonomy. This motivating effect could arise, for instance, by being allowed more space to self-organize one's studies or choose one's subject. Clearly, this is related to the research dimension of offering freedom.

Thus, the literature survey brought to light the three dimensions of honours pedagogy: creating community, enhancing academic competence, and offering freedom. Each dimension was then coordinated with a teaching approach, and each approach was assigned a cluster of teaching strategies to put it into practice. Those three teaching approaches and the clusters of teaching strategies related to them partly overlap and interconnect. It was a deliberate decision to define teaching strategies very broadly. There is wide variation among teaching strategies needed for honours classes. Indeed, as the literature suggests, and our research data confirm, honours teaching is not just about formal didactic activities (for example, giving feedback). It is equally about behaviour that reflects the teacher's personality (for example, being friendly, accessible or enthusiastic). As this study shows, experienced honours teachers apply strategies as part of a more comprehensive practice: they try to create conditions conducive to optimal learning for their honours students.

The framework for an honours pedagogy that is presented in this study appears to resonate with the daily practice of honours teachers, notwithstanding the differences in their backgrounds. Whether they are experienced honours teachers or novices; coming from different learning environments such as community colleges or research universities; or coming from an American or European context – all make a clear distinction between honours teaching and regular teaching. Are there signature procedures for teaching and learning within honours, like one's name written in one's own handwriting, that are conducted in similar ways, by all honours teachers and from one institution to the next? The answer is 'yes'. Broadly speaking, teachers agree on the teaching strategies related to the three dimensions of honours teaching: creating community, enhancing academic competence and offering freedom. On that basis, we can now turn to a discussion of the outcomes of the study, taking each of these three key pedagogical concepts in turn.

## Creating Community

The three bodies of academic literature that were used in chapter 2 of *Teaching for Excellence – honors pedagogies revealed*, allowed us to formulate three specific clusters of teaching strategies and forms of teacher behaviour under the broader approach of creating community. These three clusters, which were labeled with various words instead of one key term, are the following:

- *Interaction, (peer) feedback, active learning*: strategies for building an effective relationship between teacher and honours students and among honours students.
- *Encouragement, joy, inspiration*: strategies and forms of teacher behaviour that create a positive and supportive spirit.
- *Availability, interest in students, commitment*: strategies and forms of teacher behaviour that make the teacher part of the community in a practical and a personal sense.

The three teaching clusters related to the approach of 'creating community' formed the basis for constructing questionnaire items about this specific teaching approach. According to the survey findings, American honours teachers apply community-enhancing teaching strategies significantly more often with their honours students than in their regular classes. They believe that it is crucial to invite honours students to participate actively in class and that it is important for a teacher to be interested in honours students as individuals. The five-item community scale (chapters 5 and 6 of *Teaching for Excellence – honors pedagogies revealed*) revealed a significant difference between honours and regular teaching practices, and not only among the American teachers. Dutch honours teachers, however, are less inclined towards community-enhancing teaching strategies and forms of behaviour than American honours teachers.

The interviewers did not explicitly ask about creating community as a teaching approach, since this would have limited the opportunities to get an impression of what teachers themselves would come up with. Even so, 24 of the 30 American teachers spontaneously brought up the topic of creating community. They stressed the importance of their own engagement, and that of other honours teachers, in jointly creating a supportive atmosphere. Thanks to the reciprocal relationships between teachers and students, both parties can learn from and stimulate each other. Teachers think they know their honours students well enough to encourage them to follow their own path. Teachers consider it important that students know them well enough to ask for advice and support. Furthermore, teachers foster initiative by offering all kinds of opportunities for students to stand up and develop leadership skills. In short, teachers give students the opportunity to play their own role in the process of collaborative learning and creating an honours community.

Moreover, teachers stress the importance of institutional conditions that support the creation of an honours community. For instance, a supportive board, well-trained honours staff, and a physical honours space are considered necessary.

## Enhancing Academic Competence

Three clusters of teaching strategies related to the dimension of academic competence emerged from the review of the literature:

- *Multi- and interdisciplinary thinking, multiple perspectives*: strategies for providing context, both academic and societal, and supporting connective thinking.
- *Scholarly teaching, academic depth, involvement in research*: strategies that support the development of in-depth analytical thinking and of research skills.
- *Challenging learning tasks, difficulty, and acceleration*: the range of strategies that create challenge, both in quality (difficulty, complexity) and in quantity (pacing, size of tasks).

Teachers, from the U.S.A. as well as from the Netherlands, show a slight inclination to apply strategies for enhancing academic competence to a greater extent in honours classes than in regular classes. But overall, the analyses imply that enhancing academic competence is important for honours as well as for regular education. However, the findings reveal that the related teaching strategies to do so for honours and for regular teaching differ. Crossing traditional educational borders, offering interdisciplinary content and assigning undergraduate research are important strategies within honours. Teachers see breadth, context and perspective as important for enhancing academic competence in honours classes. Within honours classes, academic competence can also be displayed through undergraduate research and challenging assignments. For regular classes, it is considered relatively more important for a teacher, in order to enhance academic competence among students, to know his or her subject well and to explain it well.

The interviews with the American teachers show that the teachers' assumption that honours students can think at higher levels is paramount for productive honours classes. Classroom activities that stimulate *critical and independent* thinking as well as creative thinking are considered especially important. During the interviews, the American teachers also mentioned that assignments and other learning tasks should be challenging, since this leads to engagement and a richer and deeper conversation in honours classes. Independent projects, capstone projects and thesis work are seen as essential within honours. *Research teaching* and undergraduate honours research are described as important vehicles for students' cognitive growth as well as for their personal and professional development. In light of these findings, there is good reason to add a fourth cluster of teaching strategies to those already given above: those that promote critical, independent and creative thinking.

## Offering Freedom

For the dimension of offering freedom, three clusters of teaching strategies were also distilled from the literature survey:

- *Flexibility, allowing for self-regulation, openness*: strategies that create space for students' questions, choices, and initiatives' scaffolding
- *Innovative teaching, experimentation, fun*: strategies that foster the sense and excitement of experimentation
- *Professionalism, novice relationship, challenge*: strategies that treat honours students as 'junior colleagues' in research and education (activities).

The findings of the survey reveal that for honours teachers, both from the U.S.A. and from the Netherlands, offering freedom distinguishes their honours teaching from their regular teaching. The teachers included far more freedom-related items in their top-three and top-five lists for honours teaching compared to regular teaching. By splitting the results into freedom and structure, I discerned a distinct difference between honours teaching and regular teaching. Indeed, the teachers do not consider freedom an appropriate approach for regular classes. Instead, they consider offering structure as appropriate for regular classes. This entails, for instance, offering well-organized subject matter and being clear about their expectations.

Granting responsibility to honours students and allowing them freedom in choosing which topics to study and in their time management are considered appropriate teaching strategies in honours programmes. Leaving room for experimentation, creating space for the students' own initiative and encouraging questions seem to characterize honours education. In sum, they believe that a greater tailoring of honours programmes to students' needs within a strong framework of community would be appropriate.

The list of topics covered in the interviews did not explicitly include freedom. It was omitted so that the interviewers could get an unbiased impression of how teachers deal with their honours students. However, the teachers did speak readily about the importance of freedom. Their teaching is student-centered and offers a high degree of flexibility to honours students. Teachers allow room for student choice, subject focus and time-management, granting them responsibility for themselves. It also appears that teachers often see teaching strategies related to offering freedom as a means to another end. For instance, the development of an honours student's capacity for self-regulation (end) is seen as an integral part of a capstone project (means). *Encouraging choices* is often seen as a means of achieving goals such as engagement, academic depth or bonding. It appears that the way teachers apply strategies related to offering freedom has much to do with the teachers' personality and involvement in the honours community. The interviews illustrate that offering freedom goes hand in hand with trusting the students and taking them seriously. *Teachers grant honours students responsibility*, not only so that they can learn to make choices and reflect on them, but also to put the students in a position to create their own *independent learning strategy*.

Furthermore, teachers talked about their own freedom in teaching. Honours teachers use the honours class as an educational innovation room. This was also borne out by the survey, showing that this is more common in the American context than in the Dutch. When the survey was conducted, honours programmes were relatively new in the Netherlands. Only 3% of all Dutch teachers had more than ten years of teaching experience in honours, whereas 40% of American teachers had. Honours education was an experimental initiative in the Dutch situation, while it was a long-standing tradition in the American context.

## Honours Teachers

Honours teaching cannot be studied in isolation. It was assumed that attributes such as teachers' conceptions of teaching and learning, their motivation and feeling of self-determination, and their perception of students all have an impact on teaching practice in general and also on practices in honours teaching.

The outcomes of these attributes and their relationships with teaching will be discussed in this section, starting with teachers' conceptions of honours teaching and learning in higher education.

The findings give the overall impression that honours teachers are more inclined towards a student-learning orientation than a teacher-content orientation, particularly in how they organize their classes (instructional emphasis). But, irrespective of which orientation teachers prefer, there is a measurable effect on their teaching approaches, albeit not a statistically significant one. Moreover, the findings show that American teachers see their honours classes as a laboratory for educational innovation, which may involve some risk – for teachers as well as students. Dutch honours teachers do not perceive the notions of risk-taking and educational innovation as key ingredients of honours education. Dutch teachers also place more importance on learning products, such as grading.

During the interviews, American teachers reflected spontaneously on what they believe to be the core of honours education. Their reactions led to the identification of several main themes: outstanding performance, with a strong focus on the process of learning more than on its outcomes; the notion of high expectations of a fairly homogeneous group of students with strong motivation and academic potential; and the notion of honours as being strategically important for their institution in the sense of attracting good faculty members as well as students.

Intrinsic motivation and self-determination are high factors among Dutch teachers and even significantly higher among American teachers. Does motivation make a difference? The answer is 'yes, it does'. If teachers are more motivated, they subscribe to the importance of creating community or enhancing academic competence within honours. The effect of motivation on offering freedom could not be measured.

From the point of view of teachers, it is both motivating and pleasurable to work with honours students and help them to fulfil their potential. Teachers are enthusiastic about being able to share in depth much of their academic field of interest with the students. Motivation helps to create an informal, relaxed yet demanding class atmosphere – and the other way around. Many American teachers perceive honours teaching as a challenge, finding this inherently exciting and rewarding.

American and Dutch teachers include the same five student qualities in their top-five for honours students (although in a different order): enterprising in the sense of taking initiatives; curious; creative thinking; motivated; willing to invest effort in their studies. Compared to their Dutch colleagues, American teachers attach significantly higher importance to the following qualities of honours students: risk-taking; involvement in the academic community; and being stimulating for fellow students. Risk-taking is perceived as engagement in original, out-of-the-box and open-ended tasks; as such, it is related to the teaching approach of offering freedom. Student qualities of involvement and stimulating fellow students are linked to the teaching approach of creating community. This is in line with the finding that both approaches are important in American honours education. Dutch teachers place significantly more emphasis on qualities of honours students that reflect academic competence: a passion for research and getting good grades.

Both American and Dutch teachers believe that their regular students need clear goals, clear class structure and well-explained subject matter. The interviews with American teachers also illuminated their concerns about some of their honours students: various teachers reported that honours students may be over-competitive or over-committed. This may result in losing track of the honours learning experience while focusing on the output instead of on the process. Furthermore, American teachers experience honours students as engaged and both academically and personally more mature than students in regular programmes. They perceive their honours students as young people who are willing to work harder than students in regular programmes. Honours students are seen as people who approach learning differently compared to regular students and are generally stronger communicators, often skilled in debate and other forms of verbal communication.

## Discussion

It was my ambition to examine reported strategies in honours education systematically, together with their contrast to teaching strategies in regular classes, on the basis of a conceptual framework that draws upon multiple perspectives (honours literature, giftedness research, self-determination theory) and multi-institutional survey data from two countries, supplemented by qualitative interview data from experienced U.S. honours teachers. Some limitations of the conceptual and methodological choices that were made in this study are discussed in the seventh chapter of the book *Teaching for Excellence* (Wolfensberger, 2012). For instance, it is obvious that studies of actual teaching practices (classroom observations) and of students' perceptions of teaching practices in honours would enrich the picture (Pascarella & Terenzini, 2005).

## Implications

The findings presented in this study have several implications for both practice and future research activities. First and foremost, the findings can contribute to the fostering of faculty development initiatives for honours. The findings reveal that teaching in honours is deemed different from teaching in regular classes; in short, the teacher can make a difference. The extent to which teachers in higher education are equipped to facilitate the creation of this kind of honours environment is a matter that certainly requires further debate and analysis. However, as more students and teachers become involved in honours programmes, it is important to invest specifically in this area of faculty development. I agree with Yair (2008) that the scholarship of teaching is not simply amenable to transfer or distribution, but steps can be taken to encourage the proliferation of good teaching practice in honours. This should have already started with teacher education. Having said that, this study showed striking similarities between American and Dutch honours teachers in their perception of honours teaching. These shared understandings allow for an international exchange of honours teachers and international collaboration among institutes. It should be noted, however, that educational contexts differ between Europe and the U.S.A., so obviously that must be taken into account.

Second, the outcomes from the interviews suggest that institutional conditions for creating an honours community and back-up for teachers are crucial. The outcomes reveal that teachers are motivated and committed to their students and, as such, honours teachers may function as role models for an institution's faculty. Institutions should cherish and nurture their motivation and commitment. Honours education can thrive in the right institutional conditions and, vice versa, institutions can mirror the honours experience by building an academic environment that stimulates personal relations, personal and professional growth and passion for teaching amongst all faculty members.

With respect to future research activities, the implications of the present study are numerous. Three avenues for further research are described in the next section.

## Avenues for Further Research

The book *Teaching for Excellence – honors pedagogies revealed* attempted to substantiate key components of an honours pedagogy, based on an extensive literature review and empirical research among honours teachers. I see three main avenues for further research that could build on the findings of this study as well as some reasons for debate/reflection.

The study reveals that teaching strategies that are generally seen as essential in honours education fall under the three main teaching approaches, namely: creating community, enhancing academic competence, and offering freedom. These three approaches stand out as essential in honours teaching and were explored through teachers' self-reported teaching practices.

Our findings could be used as a basis for further research into what teachers actually do in their daily practice in honours classes – by conducting classroom observations, for example. The validity of our three approaches could then be further tested and possibly enriched by reference to actual practice. This could lead to practice-based honours course descriptions focused on effective honours teaching strategies, in line with the work of, for instance, Dixon, Prater, Vine, Wark, Williams, Hanchon and Shobe (2004) and Wiegant, Scager and Boonstra (2011). The findings of this study reveal the importance of offering freedom within honours pedagogies. Teachers' practices related to offering freedom and structure within honours and regular courses could be further investigated. An understanding of the unique dynamic between freedom and structure could lead to new methods for eliciting excellence within higher education. Examples of research into actual teaching practices include conducting a comparative content analysis of course syllabi of honours courses and courses in the regular curriculum on the same subject matter, and classroom observations on teacher-student interactions comparing honours and regular courses. These types of research allow for a further analysis of the three approaches that were developed in this study, based on actual classroom practices.

Another avenue for further research would take the students' perspectives into account. After all, the single most important difference between teaching honours and regular classes is the students. This study did not include student perceptions of honours teachers or courses. It would be interesting to discover the students' opinion of their teachers' approaches and strategies (see, for instance, Shaunessy and McHatton, 2009; Van der Valk, Grunefeld and Pilot, 2010). Doing so could indicate if the three approaches of creating community, enhancing academic competence and offering freedom also remain essential in the light of students' needs and wishes. For instance, this could be investigated by conducting interviews among students in honours programmes in comparison to students in regular programmes who take courses with the same teachers.

It is known that data for learning outcomes assessment may suffer from low validity and may fail to capture the complete essence of the complex field of honours education (Carnicom & Snyder, 2010). Yet, new insights may come from research on the effectiveness of honours teaching whereby students' learning outcomes are analyzed. While most of the teachers who participated in this study agree that honours education should be focused on eliciting excellence, in that students' outcomes were not included in this study, I do not know whether the proposed strategies are effective in reaching this goal. To take this research further, it would be interesting to investigate the effect of honours teaching strategies on students' outcomes, perceived well-being and mindset (Dweck, 2000). Research on honours alumni should then be included.

This study reveals a distinct set of teaching practices facilitating the mastery of the honours experience, envisioning the 'signature pedagogy' (Shulman, 2005a; 2005b) evolved by honours. Although this study offers a rich basis for faculty development in honours, it would be good to undertake further study on the effectiveness of such initiatives. This is the third avenue for further research that I envision. The role of teachers is pivotal, certainly for highly talented and motivated students, in creating community, scaffolding, and balancing freedom and structure. However, faculty development for honours is in its initial phase in the Netherlands. It is largely absent in teacher education, which is a gap in provision. As noted by Segers and Hoogeveen (2012), there is a need for research into the quality of faculty development for honours. Specifically, further research is needed into the design and effects of faculty development (Van Veen, Zart, Meirink & Verloop, 2010). Honours programmes have been shown to serve as laboratories for innovation (Denisson, 2008), so faculty development should cover effective ways of integrating room for experimentation by honours teachers. With regard to the effects, we need more insight into the relation between faculty development interventions and the effectiveness of teachers' strategies as well as students' outcomes. Specifically, such studies should address faculty development that integrates the approaches of honours pedagogies as described in this study: creating community, enhancing academic competence, and offering freedom.

Besides these three avenues for further empirical research, the outcomes of this study warrant a conversation about ethical issues concerning honours education, reflecting on its purposes and on educational policies.

What should be our goal in honours education and how are we to reach it? Do teachers have a special responsibility for inspiring honours students to respect other humans, disciplines and cultures through genuine conversations, interactive learning and international exchange? Do honours students have specific moral and ethical sensitivities (Tirri & Nokelainen, 2011) that honours programmes should address? And why would this be truer for students in honours programmes than for students in regular programmes?

I believe that the purpose of education must be to enhance, not compromise, human difference and dignity (Sacks, 2007). Education in a democratic society must provide *all* students with opportunities to develop their talents, taking into account all of the differences between them. This requires differentiation among students, including, by consequence, the allocation of resources specifically for talented and motivated students, allowing them to elicit excellence. Reflection on why and how to evoke excellence for these students, and whether we succeed in sufficiently addressing their moral and ethical questions, is crucial. In honours courses, one of the important questions should be, what makes a life well-lived? The answers have everything to do with moral principles and values that give continuity and dignity to life. The answers relate education to contribution, fulfillment and happiness. Teachers should be educating critical and creative young people who thereby develop a desire, capacity and confidence to make a difference in society and science. Reflection is needed to provide direction for the design of social and ethical themes in honours programmes and higher education. Further research could explore how teachers provide such an education.

## References

Carnicom, S., & Snyder, Ch. A. (2010). Learning outcomes assessment in honors: An appropriate practice? *Journal of the NCHC, 11*(1), 69–82.

Clark, L., & Zubizarreta, J. (Eds.). (2008). *Inspiring exemplary teaching and learning: perspectives on teaching academically talented college students*. Lincoln, NE: NCHC.

Cosgrove, J. R. (2004). The impact of honors programs on undergraduate academic performance, retention, and graduation. *Journal of the NCHC, 5*(2), 45–53.

Denisson, G. M. (2008). Honors education and the prospects for academic reform, *Innovative Higher Education, 33*, 159–168.

Dixon, F. A., Prater, K. A., Vine, H. M., Wark, M. J., Williams, T., Hanchon, T., & Shobe, C. (2004). Teaching to their thinking: A strategy to meet the critical-thinking needs of gifted students. *Journal for the Education of the Gifted, 28*(1), 56–76.

Dweck, C. S. (2000). *Self-theories: Their role in motivation, personality and development*. Philadelphia, PA: Psychology Press.

Pascarella, E. T., & Terenzini, P. T. (2005). *How college affects students: A third decade of research* (Vol. 2). San Francisco, CA: Jossey-Bass.

Rinn, A. N. (2007). Effects of programmatic selectivity on the academic achievement, academic self-concepts, and aspirations of gifted college students. *Gifted Child Quarterly, 51*(3), 232–245.

Sacks, J. (2007). *The dignity of difference. How to avoid the clash of civilizations.* Londen, UK: Continuum.

Segers, E., & Hoogeveen, L. (2012). *Programmeringsstudie. Excellentieonderzoek in primair, voortgezet en hoger onderwijs.* Behavioural Science Institute & Centrum voor Begaafdheidsonderzoek, Radboud Universiteit Nijmegen. Retrieved from http://www.nwo.nl/files.nsf/pages/NWOP_8SRC2K_Eng/$file/PROO%20Excellentie%20Programmeringsstudie.pdf.

Shaunessy, E., & McHatton, P. A. (2009). Urban students' perceptions of teachers: views of students in general, special, and honors education. *Urban Rev, 41,* 486–503.

Shulman, L. (2005a). Pedagogies of uncertainty. *Liberal Education 91*(2), 18–25.

Shulman, L. (2005b). Signature pedagogies in the professions. *Daedalus 134*(3), 52–9.

Shushok, F. Jr. (2002). *Educating the best and brightest: Collegiate honors programs and the intellectual, social and psychological development of students.* Dissertation, University of Maryland. College Park.

Tirri, K., & Nokelainen, P. (2011). *Measuring multiple intelligences and moral sensitivities in education.* Rotterdam, Netherlands: Sense Publishers.

Van der Valk, A. E., Grunefeld, H., & Pilot, A. (2010). Empowerment en leerresultaten bij getalenteerde bètaleerlingen in een verrijkte onderwijsleeromgeving. *Pedagogische Studien, 88,* 73–89.

Van Veen, K., Zart, R., Meirink, J., & Verloop, N. (2010). *Professionele ontwikkeling van leraren. Een reviewstudie naar effectieve kenmerken van professionaliseringsinterventies van leraren.* ICLON/Expertisecentrum Leren van Docenten.

Wiegant, F., Scager, K., & Boonstra, J. (2011). An undergraduate course to bridge the gap between textbooks and scientific research. *CBE Life Sciences Education, 10*(1), 83–94.

Wolfensberger, M. V. C. (in press). *Honors in northern Europe. Talent Development and Culture towards Excellence in Higher Education in a Networked Society.* Springer.

Wolfensberger, M. V. C. (2012). *Teaching for Excellence – Honors Pedagogies Revealed.* Münster, Germany: Waxmann.

Yair, G. (2008). Can we administer the scholarship of teaching? Lessons from outstanding professors in higher education. *Higher Education, 55,* 447–459.

# Fostering Honours Communities among Commuter Students

*Stan van Ginkel, Pierre van Eijl, Albert Pilot and John Zubizarreta*

## Introduction

Research has shown that honours programmes often involve networks of students that contribute to the development of the students' talents (Van Ginkel, Van Eijl, Pilot, & Zubizarreta, 2012). These networks are also described as *"learning communities"* (Wilson, Ludwig-Hardman, Thornam, & Dunlap, 2004) and *"honours communities"* (Van Eijl, Wolfensberger, & Pilot, 2008). Such communities foster productive interaction among students, teachers, and other professionals during their affiliation with the programme. As a result of such connections, students discover new learning opportunities and gain experience in organizational and leadership skills. In honours programmes, in particular, these contacts are an essential component of what defines honours activities as special enhancements of a student's overall educational experience. Our study focuses on strategies for the development of honours communities.

We focus particularly on commuter students because they comprise the majority of honours students in the Netherlands. One of the challenges for an honours director is to create a vibrant honours community within this specific context. We make the assumption that, for commuter students, a more careful and intentional implementation of an honours community is necessary because most students leave campus when classes are finished (Jacoby, 2000). And, as Kuh, Gonyea and Palmer (2001) found in their research, commuter students are overall less engaged than students who live on campus. Extra activities have to be organized and strategically timed to suit these students, and the challenge is complicated by competition with numerous other events taking place in the city. Our study analyses five different honours communities of commuter students in order to suggest some best practices for creating maximum benefits for students.

## Theoretical Background

Our focus on communities in education is supported by constructivist learning theories, which assume that learners by preference construct knowledge in an active manner within an authentic context (Brown & Campione, 1994). Socio-constructivist learning theories further suggest that learning is more effective when it occurs in a social context (Wenger, 1998) rather than as an individual, isolated activity as frequently occurs in a classroom. The related learning theory of situated cognition (Greeno, 1998) states that, if learning is embedded in social interactions among people in a specific situation, then it has a positive effect on personal development.

McMillan and Chavis (1986) describe a community in general as characterized by *"a feeling that members have of belonging, a feeling that members matter to one another and to the group, and a shared faith that members' needs will be met through their commitment to be together"* (p. 9). Cross (1998) defines learning communities more specifically as *"groups of people engaged in intellectual interaction for the purpose of learning"* (p. 4). Cross combines the concept of learning communities with the design of a curriculum and cites the structuring of the programme and the frequency of contacts between students as important factors.

Wilson and colleagues (2004) also stress the connection with the curriculum by introducing the concept of a *"bounded learning community."* According to these researchers, a learning community is bounded by a particular course or curriculum. Participating students collaborate with other students and a teacher, working together within a fixed timetable and with an explicit requirement to seek contact with others by communicating and working online; the teacher plays a crucial role in facilitating the creation of such a learning community. Besides factors such as *"shared goals of the community"* and *"safe and supporting conditions,"* teachers are a critical component of learning communities (Sherin, Mendez, & Louis, 2004; Shulman & Sherin, 2004); their task is to provide the infrastructure for work and interaction, model effective collaboration, monitor and assess learning, provide feedback, troubleshoot and resolve problems, and establish trusting relationships with students (Wilson et al., 2004).

Such communities can enhance learning outcomes (Lankveld & Volman, 2011; Tinto & Russo, 1994), increase the pace of study (Eggens, 2011), raise the level of reflection (Cross, 1998; Tinto, 1995), improve the attitude of students (Tinto & Russo, 1994), and strengthen emotional support among students (Lankveld & Volman, 2011). Furthermore, these contact networks can influence the extent to which students interact outside classrooms (Tinto &

Russo, 1994), and create a *"sense of community"* (McMillan & Chavis, 1986). This latter aspect is a challenge for many honours directors and teachers (Koh, Chaffee & Goodman, 2009) because education tailored to high-achieving, motivated, and talented students – particularly those in honours programmes – should also take place in a culture of excellence in order to empower students (van der Valk, Grunefeld & Pilot, 2010). This culture of excellence is frequently mentioned as an important characteristic of an honours programme (Ford, 2008; Mariz, 2008; Slavin, 2008).

Previous research has shown that communities are essential to many honours programmes (De Boer & Van Eijl, 2010), but we know little about the specific factors and mechanisms for success. This new knowledge we aim for in this study is needed to establish strategies for community development of commuter students in honours.

## Method

In this exploratory study, a mixed methods approach was used for data collection and data analysis (Creswell & Plano Clark, 2007). Within this approach, qualitative and quantitative methods are combined because the aim of this study requires a combination of different types of data. To achieve a set of strategies for community building among commuter students, we conducted a cross-case analysis in the Netherlands. From four universities, the following five cases were selected: Utrecht Law College (ULC); Professional School of Arts (PSAU); Top Class Healthcare; Honours Programme in Biology; and Interdisciplinary Honours Programme. Our data collection was based on interviews, questionnaires, and documentary analysis. Furthermore, we interviewed teachers and students from different American honours programmes to gain insight into (1) key characteristics and additional qualities of honours communities, (2) their functions, and (3) development strategies. The results of these interviews and insights were arranged to present a basic set of strategies to develop honours communities. This framework was used to conduct an interpretative analysis of the five Dutch case studies with a member check for confirmation and case details.

## Seven Strategies for Implementing Communities

From our study, seven strategies can be distinguished for the development and maintenance of communities within the special population of commuter students in honours programmes. Both teachers and students can use these strategies; the teachers are often in the best position to initiate them, even though the ultimate goal is that students own their community and take initiatives themselves. The seven strategies are listed in Table 1.

*Table 1:*    *Strategies to stimulate honours communities for commuter students in honours programmes*

| Strategies |
| --- |
| 1    Matching students based on willingness and capabilities for cooperation |
| 2    Programming challenging teamwork activities that are student-regulated |
| 3    Facilitating students' initiatives without taking the lead |
| 4    Creating an intense period of interaction to deepen and enhance bonding |
| 5    Organizing a series of interactive activities during the programme to stimulate the community |
| 6    Highlighting the performance of a teacher as a role model for development of talent and as a coach for community-building |
| 7    Involving community activities in feedback procedures and student evaluations |

*First*, the matching of students is important because students need to be informed beforehand about the content and intentions of the programme. The selection procedure should focus on the extent to which students would like to work actively with other students or interact with teachers and professionals. For example, at ULC the following criterion played an important role: *"students need to contribute to the programme, instead of only following the programme"*. At the start of the programme, arranging the students into groups is important. Depending on the type of assignment, teachers need to encourage interdependence among students by matching students' complementary passions or disciplines in order to fulfil a particular goal. At PSAU, for example, students can design games for real clients only by combining their expertise as game designers, graphic designers, and programmers.

*Second*, the programming of challenging teamwork activities that are student-regulated focal events, as in the case of PSAU, can enhance collaboration among students. Furthermore, the interaction among students and between students and faculty can be improved by facilitating a physical project space, providing a budget, and supporting the use of social media and communications platforms. Interdependence in producing an actual product is another strategy that promotes teamwork among students, as demonstrated in the Honours Programme in Biology where students write a book together, and mutual interaction can be further enhanced by the use of peer feedback. Interviews with American teachers and students showed that *"common ground"* is an important prerequisite for stimulating student interaction, but the study of the interaction patterns among students of PSAU showed us that not every student is equally active in a community and that this pattern may change during the year.

*Third,* facilitating student initiatives that fit into the aims of the honours programme and its culture can be a powerful way of strengthening student ownership of an honours community, as demonstrated in the cases of ULC and Top Class Healthcare. The staff can encourage such initiatives through contacts with industry, project budgets, or appropriate facilities (including physical spaces) for the honours students.

*Fourth,* implementing an intense period of interaction in the initial phase of a programme is important for creating a sense of community. Some programmes start with a workshop or an orientation weekend, as in Top Class Healthcare with its course on leadership skills. The Interdisciplinary Honours Programme in Leiden is another example where interaction among students was noticeably stronger after an international seminar in Brussels.

*Fifth,* organizing a series of interactive activities with formal and informal meetings during the programme stimulates community-building in honours programmes. ULC and PSAU also provide important stimuli to an active community life through fixed groups in classes and regular meetings within the programme over a long period. A site visitor to an American honours programme described this point as follows: *"shared experiences are the key issue."* Ideally, a strong sense of community leads to continued mutual contacts after the termination of the programme, as in the PSAU programme where students continue meeting with each other on a monthly basis.

*Sixth,* the performance of the teacher as a role model is indispensable. In honours programmes, contacts between students and teachers are extremely important. A site visitor highlighted the following: *"the interchange between faculty and students is one of the hallmarks of honours."* The teacher is expected to give individual attention to the learning process, provide students with the opportunity to pose questions, and challenge students to find new paths. The teacher must involve students in decisions about the content of the programme, give students responsibility for specific tasks, emphasize cooperation instead of competition, stimulate presentations to a relevant public, and take initiative in providing feedback to community members. Thus, the teacher functions mainly as a catalyst in order to promote and coach the community. An American honours student described this dimension of a faculty member's role in helping to build community: *"The faculty should help to shape the ideas, but not originate the ideas."*

*Seventh*, community activities can be considered as part of the honours diploma. Some programmes use honours portfolios and meetings with tutors or coaches to review the involvement of individual students in the programme and in community activities.

Finally, these strategies for building a vibrant community should be more than separate interventions; the combination of these strategies produces a well-functioning honours community.

## Concluding Remarks and Future Research

Our research and the literature underscore that honours communities enhance learning and interaction. Furthermore, they fulfill multiple social and emotional functions for participants, encouraging them to support each other and undertake initiatives while providing a platform for collaboration on academic and social fronts. Depending on the stage of the community's development, three main factors improve honours education for a given group of students: the honours programme itself, the staff, and the resources. Our study suggests seven strategies for developing an honours community among commuter students. Empirical research is needed to determine conclusively if these strategies provide the intended results.

## References

Boer, D. de, & Eijl, P. J. van (2010). Naar een onderzoeksagenda voor talentontwikkeling in het hoger onderwijs. *(Towards a research agenda for talent development in higher education). Tijdschrift voor Hoger Onderwijs (Journal for Higher Education)*, 28(4), pp. 239–250.

Brown, A. L., & Campione, J. C. (1994). Guided discovery in a community of learners. In McGilly, K. (Ed.) *Classroom lessons: Integrating cognitive theory and classroom practice*, pp. 229–270. Cambridge, MA.: Massachusetts Institute of Technology.

Creswell, J. W., & Plano Clark, V. L. (2007). *Mixed Methods Research.* Thousand Oaks, CA: Sage Publications Inc.

Cross, P. (1998). Why learning communities? Why now? *About Campus*, 3(3), pp. 4–11.

Eggens, L. (2011). *The student X-factor: social and psychological determinants of students' attainment in higher education.* PhD thesis, University of Groningen, the Netherlands.

Eijl, P. J. van, Wolfensberger, M. V. C., & Pilot, A. (2008). Talentontwikkeling bij Amerikaanse honoursprogramma's en honours colleges. Site visitors van de National Collegiate Honors Council over talentontwikkeling (Talent development in American honors programs and honors colleges. Site visitors of the National Collegiate Honors Council about developing talent). *Mededeling 83.* Interfacultair Instituut voor Lerarenopleiding, Onderwijsontwikkeling en Studievaardigheden (Institute of Education), Universiteit Utrecht, Utrecht, pp. 1–29.

Ford, J. (2008). Creating an honors culture. *Journal of the National Collegiate Honors Council,* Spring/Summer 2008, pp. 27–29.

Ginkel, S. van, Eijl, P. van, Pilot, A., & Zubizarreta, J. (2012). Building a Vibrant Honors Community among Commuter Students. *Journal of the National Collegiate Honors Council,* 13(2), p. 197–218.

Greeno, J.G. (1998). The situativity of knowing, learning and research. *American Psychologist,* 53(1), pp. 5–26.

Jacoby, B. (2000). Why involve commuter students in learning? In Kramer, M. (Series Ed.), & Jacoby, B. (Vol. Ed.). *New directions for higher education: Number 109.* Involving commuter students in learning (pp. 3–12). San Francisco: Jossey-Bass.

Koh, K., Chaffee, J., & Goodman, E. (2009). Networking an honors community out of fragmentation. *Honors in Practice,* 5, pp. 161–170.

Kuh, G. D., Gonyea, R. M., & Palmer, M. (2001). The disengaged commuter student: fact or fiction? *National Survey of Student engagement.* Indiana University, Center for Postsecondary Research and Planning.

Lankveld, T. A. M., & Volman, M. L. L. (2011). Ondersteuning van docenten bij onderwijsvernieuwing: de rol van communities of practice. (Supporting teachers in educational reform: the role of communities of practice). *Tijdschrift voor Hoger Onderwijs (Journal for Higher Education),* 29(1), pp. 41–53.

Mariz, G. (2008). The culture of honors. *Journal of the National Collegiate Honors Council,* Spring/Summer 2008, pp. 19–25.

McMillan, D. W., & Chavis, D. M. (1986). Sense of community: A definition and theory. *Journal of Community Psychology,* 14(1), pp. 6–23.

Sherin, M. G., Mendez, E. P., & Louis, D. A. (2004). A discipline apart: The challenges of "fostering a community of learners" in a mathematics classroom. *Journal of Curriculum Studies,* 36(2), pp. 207–232.

Shulman, L. S., & Sherin, M. G. (2004). Fostering communities of teachers as learners: Disciplinary perspectives. *Journal of Curriculum Studies,* 36(2), pp. 135–140.

Slavin, C. H. (2008). Defining honors culture. *Journal of the National Collegiate Honors Council,* Spring/Summer 2008, pp. 15–18.

Tinto, V. (1995). Learning communities, collaborative learning and the pedagogy of educational citizenship. *American Association of Higher Education Bulletin,* 47(7), pp. 11–13.

Tinto, V., & Russo, P. (1994). Coordinated studies programs: Their effect on student involvement at a community college. *Community College Review,* 22(2), pp. 16–25.

Valk, A. E. van der, Grunefeld, H., & Pilot, A. (2010). Empowerment en leerresultaten bij getalenteerde bètaleerlingen in een verrijkte onderwijsleeromgeving. (Empowerment and learning results with talented upper-secondary science students in an enriched learning environment). *Pedagogische Studiën (Educational Studies),* 88(2), pp. 73–89.

Wenger, E. (1998). *Communities of Practice. Learning, Meaning and Identity.* New York: Cambridge University Press.

Wilson, B. G., Ludwig-Hardman, S., Thornam, C. L., & Dunlap, J. C. (2004). Bounded community: Designing and facilitating learning communities in formal courses. *The International Review of Research in Open and Distance Learning,* 5(3).

# Creating Honours Community within a Large Inclusive Public University

## Innovative Practices in the Development of Barrett, The Honors College at Arizona State University

*Kristen Joy Hermann*

Barrett, The Honors College at Arizona State University (ASU), a model United States honours college, has its own faculty and staff, a ten million dollar endowment, a high concentration of national merit and Fulbright scholars and a new campus that stands alone for its size and comprehensiveness of services.

In 2009, ASU reconceptualized the model for an American honours college that infers greater organizational complexity within the structure of a university when it entered into a public-private partnership to build the nation's premier $140 million honours residential college campus. The eight acre honours complex on the Tempe site includes: 1700 beds in a variety of units, Faculty Fellow and Barrett administration offices, 12 classrooms, an honours community centre (with student lounges, activity rooms, computer and writing labs and a fitness centre); a comprehensive sustainable living and learning community and organic garden, and a multi-room dining centre and signature refectory.

This best practices presentation is about how the unique development of this honours college impacted the university, the state of Arizona, the nation and the world in creating a culture of excellence and an honours campus community that presents a new paradigm for honours communities within large American universities. Many honours colleges have elements in common with Barrett, such as a central freshmen seminar course, an honours thesis requirement, dedicated space to operate and, in some cases, designated residential space, but Barrett has a combination of elements that makes it a unique and innovative centre of academic excellence in the U.S. The study outlined below explores the milestones in the development and trajectory of Barrett at ASU over the last twenty-five years through the experiences of five senior administrators instrumental in shaping Barrett's identity. It documents the elements that set Barrett on a path to evolve in a distinct and extraordinary way and provides a blueprint for those working in honours colleges and programmes who wish to replicate, implement and develop a similar centralized honours residential college model.

## Methods

This action research study is a qualitative in-depth case analysis of a bounded system (Barrett) with a finite duration looking at the development of the college from its inception in 1988 to the opening of the new Barrett, The Honors College residential campus in 2009 (Yin, 1994). Action research is the method used to explore the effectiveness of the decisions, execution and outcomes central to Barrett's development. The research question in this best practices adaptation is: what are the decisions, executions and outcomes central to Barrett's development? The five participants in the study were selected based on their role in the development of the college and include a university president, the founding honours college dean and associate dean, and the current dean and vice dean.

## Findings

The findings reveal several innovative practices in the evolution of Barrett, The Honors College. There were components of the college's infrastructure and physical structure that shaped Barrett's development. They include the creation of an honours faculty cohort, giving the college a legal and stand-alone identity, providing an appropriate leadership structure, acquiring a named endowment, recruiting top students, developing a national scholarship office and establishing Barrett as a true residential honours college with the construction of the $140 million honours campus. These findings verified the innovative decisions and strategies used by senior administrators in actualizing a new vision for an honours college at the nation's largest institution.

### Faculty Role

The original and ingenious concept of a distinct full-time faculty cohort within the honours college that would develop a faculty identity outside the disciplinary home was the antithesis of most honours programmes and even honours colleges where the faculty is distributed throughout campus with a home in the college of their discipline. Developing a faculty cohort and organizing the resources of the institution in this way maximized the strength of the Barrett honours experience by providing more access to the teaching faculty within a small college environment in tandem with the students' access to the faculty of a major large public research institution.

It was important that the Barrett faculty's essential function was to teach *The Human Event* course, a core element of the honours curriculum integral to Barrett's identity and function. The role of the required freshmen seminar course was to provide intellectual connectivity between faculty and students organized around a central theme or objective in providing a rich academic experience for honours students. Long (2002) emphasized the importance of access to honours faculty and curriculum opportunities like special courses and seminars. At Barrett, there are now 28 faculty fellows and over 1400 faculty teaching honours classes on all four campuses. The larger ASU as a result of the honours curriculum inherits highly trained undergraduates who elevate the classroom experience.

## Legal Stand-Alone Identity

The decision of senior administrators to develop an honours college with a legal stand-alone identity demonstrated immense foresight and overhauled ASU's institutional standing in the state. The legal creation of the honours college was approved by the Arizona Board of Regents on July 16, 1989. Many United States honours colleges at the time were created by fiat decision of the institution's president. ASU's leadership wanted the college created by a legal process so that, if anyone wanted to decommission the college, the decision would be subject to a legal process. The founding dean explained that, while some institutions appear to have stand-alone honours colleges, these colleges are often in name only with no central community of faculty and staff that work for the college and serve students within a central residential college community. Honours colleges are organized to "infer greater organizational complexity, programmatic diversity, physical identity, size and resources, than would be commonly associated with an honours programme" (Sederberg, 2008, p. 30). The university president believed that a stand-alone college-centric model created a clear definition of an honours student and allowed for the creation of an intellectual community which has identity, a location, and students that are clearly Barrett students, but also very much citizens of the university.

## Endowment

Another milestone central to Barrett's development was in acquiring a named endowment. When business and education leaders Craig and Barbara Barrett provided the honours college with a $10 million endowment and name for the college in 1989, they gave the college an identity. The endowment and naming of the college were central to Barrett's institutional identity and gave Barrett the resources to expand academic and student support services.

## Leading the College

Structuring the college with a "dean" rather than a "director" was another example of the foresight of the five senior administrators that contributed to the study. Sederberg (2008) emphasized how much the dean title means to faculty members because "when the leader of honours education becomes a dean, he or she now 'sits at the table' with other deans and more directly participates in university decision-making" (p. 31). It was important for the dean of the college to have direct access to those responsible for allocating university resources.

## Recruiting National Merit Scholars

The idea of recruiting National Merit Scholars was a new concept and influenced the trajectory of Barrett. Barrett was predominantly comprised of Arizona students. Recruiting National Merit Scholars nation-wide increased the ability to attract the best in-state Flinn[1] scholars and made for a richer college experience for Arizona students. The record number of National Merit Scholars coming to ASU gave the institution national recognition and improved overall academic quality. Bohnlein (2008) maintains honours colleges were established to recruit strong students, raise the profile of the institution, and improve overall campus academic quality. The strategic recruitment of National Merit Scholars where the founding dean sometimes went from farmhouse to farmhouse further shows how senior administrators were using innovative approaches and just plain hard work to grow the new concept of an honours college.

---

1   Scholarship awarded to Arizona's highest-achieving high school students. The programme is managed by the Flinn Foundation.

*A National Scholarship Office*

The establishment of the Lorraine Frank Office of National Scholarships and Advisement (LFONSA) demonstrated how senior administrators organized the resources of the university to support students seeking exceptional scholarship opportunities. The LFONSA office was an essential function and operation of Barrett with operations within the college to benefit all ASU students. Recipients of national scholarships, like Rhodes, Fulbright, Marshall, Truman, Goldwater, NSEP, and Udall are highly-trained individuals sent to other parts of the world to engage in service projects that impact the international community. The founding dean recalled that, until 1991, ASU had little distinction in terms of competing for national fellowships. Students now enter the university with a truly distinguished record and are considered for admission into any top programme in the world. Last year, ASU ranked fifth in the number of Fulbright scholars with a higher yield than any United States institution.

*Reconceptualized Honours Campus*

The development of the $140 million Barrett honours residential campus established a new metric for thinking about an honours residential college in a large university. The new campus was the product of the vision of a new university president and new honours college dean who both wanted to develop a new standard for honours colleges. The Dean's vision was to place Barrett in a peer relationship with small private colleges like Swarthmore (where he spent 30 years), Williams, and Amherst, rather than viewing Barrett as a peer to other honours. The college entered into a public/private partnership with American Campus Communities – the largest developer of residential communities in the United States – to build at the developer's expense upfront – the nation's most highly evolved 4 year honours residential college. In 2003, the new ASU President and honours college dean reconceptualized the college and started planning infrastructure, services and programmes so as to be more like a top private college. At the time of the current dean's arrival, every dean and director of the 65 honours colleges in the United States were public university faculty members. Competing with private schools in terms of the quality of students, services and facilities expanded the perception of what is traditionally available to students at a public university. The new college now offered services that could compete with small privates while still offering a much richer educational opportunity than most small privates. The new dean envisioned a combination, that did not exist anywhere in the country, of a great residential college within a large public research-intensive university. Barrett's presence on four campuses was a logical part of the college's progression and another milestone. It helped fulfil an institutional vision of inclusiveness and full opportunity on all campuses and resonates a highly complex and evolved model of administrative oversight on four campuses.

## Conclusion

This study shares insight into the role and contribution of an honours college in meeting the challenges facing American universities today of creating a new set of assumptions that encourage institutions to establish innovative practices (Crow, 2010b; Duderstadt & Farriss, 2002; Fitzpatrick, 2009; Rhodes, 2001; Tierney, 1999). The study highlights that the brightest and most engaged students can be educated in a public environment rather than having to give up a large university by going to a small college or having to give up the engagement of a community of scholars by going to a large university. Barrett has proven that even the largest university can not only provide a place for students just beginning to realize their academic potential but also for the top students in the country. Barrett at ASU has proven that academic excellence thrives in an inclusive environment. This is a message of vital importance for large American universities. Barrett has set forth a new understanding and structure for honours colleges in the United States, and has created a culture of excellence and a first-of-its-kind honours campus community to support a reconceptualized model for an American Honors College.

## References

Bohnlein, I. B. (2008). *Honoring our promise: Honors college practice and the student experience* (Doctoral dissertation). Available from Dissertation and Theses database. (UMI 3338397).

Crow, M. (September-October 2010b). Differentiating America's colleges and universities: Institutional innovation in Arizona. *Change: The Magazine Of Higher Learning,* 34–39.

Duderstadt, J. J., & Farriss, W. W. (2002). *The future of the public university in America: Beyond the crossroads.* Baltimore, MD: Johns Hopkins University Press.

Fitzpatrick, L. (2009). The 10 best college presidents. *Time Online*. Retrieved from http://www.time.com/time/specials/packages/article/0,28804,1937938_1937933_1937940,00.html

Long, B. (2002). Attracting the best: The use of honors programs to compete for students. Chicago, IL: Spencer Foundation. (ERIC Reproduction Service No. ED465355).

Rhodes, F. H. T. (2001). *The creation of the future: The role of the American university*. Cambridge: Harvard University Press.

Sederberg, P. (2008). Characteristics of contemporary honors colleges. In P.C. Sederberg (Ed.), *The Honors College Phenomenon* (pp. 25–44). Lincoln, NE: National Collegiate Honors Council.

Tierney, W. (1999). *Building the responsive campus*. Thousand Oaks, CA: Sage Publications.

Yin, R. K. (1994). *Case study research: Design and methods* (2nd ed.). Thousand Oaks, CA: Sage Publications.

# The Construction of Excellence Education in Time and Space within the University

## Research Proposal into Spin-off Effects

*Nelleke de Jong*

## Introduction

Within educational policy in the Netherlands, more and more attention is being given to providing academic challenges for talented students. Promoting excellence has also become a goal of the Dutch government, which has developed and funded two initiatives in order to promote excellence in higher education. To promote excellence and talent development, higher education institutions increasingly offer excellence programmes for talented students who want and are able to do more than is offered in the regular programme. Much research has been carried out on what these talented students want and need (Achterberg, 2005; Dai, Swanson, & Cheng, 2011) and how these excellence programmes can provide the best education for them (Cosgrove, 2004; Kiley, Boud, Manathunga, & Cantwell, 2011; Mack, 1996; Zeegers & Barron, 2009).

## Spin-off Effects

An additional goal of excellence programmes is that they should not only be for the benefit of the 'happy few' talented students, but that they should also be beneficial for all students in the regular curriculum. This intention is often cited as an additional goal of honours programmes – in the Netherlands as well as in the USA, for instance – where excellence education is seen as a kind of laboratory, where education innovations take place and are then transferred to the regular curriculum. Dennison (2008) suggests that honours education has the potential to act as the foundation for academic reform in undergraduate education and Wolfensberger, Van Eijl and Pilot (2004) discuss various spin-off effects that may occur, such as innovations in course content, pedagogy, educational instruments and programme structure. Renzulli (2005) argues that gifted programme know-how may be used for total educational improvement and that it can also be used to provide opportunities for all students with a broad range of advanced-level enrichment experiences (p. 81). However, little research has taken place into *how* these spin-off effects may occur and, therefore, into the added value of excellence education for the whole educational institution.

## Construction of Excellence Education: A Spatial Reading

Excellence education is constructed within an educational institution and, thereby, becomes part of the curriculum and educational programme of that institution as a whole. However, when considering the spin-off effects of excellence programmes, what also needs to be taken into account is the *space* in which the construction of excellence education takes place, since excellence education does not take place in a vacuum, but is constructed in space. Growing use has been made of geographical ideas in education research (Taylor, 2011). What is important to recognize when including spatiality in the debate about excellence education is that space is not only socially constructed but is also constructing the social (Beyes & Michels, 2011; Chappell & Craft, 2011; Taylor, 2011). There are not 'things simply happening in space' but space is constituted by social relations and processes (Leary, 2009, p. 195). These processes are in turn constituted by space.

Lefebvre (1991) works out this idea of the production of space through the concept of the spatial triad, three modalities that together trace the production of space (Beyes & Michels, 2011): the perceived space (the production and reproduction of practices in space), the conceived space (the conceptually constructed space), and the lived space (the space that is actually lived and embodied). The lived space can also become a space of contradiction where unexpected and unanticipated encounters and connections can take place (Beyes & Michels, 2011). By taking these different levels into account, the idea that space is natural, neutral and empty is challenged. Space is not something that exists prior to people or objects and it does not take a singular and fixed form (Mulcahy, 2007). Rather, space is a product of relations and interactions that are embedded in material practices. Harvey (2007) argues that space is neither absolute, relative nor relational in itself, but that it can become one or all at the same time, depending on the circumstances. Together, these conceptions about space make clear that space and the social construct act upon each other reciprocally and that, therefore, the relations between space and the social are very important.

## Actor-Network Theory

Based on the idea that networks are constructed through these relations, actor-network theory (ANT) (Latour, 2005) traces the ways in which human
and non-human elements interact and become actors in a network. These
complex networks spread across space and time, and produce policies,
knowledge, identities, rules, routines and practices (Fenwick, 2010, p. 120).
Actor-network theory provides a framework for studying the interactions
through which this is happening.

Actor-network is an open concept (Dolwick, 2009) with its own set of
terms. The term actor (or actant) is used to describe someone or something
that acts or to which activity is granted by others. It is something that modifies
a state of affairs by making a perceptible difference. A network is an interactive assembly of actors which leaves a physical trace of some prior activity and
which can be followed by a researcher and recorded empirically (Dolwick,
2009, p. 39). In general, the terms 'actor' and 'network' can be used inter-
changeable: an actor can be seen as a network and a network as an actor (ibid).

The central concern of the ANT approach is about how actors mobilize,
come together and hold together the pieces of the network of which they are
composed (Ruming, 2009). Studies that are inspired by ANT trace the interactions through which elements or 'actants' come together and manage to stay
together in networks that can act (Fenwick, 2010). To study actor-networks is
to study the associations between different materials and relations through
which orders and hierarchies are made. The emphasis is on complexity and it
is necessary to look at the detail of interaction (Ruming, 2009). Through the
process of 'looking down', the specific and concrete are explored by which it is
possible to locate and explore heterogeneity (Law, 2002, as cited in Ruming,
2009).

ANT argues that social relations only count if they are held together by
durable and resilient materials. Therefore, agency could be characterized by
'...the collective capacity of heterogeneous networks, in which the activities
of the non-human may count for as much, or more as the activities of humans' (Ruming 2009, p. 456). Research should therefore recognize the role of
non-human actors and engage in studying them, since the role and impact of
the non-human actors would remain under-analyzed by an approach focused
solely on human interaction and organizational structure (ibid, p. 461).

If we apply actor-network theory to the construction of excellence programmes at the university, these programmes can be seen as networks consisting of human and non-human actors that engage and connect in different
ways. Human actors within the network of the excellence programme can

be students, teachers, honours directors etc. Non-human actors can be ICT, books, classrooms etc. By studying the relational strategies that make up the excellent programme as a network, it becomes clear how actors are invited or included, how some linkages work and others don't, and how connections are made stable and durable by linking to other networks and things (Fenwick, 2010). By studying excellence programmes as a network within the network of the university, we can go further than only studying human interaction and organizational structure by also studying the impact of non-human actors and the relationship between the actors that together compose the actor-network. By following the actor-network of the excellence programme (Murdoch, 2006), it is possible to study the process that constructs space (and time) and also the relations that are made with other actors and networks. In that sense, it is particularly useful when studying the spin-off effects of excellence programmes. By following the network of the excellence programme and ana-lyzing the connections with other networks and actors, the possibilities and constraints for spin-off effects that can happen are made visible. By studying the actors (both human and non-human!) in the network, it can also become clear which actors are particularly important in regard to spin-off effects.

## Relevance

From a scientific point of view, this research will contribute to the educational research of excellence education and the use of excellence programmes as a means of improving the educational programme of an institution by bringing spatial thought into the debate on excellence education. The societal relevance of this research lies in the need for understanding what the effects of excel-lence programmes are on the institutions and educational programmes by evaluating different kinds of excellence programme. This can be used to guide the implementation of new excellence programmes including the allocation of money to programme them, so that the programmes have the most positive effects possible.

## References

Achterberg, C. (2005). What is an honors student? *Journal of the NCHC*, 6(1), 75–83.
Beyes, T., & Michels, C. (2011). The production of educational space: Heterotopia and the business university. *Management Learning*, 42(5), 521–536.

Chappell, K., & Craft, A. (2011). Creative learning conversations: producing living dialogic spaces. *Educational Research, 53*(3), 363–385.

Cosgrove, J. R. (2004). The impact of honors programs on undergraduate academic performance, retention, and graduation. *Journal of the NCHC 5*(2), 45–53.

Dai, D. Y, Swanson, J. A., & Cheng, H. (2011). State of research on giftedness and gifted education: a survey of empirical studies published during 1998–2010. *Gifted Child Quarterly, 55*(2), 126–138.

Dennison, G. M. (2008). Honors education and the prospects for academic reform. *Innov High Educ, 33*, 159–168.

Dolwick, J. S. (2009). 'The social' and beyond: introducing actor-network theory. *J Mari Arch, 4*, 21–49.

Fenwick, T.J. (2010). un(Doing) standards in education with actor-network theory. *Journal of Education Policy, 25*(2), 117–133.

Harvey, D. (2007). Space as a keyword. In N. Castree, & D. Gregory (Eds.), *David Harvey: A critical reader* (pp. 270–286). Malden, MA: Blackwell.

Kiley, M., Boud, D., Manathunga, C., & Cantwell, R. (2011). Honouring the incomparable: honours in Australian universities. *High. Educ., 62*, 619–633.

Latour, B. (2005). *Reassembling the social: an introduction to actor-network theory.* Oxford: Oxford University Press.

Law, J. (2002) *And if the global were small and non-coherent? Method, complexity and the Baroque.* Centre for Science Studies and the Department of Sociology, Lancaster University, Lancaster. In Ruming, K. (2009). Following the actors: mobilising an actor-network theory methodology in geography. *Australian Geographer, 40*(4), 451–469.

Leary, M. E. (2009). The production of space through a shrine and vendetta in Manchester: Lefebvre's spatial triad and the regeneration of a place renamed Castlefield. *Planning Theory and Practice, 10*(2), 189–212.

Lefebvre, H. (1991). *The production of space.* Oxford/Cambridge, MA: Wiley-Blackwell.

Mack, M. (1996). These things called honors programs. *Liberal Education, 82*(2), 34–39.

Mulcahy, D. (2007). Managing spaces: (re)working relations of strategy and spatiality in vocational education and training. *Studies in Continuing Education, 29*(2), 143–162.

Murdoch, J. (2006). *Post-structuralist geography.* London, England: Sage.

Renzulli, J. S. (2005). Applying gifted education pedagogy to total talent development for all students. *Theory into practice, 44*(2), 80–89.

Ruming, K. (2009). Following the actors: mobilising an actor-network theory methodology in geography. *Australian Geographer, 40*(4), 451–469.

Taylor, C. (2011). Towards a geography of education. *Oxford Review of Education, 35*(5), 651–669.

Wolfensberger, M. V. C, Eijl, P. J. van, & Pilot, A. (2004). Honours programmes as laboratories of innovation: a perspective from the Netherlands. *Journal of the NCHC, 5*(1), 115–142.

Zeegers, M., & Barron, D. (2009). Honours: a taken-for-granted pathway to research? *Higher Education, 57,* 567–575.

# Do Honours Programmes Create a Culture of Excellence?

*Lammert Tiesinga*

## Introduction

Honours programmes (or *excellence programmes*) in the Netherlands are designed to challenge talented students and to stimulate ambition and excellence in higher education (Ministerie van OCW, 2007, 2011). Literature on honours education suggests that communities of honours students create their own culture, with a strong emphasis on motivation and excellence. The goal of this study is to gain more insight into the nature of the culture within communities of honours students, if it exists, and into the way in which honours teachers encourage that culture.

## Theoretical Background

Culture is generally seen as important in several respects. Culture is what knits the members of a community together. It is a pattern of beliefs and expectations which produces norms that powerfully shape the behaviour of individuals and groups (O'Reilly, 1989). Culture is our mental software (Hofstede, Hofstede and Minkov, 2011). The cultural perspective puts the individual in his social and cultural environment. Students have a history and background related to family, education and upbringing. When they grow older and leave their homes to study at university, they enter into a new academic environment of university staff and peers that influences them (Pascarella and Terenzini, 2005).

An honours community might have specific features that distinguish it and its culture from the academic community and dominant culture as a whole. The culture of honours communities is generally characterized as excellence-oriented. Students have high expectations and impose high demands on themselves and each other; a culture of working hard, getting the best out of themselves. Students experience their honours community, with its motivated and talented peers, as stimulating (Van Eijl, 2007). Honours students have a strong intrinsic motivation; they highly value courses that fit in with their own personal interests, courses that are challenging and awaken their curiosity (Wolfensberger and Offringa, 2012). Intrinsic motivation is strongly associated with self-regulation (Ryan and Deci, 2000), and self-regulated learning with the use of metacognitive strategies (Zimmermann, 1990).

Creativity, 'thinking out of the box', is often mentioned as a characteristic, based on theories of Renzulli (1978) and Sternberg (2003). Sternberg mentions the creative innovator, who stands up to vested interests and defies the crowd. Mariz (2008) defines honours culture as a culture of intellectual challenge, inquiring and fearless questioning. Slavin (2008) stresses the importance of taking intellectual risks.

Based on literature on honours students and honours education, four elements of a culture within an honours community can be distinguished. Honours students are directed towards:

- their personal development, driven by intrinsic motivation, self-regulation and reflection;
- cooperation within their community, working together with like-minded others and sharing knowledge;
- innovation: displaying curiosity, asking questions and searching for creative and innovative solutions;
- excellence: setting high standards and striving for the best result.

In this way, honours culture can be regarded as a model of a culture of excellence.

## Research Questions

Research questions (summarized) are:

- Which features characterize the culture of an honours community, according to honours students and honours teachers?
- How do honours students experience interaction with the environment outside their honours community?
- What do honours teachers do in order to encourage an 'honours culture' and stimulate the four elements of honours culture?

## Method

Students were interviewed in small groups. Five groups of honours students (3–5 persons) from different faculties (*schools*) of Hanze University, Groningen, were interviewed on the basis of a schedule with five components:

- What I think is important … (related to honours)
- What the group thinks is important …
- The way of acting within the honours community
- Influence of/ influence on the honours teacher
- Influence of/ influence on the environment outside honours

Students were asked to write down their observations on these issues on 'post-it notes' (individually) and to stick them on to a large sheet. Their observations were then discussed. Eighteen students in total signed up for the interviews and participated voluntary.

Transcripts of the interviews with students were analyzed with Atlas.ti (software for qualitative data analysis). Text segments of students were encoded by two researchers, independently at first, followed by discussion in order to reach consensus. Codes were attached on the basis of student text segments independent of theoretical frames. Codes were linked to the elements of the theoretical framework afterwards only.

Ten honours teachers of Hanze University Groningen were interviewed individually by means of a semi-structured interview. Honours teachers were selected randomly from a list. Transcripts of the interviews were summarized afterwards.

## Results

Interviews with students and teachers confirmed the existence of several features of an honours culture. What students value as important is the challenge that the honours programme offers them and their freedom to work on their own personal and professional development. They also appreciate the chances they are offered in connection with the working field.

They experience their honours community as very stimulating and experience their fellow honours students as like-minded in various ways: in motivation, in helping each other, in sharing the same goals and interests and in appreciation of quality. They trust each other and value collaboration in a good atmosphere, sharing knowledge and learning together, respect, and being critical and honest. Data-analysis showed that features connected to the elements *personal development* and *community* were mentioned more often than features concerning *excellence* and *innovation*. The aspects related to *innovation* in particular were not mentioned very often by students. However, the fact that students did not mention these aspects spontaneously does not necessarily prove that these aspects are of no importance.

Students mentioned several characteristics of honours teachers. Honours teachers enforce critical thinking, reflection and personal development, help to create new insights and to draw connections. Teachers tend to be supportive, enthusiastic and open, contributing their own ideas and thoughts. The relationship between students and teachers is more equal than in regular education. The environment can have an influence on honours students in different ways: sometimes stimulating and appreciative, sometimes negative. Honours students often feel that they are regarded as show-offs ('strebers') or eager beavers. High expectations from teachers and others often put a lot of pressure on honours students. Honours students, however, evoke a sense of enthusiasm and pride, particularly from the part of their honours teachers.

Honours teachers characterize honours students as being open, responsible, good at giving and taking feedback, having the courage to tell the truth. They stimulate each other, are creative, enjoy working together, operate as a team, and so on. They are also motivated and ambitious and look for quality. They have the capacity to reflect on their activities and their development and are more self-regulating in learning than regular students. Teachers support the elements of 'honours culture' in a number of ways:

- Personal development, by asking the right questions, stimulating reflection on student personality profiles or personal development plans, by respecting the student's choices, without prescribing what the student should do.
- Community activities are encouraged by group meetings, group facilities, the use of social media and informal meetings.
- The search for creative and innovative solutions is stimulated by complex real-life assignments that call for research and creativity, by critical questioning or even by techniques of creative thinking.
- Honours teachers indicate that students make great demands on themselves as a student and work hard to get the best results. Teachers have high expectations, but in many cases they feel the necessity of 'cooling down' the high aspirations of students.

## Conclusions and Discussion

The results of this survey appear to be unambiguous and in line with literature on gifted students and honours education. A culture of excellence (as defined by the four elements) clearly seems to develop within honours communities and is stimulated by honours teachers. The same features of honours culture are mentioned spontaneously by students as well as teachers, and are encouraged by teachers in several ways.

Conclusions should be drawn with care, however. The interviews concern a relatively small number of students and teachers. The honours students participating in the interviews had not been selected for the interviews at random, but willingly signed up: therefore, the group as a whole could have been more varied. The interviews were held exclusively with students and teachers from Hanze University of Applied Sciences in Groningen and the results, therefore, might not necessarily be applicable to other universities. Nevertheless, the results indicate that:

- Honours programmes should combine individual freedom and self-regulated activities for students with the forming of an inspiring honours community;
- Honours students should be matched with special types of teacher; those who can coach students by contributing to the thinking process, asking questions, stimulating reflection and critical thinking;
- Honours programmes should pay attention to time management and the handling of high, often unrealistic, expectations;
- It is important to create a safe environment in which students dare to express themselves, ask questions and take risks.

If indeed a distinct honours culture (or culture of excellence) is established as a result of honours programmes, it might contribute to a culture of excellence on a larger scale, especially by establishing new role models for *all* students. More research on this issue will be carried out.

## References

Eijl, P. J. van. (2007). *Honours, tool for promoting excellence. Eindrapport van het project "Talentontwikkeling in Honoursprogramma's en de meerwaarde die dat oplevert".* Utrecht: Universiteit Utrecht, IVLOS-Mededeling nr. 82.

Hofstede, G., Hofstede, G. J., & Minkov, M. (2011). *Allemaal andersdenkenden. Omgaan met cultuurverschillen.* Amsterdam/Antwerpen: Uitgeverij Contact.

Mariz, G. (2008). The Culture of Honors. *Journal of the National Collegiate Honors Council, 9* (1), 19–25.

Ministerie van OCW (2007). *Strategische agenda voor het hoger onderwijs-, onderzoek- en wetenschapsbeleid.* Den Haag: Ministerie van OCW.

Ministerie van OCW (2011). *Kwaliteit in verscheidenheid. Strategische Agenda Hoger Onderwijs, Onderzoek en wetenschap.* Den Haag: Ministerie van OCW.

O'Reilly, Ch. (1989). Corporations, Culture, and Commitment: Motivation and Social Control in Organizations. *California Management Review,* Summer 1989: 9–23.

Pascarella, E. T., & Terenzini, P. T. (2005). *How College Affects Students. Volume 2. A Third Decade of Research.* San Francisco: Jossey-Bass.

Renzulli, J. S. (1978). What makes giftedness? Reexamining a definition. *Phi Delta Kappan, 60,* 180–184.

Ryan, R. M., & Deci, E. L. (2000). Intrinsic and Extrinsic Motivations: Classic Definitions and New Directions. *Contemporary Educational Psychology 25,* 54–67.

Slavin, Ch. (2008). Defining Honors Culture. *Journal of the National Collegiate Honors Council, 9* (1), 15–18.

Sternberg, R. J. (2003). WICS as a model of giftedness. *High ability studies, 14,* 109–139.

Wolfensberger, M. V. C., & Offringa, G. J. (2012). Qualities honours students look for in Faculty and Courses, Revisited. *Journal of the National Collegiate Honors Council, 13* (2), 171–182.

Zimmerman, B. J. (1990). Self-Regulated Learning and Academic Achievement: An Overview. *Educational Psychologist, 25* (1), 3–37.

# Retention, Graduation and Programme Completion for Students Entering an Honours Programme at a Major Public University, 1998–2010

*Lynne Goodstein, Patricia Szarek and Frank Wunschel*

The use of honours education to recruit high-achieving students to public universities has increased in recent decades. Sederberg (2007) describes the trend among public universities to convert existing honours programmes to become what some institutions view as more elite honours colleges. Others have written about the pressures from higher administration to expand the size of existing honours programmes, thereby increasing the proportion of the overall student body comprised of honours students (Sederberg, 2007; Lanier, 2007; Goodstein, 2012).

Most honours programmes utilize quantitative measures, in whole or in part, as determinants of the admissions process. Standardized test scores, high school grade point averages, and class rank are generally correlated with likelihood of admission to an honours programme.[1] These "input" measures reflect the academic achievement of entering students and may contribute to higher institutional rankings. However, they do not, in and of themselves, provide information on the impact of the presence of these high-achieving students on the institution to which they are admitted, nor do they reflect the significance of this elite status on the honours students themselves.

A premise of most honours programmes is that the presence of a cohort of higher-achieving students on campus will enhance the general intellectual environment of the university and improve the overall level of student success, as indicated by, for example, retention and graduation rates. College persistence and completion have been extensively theorized about (Pascarella & Terenzini, 1980; Tinto, 1993) and empirically studied in general college populations (Astin, 1975) in efforts to identify predictors. Some of the most significant predictors of both persistence and completion are the same measures used to admit students to honours programmes (Astin, 1975; Beecher & Fischer, 1999; Smith, Edminster & Sullivan, 2001). Therefore, it is logical that honours programmes would provide universities with the ability to retain and graduate students at higher overall rates.

---

1    In the interests of brevity, "honours programme" will be used in this paper to refer also to honours colleges.

## University Retention and Graduation Rates among Honours and Non-Honours Students

There have been no published studies explicitly assessing the impact of the presence of honours students on overall retention and graduation rates, but some comparisons of honours and non-honours students on retention and graduation have been performed. As would be expected, when statistical controls are not applied, honours students do persist in college and graduate at higher levels than the general population of undergraduates. Pflaum, Pascarella and Duby (1985), studying one-year retention rates without controlling for academic variables, reported higher one-year retention rates for students enrolled in an honours programme compared with non-honours students. Slavin, Coladarci and Pratt (2008) also reported higher one-year retention rates for students who had completed honours requirements compared with non-honours students.

A stronger argument for the value of honours education requires the use of statistical controls to compare similarly situated honours and non-honours students on retention and graduation rates. Honours education can be time- and resource-consuming, and it would be logical that honours students would succeed at higher rates than similarly situated non-honours students. There are a few studies that address this question, and the results are mixed. Controlling for SAT and high school rank, Slavin and colleagues (2008) reported that participation in an honours college increases the likelihood of one-year retention but does not increase the likelihood of graduation. Wolgemuth, Whalen, Sullivan, Nading, Shelley and Wang (2006–2007), in a large-scale multivariate study of predictors of retention and graduation at a public research university, found that participation in honours did not show a difference in one- and two-year retention rates but *reduced* the likelihood of retention in years 3 and 4, possibly because of increased likelihood of transferring out among high-achieving students in the study. Like Slavin and colleagues (2008), they found that participation in honours was not related to the likelihood of graduation, controlling for demographic and academic variables.

It is somewhat surprising that evidence for stronger and more consistent impacts of honours programmes on retention and graduation have not been found in existing studies, given the mission of honours education. One would expect that involvement in an honours programme would result in students experiencing greater collegiate success than similarly situated peers who do not receive the benefits of an honours education. This is indeed the finding of Slavin and colleagues (2008) with respect to one- and two-year retention, but not for graduation rates. Given that significant resources are invested in the smaller classes, interdisciplinary seminars, supplemental advising, special-ized programming, residential communities, required honours theses, and the like, it seems important to further explore the academic benefits students obtain by virtue of their participation in an honours programme.

## Retention and Completion within Honours Programmes

What is necessary for students who are admitted to an honours programme to have a true "honours experience?" The benefits of membership in an hon-ours programme can only be delivered if students actively participate in the programmes and services available to them. Some students may accept a spot in an honours programme because of encouragement from parents or as a credential for their résumés, but then they might choose not to take full ad-vantage of opportunities offered. Students who are not fully involved in the curriculum or programming of honours programmes cannot obtain all the academic, intellectual, social or cultural benefits available. They may do the minimum to remain on the programme as long as possible as "freeloaders," enjoying the perquisites of membership while avoiding the responsibilities.

Perhaps more importantly, there are university-wide implications of non- or under-participating honours students in the form of empty seats in honours classes or less than full programme audiences. There is also an opportunity cost because other honours-eligible students who would have been fully participat-ing members could not be admitted to the programme due to a lack of space.

Ultimately, underperforming honours students are most likely to drop out or be dismissed from the programme by virtue of their failure to fulfil require-ments for participation in coursework or thesis completion. This non-com-pletion, as Campbell and Fuqua (2008–2009: 130) note, "carries personal, family, and institutional consequences. An element of pride and self-worth is associated with a new college student's acceptance into an honours pro-gramme and the accompanying label of "honours student." When a student ceases to participate in the programme and the label is removed, feelings of academic-related inadequacy and family disappointment often result."

In this way, one can think of nonparticipation or minimal participation in the curriculum and services of an honours programme as a retention and graduation issue. Just as persistence through four, five or six years and gradu-ation from the university are viewed as indicators of success for non-honours students, one could look at remaining in good standing in an honours pro-gramme and graduation as an honours scholar, or with honours, as indicators of success.

The question of retention and completion rates within honours programmes has received even less research attention than overall university
retention and graduation rates. There are two published studies that focus on
retention and completion of college honours programmes. Cosgrove (2004)
investigated academic performance and time to degree for three groups –
honours programme completers, non-completers and high-ability non-honours students – who entered three public comprehensive universities in
Pennsylvania. He found that students who completed honours programmes
had higher academic performance and shorter time to degree than both
partial completers and high-ability non-honours students. Hence, students
who completed their honours requirements demonstrated greater academic
success than students who began but did not complete in honours. It is critical
to note, however, that of the 113 honours students included in Cosgrove's study
(2004), only 30, or 27%, actually completed programme requirements.

The most comprehensive study of retention and programme completion
among honours students was conducted by Campbell and Fuqua (2008–
2009). The focus of their study was on predictors of student completion of
a collegiate honours programme at a major mid-western research university.
Researchers examined the most effective variables in discriminating among
three groups: honours programme completers, partial-completers and
non-completers. Campbell and Fuqua (2008–2009) found that high school
GPA, class rank, first semester college GPA, gender, and freshman honours
housing were the most important predictors of programme completion. Honours freshman housing was found to be one of the only variables that can
be reasonably easily influenced by programme administrators as a contrib-
utor to programme completion. Again, however, it is noteworthy that, of the
336 honours entering freshmen in the study, only 62, or 18.45%, completed
all honours degree requirements by the end of five years. An additional 73,
or 22%, completed the General Honours Award, while 201 (60%) earned no
honours awards.

The completion rates as reflected in these two published studies appear
quite low. Essentially, these researchers' findings are that, of those students
who begin in honours programmes as freshmen, the vast majority (over 70%)
do not obtain full programme benefits. As the honours equivalent of the
overall university graduation rate, these low rates are of concern; yet, there is
little published information regarding honours completion rates. Given the
considerable investment made by universities in their honours programmes,
it is important to know more about retention and completion in honours.

The two cited studies provide indicators of the variables administrators
should look for during the admissions process but, with the exception of

initial honours housing (Campbell and Fuqua, 2008–2009), these predictors are (or are highly correlated with) the same input variables already used in honours admission decisions. Therefore, these studies, while they are important efforts to shed light on an understudied subject of great importance to honours programmes, offer little help in identifying strategies that may result in increased programme completion rates.

## Programme Factors Affecting Honours Retention and Completion

Both Cosgrove (2004) as well as Campbell and Fuqua (2008–2009) acknowledge that, theoretically at least, retention and completion in honours should be associated with specific programme characteristics. Among honours programmes nationally, wide variability exists with regard to specific admissions criteria, curricular, programme and residential offerings, academic and participation criteria for remaining in good standing, and academic, curricular, and independent research requirements for earning official recognitions. There is no accrediting body for honours programmes; the primary means for promoting some degree of standardization are documents published by the National Collegiate Honors Council (NCHC, 2010, 2010a) outlining "Basic Characteristics of a Fully Developed Honours Program" and a similar document for honours colleges. At the same time, honours programmes pride themselves in their unique offerings, climate and character, and considerable discretion across schools and colleges exists with respect to how the NCHC guidelines are followed.

If an institution's goal were to increase honours completion rates, what are some of the actions it could take? Based upon the study of Campbell and Fuqua (2008–2009), admissions selectivity is probably the most effective strategy to lead to greater program completion. Admitting only students with extremely high scores, however, may come into direct conflict with the interests of the university in increasing the overall academic caliber of incoming students. Other programmatic initiatives such as honours freshman housing and promotion of honours community through student organizations, community service, and effective co-curricular programming may strengthen students' identification with honours and reinforce awareness of honours requirements and expectations for fulfilling them. On the curricular side, easy availability of coursework for fulfilling honours requirements, informed honours advising, and clear communication of "roadmaps" for fulfilling requirements may foster retention and completion. Merit scholarships may also play a role as both "carrot and stick" in retention and graduation. A merit scholarship acts as a carrot by attracting students with higher academic ability who might not otherwise attend the institution and, in the case of universities that tie scholarship to programme participation, a stick through its threat of removal if students do not conform to honours requirements.

The level of rigour of specific honours requirements is likely to influence programme completion rates. Most honours programmes require students to maintain a specified grade point average while some also require enrollment in a specified number of honours credits per year. Some programmes require the completion of an honours thesis or project for programme completion. Virtually all programmes specify the completion of a minimum number of honours course credits for programme completion. Higher grade point averages, more demanding annual participation requirements, higher numbers of required honours credits earned, and a mandatory honours thesis are most likely related to lower programme completion rates.

Another strategy used by some universities that might be related to programme completion rates is the mid-career honours award. This award recognizes students' fulfillment of honours coursework and other requirements during their first two years, generally prior to engaging more deeply in work in the major subject of study and independent research. It is unclear how this mid-career award would impact retention and, more importantly, completion of the four-year honours award. Some students may view the receipt of the mid-career award as an appropriate stopping point and be less likely to persist in honours beyond the receipt of this award. On the other hand, working toward the mid-career award may result in students becoming more engaged in the honours community and more knowledgeable about the benefits of honours work. Therefore, it is possible that receipt of a mid-career award would increase a student's likelihood of full programme completion.

The current study focuses on retention and programme completion rates of multiple cohorts of entrants to an honours programme at a major public university. There are few published studies on this topic, and none with as extensive a study population; so this work provides baseline data that hopefully will be of use to other institutions pondering their own retention and completion rates. The fact that the study follows multiple cohorts of entrants throughout their college careers also enables researchers to track changes in retention and graduation rates over time. Changes in these rates may be associated with programmatic interventions that were put in place over the study period.

While the primary focus of the study is on students' retention and completion within the honours programme, the research also addresses these students' retention and graduation rates within the university at large. There are two reasons for assessing rates of university retention and graduation of honours entrants. First, the benefits of recruiting high-achieving students rely upon their participation in the university's academic and community life. If these students transfer out, the opportunity for them to elevate the overall academic life of the university is lost. Second, university retention and graduation are a gauge of honours students' satisfaction with the education offered by the university, as most would have other attractive options if they were not satisfied.

In summary, the current study focuses on three major questions. First, what are overall university retention and graduation rates for students who begin university life enrolled in an honours programme? Second, what proportion of entering honours students fulfil requirements to receive honours awards mid-career and at graduation? Third, do students who receive mid-career honours awards earn four-year honours at graduation at higher or lower rates than their peers who choose not to earn the mid-career award? A further focus of our analysis will be to examine whether there were changes in retention and programme completion rates among the multiple cohorts over time and, if so, whether those changes appear to be associated with changes put in place to strengthen the quality of the honours programme during the years in question.

## Methodology

*Participants and Institutional Context*

Participants in this study consist of cohorts of all freshmen entering the honours programme at a major public research university in the Eastern United States during fall terms from 1998 through 2010. To be included in the cohort, entering freshmen were coded in the university system as a "member" of the honours programme on the 10th day of the fall semester. They were then tracked for up to 6 years or until graduation, whichever came first. Table 1 indicates demographic and academic characteristics of each cohort. The extent of diversity in the cohorts ranged from 15% to 33% underrepresented minorities, with their proportions gradually increasing over time. The gender balance of entering honours students shifted from slightly more females from 1998 to 2003 to slightly more males in 2004 and beyond. Class rank remained constant throughout the study period, with cohorts averaging in the top 5% of their high school classes. Average SAT scores (critical reading + quantitative reasoning) trended upwards during the study period, from 1341 in 1998 to 1393 in 2010. The institution from which data were gathered is a public research extensive land-grant residential university in the eastern United States with a population in 2009 of approximately 16,000 undergraduates and 5,000 graduate students.

*Table 1:      Demographics and Academic Characteristics of Entering Honours Freshmen, 1998–2010*

|  | 1998 | 1999 | 2000 | 2001 | 2002 | 2003 | 2004 |
|---|---|---|---|---|---|---|---|
| # Freshmen | 205 | 241 | 268 | 305 | 263 | 247 | 257 |
| % Female | 55% | 57% | 53% | 52% | 54% | 52% | 47% |
| % Minority | 17% | 15% | 18% | 15% | 16% | 15% | 18% |
| Avg SAT (CR+M) | 1341 | 1351 | 1333 | 1345 | 1351 | 1356 | 1382 |
| Avg HS Rank | 95 | 95 | 94 | 94 | 95 | 96 | 96 |

|  | 2005 | 2006 | 2007 | 2008 | 2009 | 2010 | |
|---|---|---|---|---|---|---|---|
| # Freshmen | 263 | 301 | 291 | 337 | 389 | 443 | |
| % Female | 50% | 44% | 50% | 47% | 46% | 45% | |
| % Minority | 22% | 26% | 33% | 26% | 26% | 28% | |
| Avg SAT (CR+M) | 1398 | 1397 | 1402 | 1388 | 1395 | 1393 | |
| Avg HS Rank | 96 | 96 | 95 | 95 | 95 | 96 | |

Admission to the honours programme at the university under study is by invitation only and involves a holistic review process. All applicants to the university are considered, and admission decisions are based upon the following considerations: academic (GPA, SAT/ACT), high school competitiveness, diversity, and special talents, with academic criteria being most heavily weighted. It is noteworthy that, during the study period, the size of the entering freshman cohort increased dramatically, from 205 in 1998 to 443 in 2010, a 116% increase. This increase reflected a strategic decision by the university administration to improve the academic quality of the undergraduate population as a whole by targeting students eligible for honours and providing sufficient spaces in the programme to accommodate them (for further discussion of the politics of honours expansion, see Goodstein, 2012).

Once students join the honours programme, they must meet certain academic and participation standards. Annual reviews of all honours students take place over the summer, and students who fail to meet these standards are placed on probation or dismissed. To remain in good standing and receive honours awards, until 2007 students were required to earn at least a

3.2 grade point average; this criterion was raised to 3.4 for students entering in subsequent years. There is a sliding scale to allow students earlier in their college careers the opportunity to "catch up" by being placed on probation rather than being dismissed. Students are also required to enrol in at least one honours course per year to meet the participation requirement.

At the university under study, two honours awards are given: sophomore honours (mid-career award) and graduation as an honours scholar (end-career award). Criteria for sophomore honours include earning 16–18 honours course credits (including the completion of one interdisciplinary core course from 2007 on), participation in a specified number of co-curricular events sponsored by the honours programme, and the requisite GPA. Students in good standing who did not earn sophomore honours are still eligible to graduate as an honours scholar. To earn this award, students must be in good standing in the honours programme, earn at least 12 honours credits related to the major, complete an honours thesis, and fulfill any additional departmental requirements.

Beginning with the entering 2003 cohort, university and honours programme leadership implemented a strategic plan for improving the quality of the honours experience for students. Considerable effort was directed toward strengthening the quality of honours programmes, curriculum, and services, with the goal of reinforcing students' identification as members of the honours programme. These efforts took many forms, including the development of a set of interdisciplinary core courses, the creation of a freshman seminar programme, enhanced honours advising, expansion of co-curricular cultural, intellectual and social programmes, fostering student involvement in Honours Council and other student organizations, and developing a menu of honours study abroad programmes. Probably the highest impact on community-building was achieved through implementing mandatory honours housing for first year students. Whereas there had previously been no separate honours housing for first year students, by 2004 all incoming honours residential students were required to live in one residential facility on campus. Additional honours housing for upper class students was developed as a result of student demand so that, by 2010, 50% of all honours students lived in honours housing.

## Results

The data to track first and second year university retention rates were only available for the 2002 entering class onward, so data are presented for entering honours cohorts from 2002 to 2010. Figure 1 illustrates one-year university retention rates. The proportion of entering freshman honours students who returned to the university for their second years ranged from 95% to 98%. University second-year retention rates[2] for the same entering honours freshman cohorts ranged from 92% to 95%. These trend lines are essentially flat.

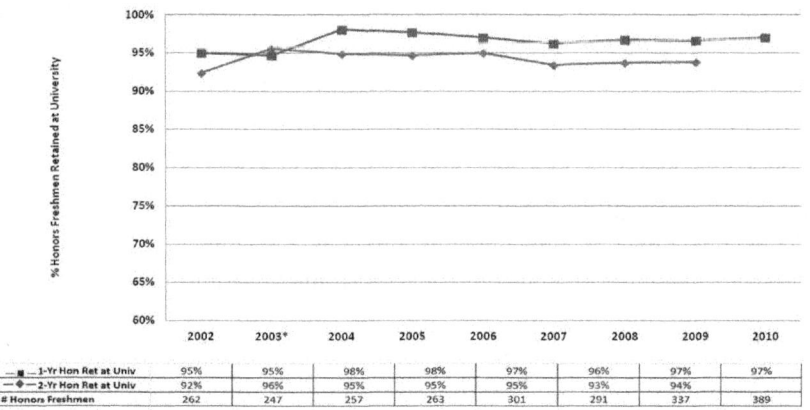

| | 2002 | 2003* | 2004 | 2005 | 2006 | 2007 | 2008 | 2009 | 2010 |
|---|---|---|---|---|---|---|---|---|---|
| 1-Yr Hon Ret at Univ | 95% | 95% | 98% | 98% | 97% | 96% | 97% | 97% | |
| 2-Yr Hon Ret at Univ | 92% | 96% | 95% | 95% | 95% | 93% | 94% | | |
| # Honors Freshmen | 262 | 247 | 257 | 263 | 301 | 291 | 337 | 389 | |

*\* A small number of students entering in 2003 were not enrolled at the university in 2004, but returned from leaves of absences in 2005. This led to a higher 2-year retention rate than 1-year retention rate.*

Figure 1:    *1- & 2-Year Retention at the University for Students Entering as Honours Freshmen, 2002–2010*

Figure 2 illustrates six-year university graduation rates for honours freshmen entering from 1998 through 2004. Students who enter the university as honours students graduate at impressively high levels. For the eight cohorts studied, graduation rates increase slightly from 88% for students entering in 1998 through 2000 to the low 90s for students entering in 2003 through 2005.

Figure 3 illustrates one- and two-year retention rates *in honours* for cohorts entering the university from 2002 to 2010. One- and two-year retention rates reflect the proportion of students in each entering cohort considered to be "in good standing" in the honours programme on the tenth day of the fall semester in their second and third years, respectively. Students would be considered not in good standing if they had been dismissed for failing to maintain the necessary grade point average, for non-participation, or for voluntarily withdrawing from the programme.

---

2   Due to the time lag in obtaining this information, only one-year retention rates for this analysis and others in the paper are available for students entering in 2010.

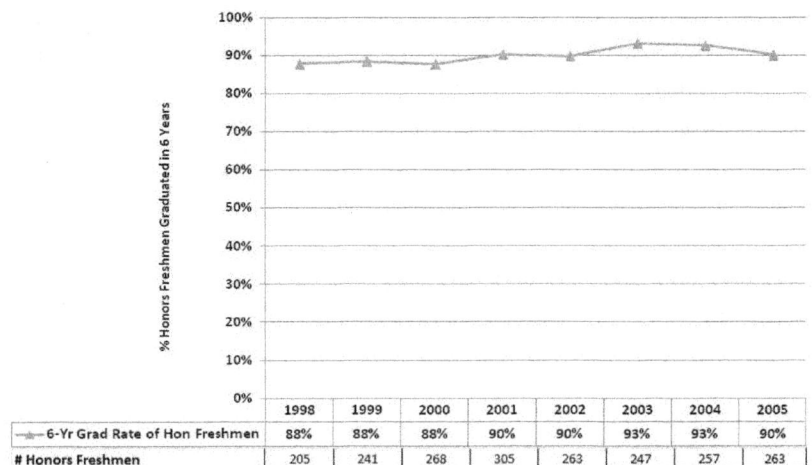

| | 1998 | 1999 | 2000 | 2001 | 2002 | 2003 | 2004 | 2005 |
|---|---|---|---|---|---|---|---|---|
| 6-Yr Grad Rate of Hon Freshmen | 88% | 88% | 88% | 90% | 90% | 93% | 93% | 90% |
| # Honors Freshmen | 205 | 241 | 268 | 305 | 263 | 247 | 257 | 263 |

*Figure 2:*   *6-Year Graduation from the University for Students Entering as Honours Freshmen, 1998–2005*

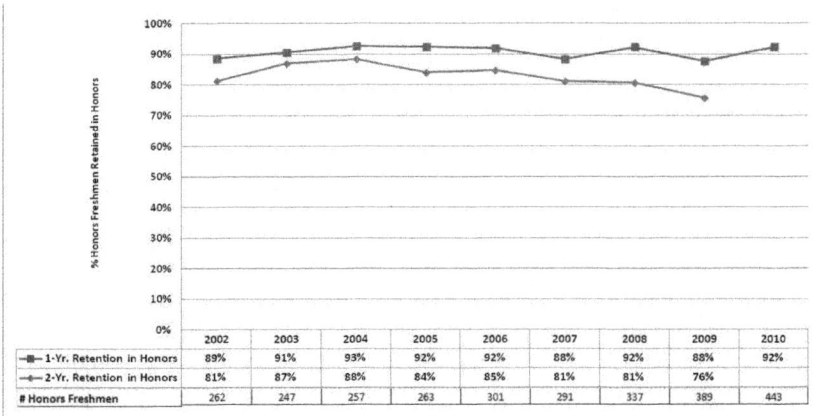

| | 2002 | 2003 | 2004 | 2005 | 2006 | 2007 | 2008 | 2009 | 2010 |
|---|---|---|---|---|---|---|---|---|---|
| 1-Yr. Retention in Honors | 89% | 91% | 93% | 92% | 92% | 88% | 92% | 88% | 92% |
| 2-Yr. Retention in Honors | 81% | 87% | 88% | 84% | 85% | 81% | 81% | 76% | |
| # Honors Freshmen | 262 | 247 | 257 | 263 | 301 | 291 | 337 | 389 | 443 |

*Figure 3:*   *1- & 2-Year Retention in Honours for Students Entering as Honours Freshmen, 2002–2010*

One-year honours retention rates varied little across the study period and were uniformly high. Between 88% and 92% of each cohort entering between 2002 and 2010 were members of the programme one year later. Two-year retention rates were also relatively strong; between 76% and 88% of cohorts entering as freshmen during this time period were still in honours at the start of their third years. The trend for two-year retention shows a slight downward slope. A partial reason for this decline can be attributed to the implementation of a more stringent grade point average requirement beginning with the 2008 cohort. Like first-year retention rates, the trend line for second-year retention rates is still relatively flat.

Figure 4 presents data on mid-career programme completion, that is, the proportion of each honours freshman cohort from 1998 to 2008 that completed all sophomore honours requirements. The trend line for mid-career programme completion illustrates a shift to a higher rate of completion starting with the 2003 cohort. For students starting in 1998–2002, the proportion earning sophomore honours hovered in the 20%–30% range. With the 2003 cohort, the proportion earning sophomore honours shifted to the high 40% to mid 50% range, with a peak of 60% for the 2006 cohort.

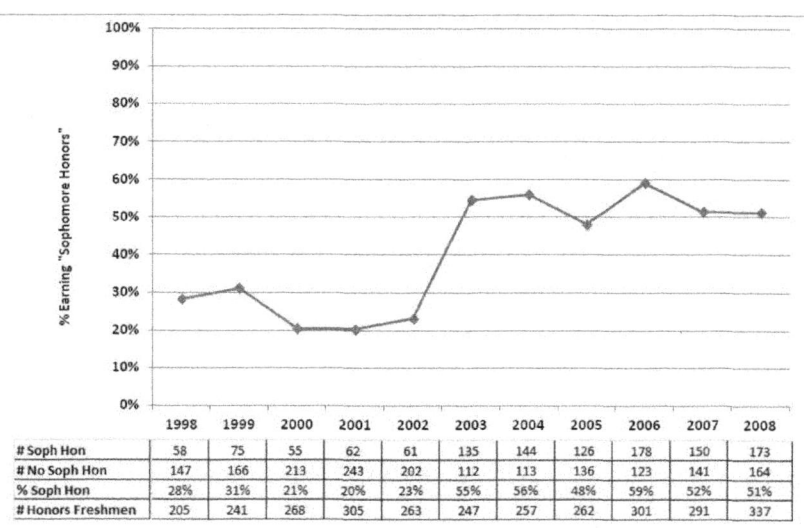

|  | 1998 | 1999 | 2000 | 2001 | 2002 | 2003 | 2004 | 2005 | 2006 | 2007 | 2008 |
|---|---|---|---|---|---|---|---|---|---|---|---|
| # Soph Hon | 58 | 75 | 55 | 62 | 61 | 135 | 144 | 126 | 178 | 150 | 173 |
| # No Soph Hon | 147 | 166 | 213 | 243 | 202 | 112 | 113 | 136 | 123 | 141 | 164 |
| % Soph Hon | 28% | 31% | 21% | 20% | 23% | 55% | 56% | 48% | 59% | 52% | 51% |
| # Honors Freshmen | 205 | 241 | 268 | 305 | 263 | 247 | 257 | 262 | 301 | 291 | 337 |

*Figure 4: Mid-career honours programme completion ("sophomore honours") for students entering as honours freshmen, 1998–2008*

Figure 5 presents data on the rates with which entering cohorts fulfilled all requirements to graduate as honours scholars, including the completion of an honours thesis, within six years for 2001 thorough 2005 cohorts and, because the data are not yet available, within four years for 2006–2007 cohorts. While the differences are less dramatic, the trend data for end-career programme completers follows the same basic pattern. This proportion is in the 20% to

30% range for 1998 to 2002 cohorts. Then, beginning with the 2003 cohort, the proportion of programme completers increases to the 40%–50% range.[3]

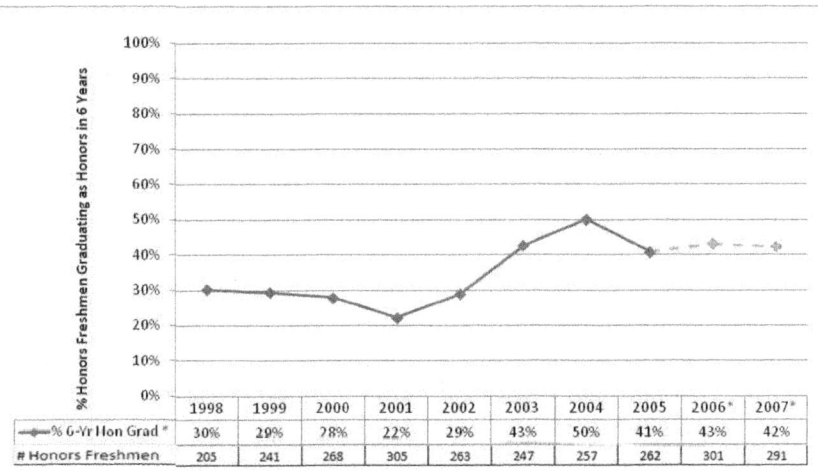

| | 1998 | 1999 | 2000 | 2001 | 2002 | 2003 | 2004 | 2005 | 2006* | 2007* |
|---|---|---|---|---|---|---|---|---|---|---|
| % 6-Yr Hon Grad * | 30% | 29% | 28% | 22% | 29% | 43% | 50% | 41% | 43% | 42% |
| # Honors Freshmen | 205 | 241 | 268 | 305 | 263 | 247 | 257 | 262 | 301 | 291 |

*y-axis label: % Honors Freshmen Graduating as Honors in 6 Years*

\* 4-Yr Hon Grad rates are shown for 2006 & 2007 cohorts.

*Figure 5:*   *End-career honours programme completion (graduation as an honours scholar) for students entering as honours freshmen, 1998–2007\**

Our final analysis was designed to explore whether the likelihood of end-career programme completion is associated with mid-career programme completion. Because some students who were part of each cohort were not eligible for the mid-career awards due to dismissal, transfer, or opting out of the programme, they were dropped from the analysis for each cohort. The reduced cohort sizes can be found in Figure 6. We have divided each cohort into two subgroups, those who completed and those who did not complete sophomore honours. For each cohort, 1998 through 2007, we then present the likelihood that students in each subgroup have earned the end-career award. The data show that, among the eight cohorts studied, between 47% and 69% of those students who earned sophomore honours went on to graduate as honours scholars. By contrast, for students who did not earn sophomore honours, the rates of end-career programme completion ranged between 24% and 35%. The trend lines for both groups are relatively flat across the entire time frame of the study.

---

3   The 6-year end-career program completion rates for the 2006 and 2007 cohorts *will* increase, although we do not know by how much. This is because some of the students in these cohorts have remained a 5th and 6th year due to double majors, change of majors, etc., and do not complete their theses until their fifth or sixth years.

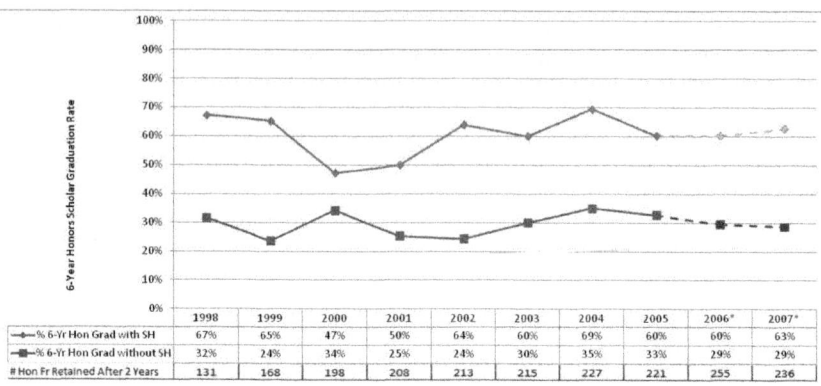

| | 1998 | 1999 | 2000 | 2001 | 2002 | 2003 | 2004 | 2005 | 2006* | 2007* |
|---|---|---|---|---|---|---|---|---|---|---|
| % 6-Yr Hon Grad with SH | 67% | 65% | 47% | 50% | 64% | 60% | 69% | 60% | 60% | 63% |
| % 6-Yr Hon Grad without SH | 32% | 24% | 34% | 25% | 24% | 30% | 35% | 33% | 29% | 29% |
| # Hon Fr Retained After 2 Years | 131 | 168 | 198 | 208 | 213 | 215 | 227 | 221 | 255 | 236 |

\* 4-Yr Hon Grad rates are shown for 2006 and 2007 cohorts.

*Figure 6:   End-career honours scholar completion ("graduation as an honours
scholar") after 6 years for students retained in honours after 2 years,
who did and did not earn sophomore honours, 1998–2007\**

## Discussion

### University Retention and Graduation rates

Study findings underscore the impressively high first and second year retention rates of students entering the honours programme as freshmen. Over 95%
of honours freshmen entering the university from 2002 through 2009 were
matriculated at the university as sophomores; for some cohorts the retention
rates were as high as 98%. These findings support the research of others who
have identified academic quantitative measures such as SAT/ACT scores and
high school grade point average, factors used in the honours admissions process, as strong predictors of first-year retention (Pflaum et al., 1985; Campbell
& Fuqua, 2008–2009).

The research demonstrates that, at the university under study, between
92% and 96% of entering cohorts of honours freshmen between 2002 and
2009 were still enrolled in the university by the start of their junior years.
This suggests that the university as a whole has been successful in retaining its
highest achieving students.

Such high university retention rates for honours students are noteworthy
because they counter arguments that high achieving students may not receive
the level of academic challenge and engagement at a public research university
that they expect, or that may be consistent with their academic and leadership

abilities. This was the inference made by Wolgemuth and colleagues (2006–2007) when they found what could be considered the counterintuitive finding of lower retention rates among honours students in the upper college years. Others have speculated that honours students may enrol in a public university because they were not admitted to an elite school or to conserve financial resources, but then they would transfer to a more prestigious institution for their junior and senior years. While tracking the destinations of the students who did leave the university is beyond the scope of this study, the authors are aware of students in the study cohorts who did choose to leave. For example, one student transferred to a nearby ivy-league institution to concentrate on international relations, a major that the public institution did not offer.

Six-year university graduation rates of entering honours freshmen cohorts from 1998 to 2004 are consistently high, showing only a two to three percentage point differential from second-year retention rates for the same students. This finding suggests that honours students who are enrolled at the university in their junior years are highly likely to graduate from the university.

These findings underscore the work of others (Wolgemuth et al., 2006–2007) who have documented the benefits of attracting high-achieving high schools students on overall university graduation rates. These data suggest that offering high-achieving high school students a spot in an honours programme may benefit the university by leading to higher overall retention and graduation rates.

Over the study period, it also appears that the proportion of entering honours students graduating from the university has increased slightly, from 88% of the 1998 cohort to 90% of the 2005 cohort. This trend toward higher graduation rates is even more marked for the general university population, with the six-year graduation rate for the same time period increasing from 71% to 83%. Honours student data are included in these general population findings and thus a portion of this increase reflects honours student persistence (Office of Institutional Research, 2010).

## Honours Retention and Programme Completion

We now switch to focus on students' participation within the honours programme. The present study shows that retention in honours remains quite high in both sophomore and junior years, with retention rates of the entering honours cohorts from 2002 through 2009 hovering at the 90% mark for rising sophomores and above 80% for rising juniors. These figures suggest that the vast majority of students in each entering cohort were both academically able and motivated to remain as members in the honours programme into their junior years.

Considering both university retention and graduation rates as well as programme retention rates for entering honours students, it is worth noting that the trend lines for these data series do not only reflect high rates; they are also relatively flat. These data series provide no evidence that the efforts to improve programme quality that were initiated in 2003 were associated with either university retention or graduation rates or programme retention rates. It is possible that the failure to detect change in these rates over the study period is due primarily to a ceiling effect; these rates are so high to begin with that there may be little room for them to move upwards.


*Mid-Career and End-Career Programme Completion*

If the present study had been completed a few years ago with cohorts entering the university prior to 2003, the results of the present study would closely mirror the findings of other published work on programme completion (Cosgrove, 2004; Campbell and Fuqua, 2008–2009). The present study found that students in the 1998 through 2002 cohorts received mid-career and end-career awards at rates between 20% and 30% per cohort. These rates correspond closely to the 27% reported by Cosgrove (2004) for the three comprehensive Pennsylvania state institutions and are only a little higher than the 18% reported by Campbell and Fuqua (2008–2009) for honours students at a more similar public state university.

It is evident, however, that there was a consistent increase in programme completion rates with the cohorts entering the university in 2003 and beyond. This increase is best seen in the mid-career award data series because the time to completion is only two years. Beginning with the class of 2003, a new plateau for programme completion was set, with between 48% and 59% of each entering cohort from 2003 through 2008 earning the mid-career award compared with rates in the 20% range for prior cohorts. End-career programme completion rates demonstrate a similar pattern. For cohorts entering the university in 2003 through 2005, 43%, 50% and 41%, respectively, of cohorts completed the programme by the end of six years; and for those entering in 2006 and 2007, 43% and 42%, respectively, completed the programme by the end of four years.

The completion of the specified honours requirements for the mid-career and end-career award signifies that programme completers have obtained specific benefits that honours students who do not earn these awards may not receive. Sophomore honours recipients have demonstrated successful completion of honours-level courses and exposure to honours co-curricular programming; the end-career award signifies success in honours course-work related to the major and the completion of independent scholarship or research. One might argue that a higher programme completion rate is an important outcome measure of the effectiveness of an honours programme.

The present research has been able to demonstrate change in the rate of mid- and end-career programme completion over a relatively short time in one honours programme at a major public university. As this is a descriptive study, the *reasons* for these changes are only speculative, and causal analyses will require different research designs in futures studies. We suggest two factors that may have led to increased rates of programme completion.

First, we did see some increase in academic qualifications of cohorts, at least as indicated by the average SAT score, during the study period. As other researchers have shown, positive outcomes in student retention and graduation are linked to the input measure of high school academic achievement (Astin, 1975; Beecher & Fisher, 1999; Smith et al., 2001). This study suggests that this finding may apply not only to persistence at the university in general but also persistence within an honours programme. Students motivated to do well on standardized tests may also be more extrinsically motivated towards other formal credentials or certificates such as sophomore honours and graduation as an honours scholar.

Second, we believe that a number of the innovations made to programme delivery beginning in 2003 also contributed critically to more successful outcomes. We believe that these programmatic changes instituted from 2003 onward collectively led to changes in honours students' attitudes about, and identification with, the honours programme and may have made them more motivated to earn awards.

Two programme elements bear special note as possibly impacting on programme completion rates. The first is the growth of honours residential housing. For freshmen, this figure grew dramatically from 0% in 2002 to 94% in 2004 and remained at or above that level in subsequent years. Housing for upper class students has increased also, such that by 2010, 49% of honours students in total lived in honours housing. Also, beginning in 2003, there was a major overhaul of the honours freshman seminar, enabling 90%–95% of honours cohorts to experience micro-communities of classmates, participate in active and engaged learning immediately after arrival, obtain mentorship from older student facilitators, and focus on successful transitions to college (Goodstein, 2004; Lease & Goodstein, 2004).

Other factors, such as interdisciplinary courses, advising, research opportunities, and co-curricular programming designed with the interests of high-achieving students in mind, have the potential of engaging students and possibly increasing their motivation for participating fully in the programme's offerings. A recent qualitative study conducted as an honours thesis underscored the value of co-curricular activities and programming in supporting programme persistence and completion (Holland, 2012).

On the other hand, it may be troubling to note that even after significant efforts to strengthen programme elements, the rates of programme completion are still relatively low. Lower than desired programme completion rates is a topic that begs more empirical research, but the authors have obtained considerable anecdotal information on this subject. Students offer a number of what might be considered "legitimate" reasons for opting out including graduating early, electing additional coursework or more than one major, not finding a thesis topic of sufficient interest, and needing the extra time to study for professional entrance exams (Holland, 2012). Other reasons for not completing the thesis may be structural inadequacies – such as a dearth of willing thesis advisors – inadequately preparing students to conduct independent scholarship, or failing to sufficiently explain the value of the thesis (e.g., to students in professional schools who feel that doing a thesis is irrelevant to their careers).

*The Value of the Mid-Career Award*

While mid-career awards are not common among honours programmes, the university under study has awarded sophomore honours since the programme's early years. Although the requirements for the award are not onerous, the award has never been terribly popular with students and, until the entering 2003 cohort, relatively few students in each entering cohort had earned this award. Even more recently, students frequently ask about the necessity and advisability of earning sophomore honours (Holland, 2012). Aware that the award will have no bearing on their being recognized as honours scholars at graduation, many do not see the value.

Nevertheless, since the university offers such an award for full participation in the honours programme during the first and second years, the honours programme staff and faculty advisors encourage students to seek it. Honours staff and faculty contend that full participation in years one and two will promote a greater level of engagement in honours education and greater academic and personal rewards. Moreover, they assume that this commitment and those rewards would keep students focused on the end-goal of graduation as an honours scholar. However, until this study, there was no evidence to support or refute this assumption.

The results of this study provide evidence that completion of sophomore honours is associated with graduation as an honours scholar. It is noteworthy that this finding is equally applicable to students entering the programme in 1998, years before the implementation of innovations in honours programme curriculum and services, as it is for the later cohorts. The trend line for end-career programme completion rates is essentially flat throughout the study period, indicating that students who earned sophomore honours earlier in the programme's history were as likely to graduate as honours scholars as students earning sophomore honours in more recent years. What is different is that a much smaller proportion of entering honours freshmen earned sophomore honours in the earlier years.

So, something happened around 2003 that led to a higher proportion of entering students earning sophomore honours and then remaining active through to programme completion. We would like to think that the strengthening of programme quality and encouraging students to fully engage in programme activities and curriculum motivated them to fulfill the requirements-starting with sophomore honours. The mid-career award helped to reinforce their involvement and build resolve to continue to completion.

It is also possible that our quality improvements were less determinative than changes in the demographics of our newly admitted cohorts. It is possible that students motivated to do well on standardized tests are also motivated to go for extrinsic rewards. If this is the case, students with higher SATs, who began to arrive in 2004 and later, might be more likely to comply with programme requirements regardless of how strong the programme. Given the descriptive nature of the study, it is not possible to definitively resolve this question; it is one for future researchers to consider.

## Conclusions

This study has presented four major conclusions about honours students' retention and graduation rates at a major university in the northeastern United States. First, at the university under study, honours students are retained at and graduate from the university at exceedingly high levels, implying that most do not transfer out. Second, while they may remain at the university, many students admitted to an honours programme never complete programme requirements. Third, over a ten-year period at the university under study, there was a substantial increase in the rates at which cohorts completed programme requirements, a change temporally associated with an increase in the quality of the programme. Fourth, the study showed that students who completed requirements for the mid-career programme were much more likely to complete the end-career programme. This suggests that earning a mid-career award may reinforce persistence toward receiving the final award, thereby enabling students to obtain the greatest value from their honours education.

### References

Astin, A. W. (1975). *Preventing students from dropping out.* San Francisco, CA: Jossey-Bass.

Beecher, M., & Fischer, L. (1999). High school courses and scores as predictors of college success. *Journal of College Admission, 163*, 4–9.

Campbell, K. C., & Fuqua, D. R. (2008–2009). Factors predictive of student completion in a college honours program. *Journal of College Student Retention, 10*(2), 129–153.

Cosgrove, J. R. (2004). The impact of honours programs on undergraduate academic performance, retention, and graduation. *Journal of the National Collegiate Honors Council, 5*(2), 45–53.

Goodstein, L. (2004). *The Honors first-year experience.* Paper presented at the National Collegiate Honors Council annual meeting, New Orleans, LA.

Goodstein, L. (2012). *A 40-Year Old Honors Program as a Start-Up: Planning for Significant Growth.* Paper presented at the Evoking Excellence in Higher Education and Beyond 2012 Conference, Hanze University, Groningen, the Netherlands, October 5–6, 2012.

Holland, A. A. (2012). Honors Retention: The Persistence of Juniors and Seniors in the Honors Program Through Examination of Commitment to Completion of Honours Thesis. *Honors Scholar Theses.* Paper 247. http://digitalcommons.uconn.edu/srhonors_theses/247.

Lanier, G. W. (2007). Growth = Bucks (?). *Journal of the National Collegiate Honors Council, 8* (1), 33–41.

Lease, J., & Goodstein, L. (2004). *Developing honors students as teachers.* Paper Presented at the National Collegiate Honors Council, New Orleans, LA.

National Collegiate Honors Council (2010). *Basic Characteristics of a Fully Developed Honors College.* (Approved by NCHC Board of Directors on February 19, 2010) http://www.nchchonors.org/basichonorscollegecharacteristics.shtml.

National Collegiate Honors Council (2010a). *Basic Characteristics of a Fully Developed Honours Program.* Approved by the NCHC Executive Committee on

March 4, 1994; amended by the NCHC Board of Directors on November 23, 2007; further amended by the NCHC Board of Directors on February 19, 2010. http://www.nchchonors.org/basichonorsprogramcharacteristics.shtml.

Office of Institutional Research (2010). *Most recent retention rates and graduation rates for entering freshmen classes by campus as of Fall 2009.* University of Connecticut Office of Institutional Research.

Pascarella, E.T., & Terenzini, P. T (1980). Predicting freshman persistence and voluntary dropout decisions from a theoretical model. *Journal of Higher Education, 51*(1), 60–75.

Pflaum, S. W., Pascarella, E. T., & Duby, P. (1985). The effects of honors college participation on academic performance during the freshman year. *Journal of College Student Personnel, 26*(5), 414–419.

Sederberg, P. C. (2007). Nothing fails like success: Managing growth in a highly developed honors program. *Journal of the National Collegiate Honors Council, 8*(1), 17–32.

Slavin, C., Coladarci, T., & Pratt, P. A. (2008). Is student participation in an honors program related to retention and graduation rates? *Journal of the National Collegiate Honors Council,* fall/winter, 59–69.

Smith, W. R., Edminster, J. H., & Sullivan, K. M. (2001). Factors influencing graduation rates at Mississippi's public universities. *College and university, 76*(3), 11–16.

Tinto, V. (1993). *Leaving college: Rethinking the causes and cures of student attrition* (2nd ed.). Chicago, IL: University of Chicago Press.

Wolgemuth, A., Whalen, D., Sullivan, J., Nading, C., Shelley, M., & Wang, Y. (2006–2007). Financial, academic and environmental influences on the retention and graduation of students. *Journal of College Student Retention, 8*(4), 457–475.

# What Motivates Pre-University Students to Excel in School?

*Hanke Korpershoek*

## Abstract

In this paper, pre-university students' school motivation is investigated in detail. Pre-university education is the highest track in Dutch secondary education. Our main aim was to investigate what motivates pre-university students to put effort into their schoolwork using an achievement-goals perspective, while paying particular attention to sex differences. School motivation was measured using an adapted version of the school motivation questionnaire of Ali and McInerney (2004), including eight subscales (first-order factors) and four dimensions (second-order factors). The study included a sample of over 1800 9th grade pre-university students from the Netherlands. Results show that sex-differences in school motivation exist. However, both boys and girls had the highest average scores on the first-order factor of task motivation (3.9 on a 5-point scale). Task motivation is one of the two subscales of the second-order factor of mastery orientation. Pre-university students' general focus on understanding, gaining knowledge, and skill improvement can be used as a starting point for stimulating excellent academic achievements.

## Aim

As compared to other European countries, few Dutch students excel in secondary education (e.g. PISA; OECD, 2010). Although 20% of the overall student population in the Netherlands pursues the pre-university track in secondary education, few students from this group have *excellent* academic achievements. The definition of excellence is beyond the scope of this paper; that is, we rather focus on pre-university students who, in our view, presumably have the potential to perform excellently. This specification of potential is broadly based on Gagné's definition of talent (1995): "high performance due to systematically developed abilities (or skills) and knowledge in at least one field of human activity, to a degree that places a student's achievements within at least the upper 15% of student-peers who are active in that field" (p. 109).

Our main aim is to investigate what motivates pre-university students to put effort into their schoolwork, using an achievement-goals perspective. To our knowledge, research in the field of school motivation has not investigated the goal orientations of students in the highest educational track in much detail. Moreover, sex differences in school motivation amongst this specific student group are unclear. To enhance school achievement among pre-university students, we need to understand what exactly motivates them to learn in school. Since these students generally perform well in school and their overall motivation for school is usually relatively high, it is important to know how we can encourage them to truly excel in their schoolwork and how we can meet their motivational needs in education.


## Theoretical Background

Numerous educational researchers have demonstrated the importance of student motivation for educational attainment. School motivation has proven to be a prominent predictor of students' academic achievement (Hustinx et al., 2009; see Brophy, 2004 and Schunk, Pintrich, & Meece, 2008 for recent reviews). According to the achievement-goal theory of motivation (e.g. Elliot & McGregor, 2001; Pintrich, 2000), students adopt different goals in learning situations. Goal orientation is suggested to influence one's interpretations of and reactions to achievement-oriented stimuli (Dweck, 1986), two highly relevant issues in classroom learning situations. Research has primarily concentrated on two types of orientations, usually referred to as mastery orientation and performance orientation (Elliot & McGregor, 2001). Mastery-oriented students attempt to understand, gain knowledge and improve their skills, whereas performance-oriented students focus on demonstrating their ability (e.g. Tapola & Niemivirta, 2008). In the present study, the *Inventory of School Motivation* (ISM; Ali & McInerney, 2004) is used to measure students' school motivation, consisting of four instead of the stated two dimensions. Taken together, these four dimensions represent students' overall school motivation. The subscales are: mastery orientation (i.e. mastery motivation) and performance orientation (performance motivation), social motivation (e.g. whether students like to work together or not) and extrinsic motivation (whether students prefer to work for rewards or not). Boys are usually more performance oriented than girls and also more extrinsically motivated, whereas girls usually have higher scores on mastery (e.g. Anderman & Anderman, 1999; Pajares & Valiante, 2001). Which students are most successful in school is part of an on-going debate.

## The Present Study

We used both first- and second-order factors to measure students' motivation. The second-order factor *mastery*, for example, consists of the two first-order factors *task* and *effort* (see Table 1). Exemplar items of the first-order factors are included in the method section below.

*Table 1:    First- and second-order factors of school motivation*

| Mastery | Performance | Social | Extrinsic |
|---------|-------------|--------|-----------|
| task | competition | social concern | praise |
| effort | social power | affiliation | token |

Most studies in the field of motivation use the second-order factors to interpret students' motivation and concentrate on mastery and performance orientation. The advantage of using first-order factors is that we are able to see which of them are responsible for high or low scores on the second-order factors (one of them or both).

## Method

The data used were collected as part of a large-scale longitudinal study in secondary education, the so-called COOL[5-18] project. In COOL[5-18], a representative sample of students is being followed in their educational career from ages 5 to 18, throughout full-time education (Zijsling, Keuning, Kuyper, Van Batenburg & Hemker, 2009). In the present study, a sample of over 1800 9th grade pre-university students from the Netherlands was used (average age: 16 years old). We used the ISM (Ali & McInerney, 2004) to measure students' school motivation. The questionnaire used here consisted of 33 translated items on a 5-point Likert scale, ranging from 1 (*strongly disagree* [in Dutch: *klopt helemaal niet*]) to 5 (*strongly agree* [in Dutch: *klopt precies*]). The ISM has strong psychometric properties (see e.g. McInerney & Ali, 2006; McInerney, Dowson, & Yeung, 2005; McInerney, Marsh, & Yeung, 2003). At an earlier stage, factor analysis was used to explore the multidimensional structure of school motivation and to reproduce the first- and second-order factors suggested from the literature. The second-order factor, Mastery, contained the first-order factors *task* (e.g. "I like to see that I am improving in my schoolwork") and *effort* (e.g. "When I am improving in my schoolwork I try even harder"). The factor Performance included the first-order factors *competition* (e.g. "I work harder if I'm trying to be better than others") and *social power* (e.g. "I often try to be the leader of a group"). The second-order factor Social consisted of *social concern* (e.g. "It is very important for students to help each other at school") and *affiliation* (e.g. "I prefer to work with other people at school rather than alone"). The second-order factor Extrinsic consisted of *praise* (e.g. "At school I work best when I am praised") and *token* (e.g. "I work hard in class for rewards from the teacher"). The reliabilities (Cronbach's alpha) of the second-order factors were: 0.77 (mastery), 0.84 (performance), 0.74 (social), and 0.86 (extrinsic). The reliabilities of the first-order factors are all above 0.68, except for the task subscale, which was 0.59.

## Results

The highest average score on the first-order factors is found on the subscale *task*. For both boys and girls, the average score on this subscale was 3.9 on a 5-point scale. Average scores on the other subscales are all ≤ 3.5. This result indicates that both sexes are particularly motivated to complete their tasks and that they are confident that they can perform the tasks successfully. With regard to sex difference, we found the following. Boys on average had higher scores on the second order factor *performance* than girls (0.2 difference). Also, on the two corresponding first order factors *competition* (0.2) and *social power* (0.2), boys score higher than girls. On the other hand, girls on average had higher scores on the second-order factors *mastery* (0.1) and *social* motivation (0.2). For *mastery*, only the sex difference on the first-order factor *effort* is significant (0.1), whereas boys and girls had equal scores on the first-order factor *task*. For *social* motivation, only the sex difference on *social concern* is significant (0.3). Boys and girls had equal scores on the first-order factor *affiliation*. Finally, no sex differences were found on the *extrinsic* motivation dimension. Boys, however, had higher scores on the first-order factor *token* (0.2), whereas girls had higher scores on the first-order factor *praise* (0.2).

## Conclusions

From these results, we can conclude that boys and girls in pre-university education differ in their school motivation to some extent. We also found that both boys and girls had the highest scores on task motivation. Therefore, although sex differences in school motivation exist, we found that the overall group of pre-university students is task-motivated. Therefore, pre-university students' general focus on understanding, gaining knowledge, and skill improvement (mastery motivation) can be used as a starting point for stimulating excellent academic achievements.

## References

Ali, J., & McInerney, D. M. (2004). *Multidimensional assessment of school motivation*. Paper presented at the 3rd SELF Research Conference, Berlin, Germany.

Anderman, L. H., & Anderman, E. M. (1999). Social predictors of changes in students' achievement goal orientations. *Contemporary Educational Psychology, 25*, 21–37.

Brophy, J. (2004). *Motivating students to learn*. Mahwah, NJ: Erlbaum.

Dweck, C. S. (1986). Motivational processes affecting learning. *American Psychologist, 41*, 1040–1048.

Elliot, A. J. & McGregor, H. (2001). A 2x2 achievement goal framework. *Journal of Personality and Social Psychology, 80*, 501–519.

Gagné, F. (1995). From giftedness to talent: A developmental model and its impact on the language of the field. *Roeper Review, 18*, 103–120.

Hustinx, P. W. J., Kuyper, H., Werf, M. P. C. van der, & Dijkstra, P. (2009). Achievement motivation revisited: new longitudinal data to demonstrate its predictive power. *Educational Psychology, 29*, 561–582.

McInerney, D. M., & Ali, J. (2006). Multidimensional and hierarchical assessment of school motivation: Cross-cultural validation. *Educational Psychology, 26*, 595–612.

McInerney, D. M., Dowson, M., & Yeung, A. S. (2005). Facilitating conditions for school motivation: Construct validity and applicability. *Educational and Psychological Measurement, 65*, 1046–1066.

McInerney, D. M., Marsh, H. W., & Yeung, A. S. (2003). Toward a hierarchical goal theory model of school motivation. *Journal of Applied Measurement, 4*, 335–357.

OECD (2010). *PISA 2009 Results: What students know and can do: Student performance in reading, mathematics and science (Volume I)*. OECD Publishing.

Pajares, F., & Valiante, G. (2001). Gender differences in writing motivation and achievement of middle school students: A function of gender. *Contemporary Educational Psychology, 26*, 366–381.

Pintrich, P. R. (2000). An achievement goal theory perspective on issues in motivation terminology, theory, and research. *Contemporary Educational Psychology, 25*, 92–104.

Schunk, D. H., Pintrich, P. R., & Meece, J. L. (2008). *Motivation in education: Theory, research, and applications* (3rd ed.). Upper Saddle River, NJ: Pearson Prentice Hall.

Tapola, A., & Niemivirta, M. (2008). The role of achievement goal orientations in students' perceptions of and preferences for classroom environment. *British Journal of Educational Psychology, 78,* 291–312.

Zijsling, D., Keuning, J., Kuyper, H., Batenburg, Th. van, & Hemker, B. (2009). *Cohortonderzoek COOL5–18. Technisch rapport eerste meting in het derde leerjaar van het voortgezet onderwijs* [Cohort study COOL5–18. Technical report of the first wave in the 9th grade of secondary education]. Groningen/Arnhem, the Netherlands: GION/Cito.

# Qualities Honours Students Look for – Revisited

*Johan Offringa and Marca Wolfensberger*

## Introduction

Wolfensberger (2004) concludes that "there are differences between honours and non-honours students in the value they place on specific qualities of teachers, fellow-students, and courses". The present paper validates the outcomes of the 2004 article, mainly by answering the question: do honours (versus non-honours) students look for different qualities in fellow students, faculty, and courses? Data were gathered in the Netherlands between 2003 and 2011. The subjects were 491 honours (bachelor) students and 908 non-honours students. Results indicate that honours students find it more important than non-honours students that teachers have high expectations of them. Furthermore, honours students want to be challenged and inspired more than non-honours students. Honours students also find it much less important than non-honours students that courses are useful for their profession or career. Instead, they put more emphasis than non-honours students on courses raising new questions. A learning context that is supportive of relatedness, provides freedom, and encourages academic competence seems to fit honours students well.

## Honours Students' Opinions over Time

Based on pilot study data obtained in 2003–2004, Wolfensberger (2004, p. 64) concludes that "there are differences between honours and non-honours students in the value they place on specific qualities of teachers, fellow-students, and courses. A learning context that is supportive of relatedness, autonomy and competence seems to fit honours students well." Since 2004, much has changed with regard to the Dutch honours situation. Many new programmes were – and are being – developed and, in line with that development, the total number of students within those programmes is increasing as well. In the meantime, slightly modified versions of the original questionnaire were repeatedly administered to honours and non-honours students from different fields and universities. The views of students themselves on the learning environment should be of interest to developers or practitioners within honours programmes. Therefore, the present paper strives to validate and expand the outcomes of the 2004 article by answering the following research questions:

1) Do honours versus non-honours students look for different qualities in
   a) fellow students,
   b) faculty, and
   c) courses?
2) How can honours students themselves be characterized?
3) Are possible differences constant over time and consistent across different fields and (types of) universities?

## Method

Repeated cross-sectional survey data were gathered in the Netherlands at Utrecht University, the University of Amsterdam, and Hanze University of Applied Sciences, Groningen, between 2003 and 2011. Subjects were bachelor students, recruited via various lecturers in honours and regular programmes. In general, students filled out a questionnaire during honours or non-honours classes. In total, 491 honours students and 908 non-honours students filled out a somewhat different, but largely overlapping, questionnaire. The items dealt with fellow students, lecturers and courses of students, and themselves, and could be answered on a 5-point scale ranging from very important to totally unimportant. Exemplar statements following the general question: "How important to you are the following characteristics of fellow students you have to cooperate with?" were: "That they obtain good study results" and "That they are motivated towards their studies". Exemplar statements following the general question: "How important to you are the following characteristics of lecturers who are teaching or supervising you?" were: "That they are friendly", "That they challenge me", and "That they have high expectations of me". With regard to courses, exemplar statements were: "That I obtain a high grade", "That it raises questions that I have never thought of before", and "That it is useful for my future profession or career". In 2011, a shortened version was integrated into a longer questionnaire.

## Results

### 1a) Fellow Students

Honours students seem to find it less important that fellow students have to work in order to obtain high grades. Also, they are less concerned with flexibility of peers. However, both differences are quite small and do not apply to the 2011 survey, since this item was not incorporated.

*1b) Teachers*

Consistently over the years, honours students find it more important than non-honours students that teachers have high expectations of them. (The effect size is around 0.5.) Furthermore, honours students want to be challenged *and* inspired more than non-honours students (effect sizes respectively are around 0.5 and 0.3).

*1c) Courses*

On average, honours students find it much less important than non-honours students that courses are useful for their profession or career (effect size is 0.7; not in 2011 questionnaire). Honours students put more emphasis on courses raising questions that they never thought of before, or bringing new ideas to mind, than non-honours students (effect size is around 0.5).

*2) Honours Students Themselves*

Honours students also indicate that they perform tasks more voluntarily and have more informal contacts with lecturers outside the classroom than non-honours students do.

*3) Constant and Consistent*

For the statements, incorporated in all three data collections, differences were found throughout the years, and in different educational contexts, i.e. type of honours programme and/or type of university.

**Conclusion**

This study indicates differences between honours and non-honours students in the value that they place on specific qualities of teachers and courses. A learning context that is supportive of relatedness, provides freedom, and encourages academic competence seems to fit honours students well.

## References

Wolfensberger, M. V. C. (2004). Qualities honours students look for in faculty and courses. *Journal of the National Collegiate Honors Council, 5 (2),* 55–66.

# Gifted Migrant-Students in Siberia

## The Experience of Development and Interaction

*Tatiana Pavlova and Anna Kushnareva*

The phenomenon of migration, despite a number of associated problems, must become a creative and intellectual potential which contributes to the strength and prosperity of the host society. So, if we want to benefit from the diversity of talents and skills of all citizens, it is worth taking a closer look at the giftedness of migrant-students as one of the components of "the intellectual reserve" who, according to the ex-President Dmitry Medvedev, "... promote programmes, modernize the state, society and economics"[1].

Having analysed the relevant literature, we have singled out the distinguishing features of this group of students:

1) a migration background, when a person is born outside the country of the current residence (first generation) or if a person is the first one in the family who is born in the country of the current residence (second generation). In some cases, it is quite relevant to speak about the third generation of migrants;
2) belonging to the minority, that is, being different (culturally, ethnically etc.) from the indigenous population;
3) a special psychological condition caused by either the state of "culture shock" or being in a permanent state of emergency (which is typical for forced migrants). Among other causes, we can mention the loss of social status and ethnic identity.

In working with gifted migrant-students, higher educational institutions have to provide types of sets of solution. The first type aims at overcoming the barriers migrant-students face which impede maximizing their academic potential. Some researchers (e.g. Vasilenko, 2002; Konstantinovsky, 2010; Dorozhkin & Mazitova, 2007) point out language, territorial and psychological barriers while others (e.g. Saksonova, 2010) believe that it is the gap in their education and the lack of effective methods that do now allow teaching diverse audience according to the principle of conformity to cultural environment,

---

1 Cited from the joint meeting of the State council Presidium, the Council for Science, Technology and Education and the Council for Culture and the Arts, 22 April 2010.

especially in the technical universities, that have a negative impact on their achievements. Other researchers (e.g. Margolis & Rubtsov, 2011) point out the lack of large-scale work carried out (and even that which has been carried out is mainly based on foundations laid in the Soviet era), and, in general, the lack of a systematic approach to this important issue affecting society and state.

The second type of solution aims at identifying and developing the giftedness of such students but where the main problem is overcoming the crises of creativity, intellectuality and motivation for achievement, which (according to psychologists e.g. Kulemzina, 2009), accompany the development of a gifted individual.

The Department of Pedagogics, NSPU, supervises the masters programme "Psychology and Pedagogics of the education of gifted children". Within the framework of this programme, we conducted a comparative study of the two largest Siberian universities: Novosibirsk State University (NSU) and Novosibirsk State Pedagogical University (NSPU) aiming at revealing the most successful approaches to working with gifted students. Both being the largest and most prestigious universities not only in the Siberian region, but also east of the Urals, they are able to select the most gifted students. The results demonstrated in various regional, national and international competitions, as well as the real competitiveness of these universities' graduates in the labour market, allow us to judge that the work carried out by these universities in this area is active and, to some extent, effective.

To achieve the goals of our comparative study, along with the analysis of psychological and pedagogical literature on the problem, we developed a questionnaire consisting of three blocks of questions. The first sought to reveal the peculiarities of the migrant-students' self-assessment within the context of the problem. The second focused on the correspondence between the real practice existing in the universities and students' expectations in terms of supporting and further development of their giftedness. The third sought to reveal the interrelation between the learning process and motivation for future work in the chosen subject discipline in the Siberian region. We encouraged 115 students from the Department of Foreign Languages, NSPU, and the Mathematics Department, NSU, to participate in the survey. 45 of them fit our definition of a migrant-student referred to above, reflecting the actual proportion between local and migrant students in the two universities. Moreover, such a sample allowed us to compare between local and migrant students.

We also strongly believe that our own experience as active lecturers in the universities under consideration contributes to a better understanding of such students' needs as we have an opportunity to get timely feedback on the results via seminars and round tables within the educational process.

In this paper about gifted migrant-students, we understand such students of a higher educational body to fit the definition referred to above and whose personalities and abilities can develop 'above average' academic potential leading to significantly positive achievement in their chosen fields.

## Case Study

As stated above, both universities have high status in the Siberian educational community. NSU is a classic university where scientific personnel training is carried out in the real scientific space of the Siberian branch of the Russian Academy of Science. This training is highly-individual. It is not the quantity of students but their focus on fundamental knowledge and participation in important research projects which is of great significance here. It is one of the few universities in our country which has demonstrated a systematic approach to working with gifted students, as part of the sequence "school-university-professional activities", since its foundation in 1959. The selection and development of potentially gifted students is carried out via the network of special schools and the system of regional and national competitions in the major subjects (physics, mathematics, chemistry, IT) long before they enter the university. Gifted youth from all regions of Siberia, the Far East, Central Asia and Kazakhstan can participate in such activities. The entrance competition is challenging, but those individuals who do finally become NSU students do not have to pay for their education. They are also provided with free accommodation. The educational process is organized so that the research which is carried out relates to topical issues which have direct relevance to their potential work and also to the real problems of science and technological progress. After they graduate, the majority of students keep on developing their expertise in their chosen areas in research institutions without losing touch with the university. They combine professional activities with teaching at their alma mater. Thus, a certain sense of belonging to the community "NSU" is created.

Migrant-students make up a significant proportion of the student community in NSU. Unfortunately, we do not have statistical data, but from our own experience we estimate the proportion to be at least 40%, depending on the department. Annually, NSU allocates quotas for 30 post-graduate students from neighbouring countries to allow them to study on a state-funded basis. They also receive a scholarship.

After Moscow and Saint-Petersburg, NGPU is the third largest institution in terms of both the number of students and its significance in practical teacher training in Russia. Its teachers' preparation solves the problem of school staffing in the Siberian region. The education here can be state-funded or commercial. Large-scale admission (there are 26,000 students, not counting post-graduate and doctoral candidates; 60% are migrant-students) impedes the selection of professionally gifted students and, as a consequence, their pedagogical support.

Despite the different profiles of students' learning, these two universities have much in common. Firstly, science has both a theoretical and practical importance. There are research laboratories, centres of applied sciences, institutions, and so on, enabling students to practise their knowledge and therefore choose more suitable specializations. Besides this, NSU students are among the most active participants in the International Youth Innovation Forum "Interra", which has been held annually in Novosibirsk since 2009. This has already become one of the most attractive international and inter-regional events in Russia at which innovative concepts, together with their application and development in economics and social life, are discussed. It not only provides students with the opportunity to meet leading experts in their fields, but also the chance to present their projects for peer review which is of importance for gifted students in general, but for gifted migrant-students in particular. Moreover, the most promising projects can get the necessary funding for implementation.

Both universities realize the importance of relevant work with their multi-ethnic and multi-religious student bodies. This is in itself significant in having a positive impact on the relationships between the various (rather than bi-ethnic) ethnic groups. There are also a number of extracurricular activities (in this regard we would like to mention *Mayevka* and *Interweeks,* NSU, being regional if not international, especially taking into account the number of European and Shanghai Cooperation Organization representatives) which aim at presenting the traditions and customs of various cultures, their interaction and mutual influence, which is the necessary condition for enabling migrant-students to "celebrate their identity". Some English researchers (e.g. Verma, Zec & Skinner, 1994; Reynolds, 2008) consider this to be one of the essential features for migrant-students' inclusion in a new educational environment.

Both universities provide their migrant-students with language courses which help to improve their proficiency in written and spoken Russian. In addition to these programmes, since 2004 the students and lecturers of the Department of Humanities, NSU, have been conducting an annual literacy contest, "Total dictation". The main aim of this event is to draw public attention to literacy issues. We also believe that the project contributes much to the popularization of the Russian language abroad as the geography of the cities/participants involved is not bounded by the Siberian region alone; it also takes in participants from Moscow, Saint-Petersburg, Basel, Vladivostok, Kazan, Cambridge, Krakow, London and other cities.

The universities' graduates are in demand in the labour market. The heads of the employment centres in NSU and NSPU confirm that about 70–80% of students start their professional activities immediately after graduation. However, many students notice, ironically, that NSU prepares personnel for 'export', which leads us to another problem accompanying successful work with gifted students – that of the "brain drain". The paradox is that, the more professional preparation and individual support the university provides for its gifted students, the higher chance there is of "losing" these graduates for further professional development from the Siberian region. We can witness such a situation in NSU when the most gifted graduates are invited to work for large companies in Europe and America, as well as in the central part of Russia.

Each university has its own campus with a well-developed infrastructure (including students' health centres, libraries, dormitories, and sports facilities).

## Outcomes

### Firstly

We assume that all participants in our survey are a priori gifted due to specific selection during the admission process as well as the necessity for possessing certain abilities for learning in their university departments. So, their self-assessment is of particular interest to us. Only 53% of the migrant-students at the Department of Foreign languages (DFL) say that they are linguistically gifted. With Mathematics Department students, the result is higher – 71% (i.e. they are mathematically-logically gifted students). We believe that such a significant gap between these two figures can be explained by the selection via olympiades, competitions, summer and winter schools organized by NSU, and studying at the Physics Mathematics School (PMS), which seems to be the very tool allowing for high accuracy in the identification of mathematically-gifted students. Actively pursued efforts aimed at developing this giftedness (prior to them entering the university) do have a strong impact on their awareness of their giftedness (without misleading them to a false perception of what they are). The majority of students who stated that they are mathematically gifted or good at programming were ex-PMS students or participants in summer-winter NSU schools in major subjects.

We also notice that migrant-students are more aware of their professional giftedness in comparison to local ones. This can be explained by the fact that migrants' motivation for education is greater than that of non-migrants, which is also confirmed by a number of studies conducted in various parts of Russia (e.g. Dyuzhakova, 2008; Yurieva, 2009). Moreover, education is often considered by migrants as a "social lift" that guarantees a certain financial and social well-being in the future. So the choice of university and qualification is made very carefully in accordance with their abilities.

Along with their major subject of study, students, traditionally, point out their creative, less sporty but, very rarely, leadership giftedness. We suppose that these results may require some additional examination as:

a) they might not be fully aware of their giftedness due to their young age, lack of experience and involvement of people who are able to contribute to their understanding of what (or who) they are. In this case, they need professional help with adaptation to university, their chosen qualification, and so on, so that in the future they are not disappointed with their occupation which may lead to more serious consequences.

   *"I want to be satisfied with what I am going to do and it will have a direct impact on the quality of my work and the quality of my life"*. (Eugenia, 21, Astana, Kazakhstan).

   In reality, migrant-students almost never ask for professional counselling or guidance, seeking instead the support of their family or friends. This fact might be a consequence of either the poor organization of such services ("I have tried many times but in vain") or the peculiarities of the mentality of the former Soviet republic inhabitants, whose representatives make up the major part of this group of students. Asking their communities or confessors for help is typical in the case of most Slavic, Asian and Highland people (living in the mountains e.g. Chechens, Dagestani, Ingush). Moreover, applying for any sort of help or support can be considered as demonstrating weakness of character.

b) on the other hand, the diversity of interests helps to avoid the "crisis of intelligence" which means, according to Kulemzina (2009), "the developing of a child's intelligence at the expense of his/her physical, emotional or personal development". So, if apart from their core (subject) interests there are other equally important interests, then the "cube of personality" (with intellectually-productive, emotional, physical and social components being its corners) will not be deformed. In this case, the university must possess some additional reserves for identifying and developing other types of giftedness in its students.

## Secondly

According to the survey, 73% of Mathematics department students and 53% of DFL students (the results almost coincide with the ones of non-migrant students, 71% and 46% respectively) believe that studying at the universities contributes to the development of their giftedness as well as their academic achievements. However, the sampling shows that the reality does not always match these students' expectations of the educational process. Furthermore, the students' expectations in these universities are partly similar. Both groups hope to develop their abilities but in different ways due to the following factors.

The future mathematicians focus on instant application of their knowledge during the first or the second course. The majority of the respondents were PMS students in their time and their subject preparation corresponded to the training of the first two years at university. However, the university does not pursue the differential approach for such students and, in the majority of cases, it results in the revision of a well-known programme of study during the initial stage. Such circumstances cannot but result in demotivation to keep on studying. A number of students also point out the necessity of choosing an individual educational route involving interactive learning tools.

DFL students draw attention to the lack of native speakers among their lecturers. They are willing to organize an English club, to perform in a foreign language, to become a "host family", but they doubt if this works efficiently without native speakers. They also mention a need for intensive teaching practice with the earlier inclusion of "language teaching methods" in the programme, counselling on specific teaching problems, and so on.

Despite the fact that the rectors of both universities speak of the opportunity for the academic mobility of their students, in reality just a few students participate in such programmes. But both groups feel the necessity for academic mobility, which, in their opinion, might contribute to achieving success in their chosen area and also to improving their competitiveness in the labour market.

Both groups point to the faculty as a factor which has an impact on the development of their giftedness. It is the giftedness of their lecturers, their proficiency in English and in language teaching methods, which is of importance for DFL students. Mathematicians would rather that their lecturers "knew their subject better and were able to explain it", that the university "had more qualified faculty (especially in programming)" and, in general, "demonstrated more interest in me".

*Thirdly*

Keeping in mind the concept of the "intellectual reserve" of our country, we believe that it is very important to track the willingness of gifted migrant-students to find work according to the qualification obtained as it further allows them to develop their giftedness in professional activities. It is also important in terms of investment recouping as there is no fee at the universities.

There are many factors which have a strong impact on the migrant-student's wish to stay in their new place of residence for further education or to job-search, such as: opportunities to maintain the traditions, customs and religious rites inherent in their origin culture; the feeling of security in their new location; the positive attitude of other people (students, lecturers, staff and local people); and, comfortable living conditions.

33% of NSU migrant-students have always been willing to work as mathematicians (in some cases they have just changed the specialization). Another 20% stated that studying at the university had an influence on their wish to work as a scientist or a programmer. Some students got new ideas of self-actualization but still closely connected with mathematics. Finally, 26.5% do not want to work as mathematicians or in a related occupation: "there is slight disappointment about specialization", "I have never understood what mathematicians do and do not now".

About 53% of NGPU students demonstrate a willingness to work as teachers: 26.5% have always wanted to work with pupils or students (in some cases, a better understanding of what a teacher is has developed during the educational process) and 26.5% mention that the motivation has changed from "do not want" to "want", mainly due to the faculty who have become a positive example and passive teaching practice during the first academic year. We must admit that a number of innovative technologies – such as project work, portfolio, and teachers' workshops – enhance the motivational aspect of their wish to keep on identifying and developing their possibilities within the framework of future professional activities and have a positive effect on students' academic achievements. 20% say that their motivation is changing in a reverse direction (from "want" to "do not want") as: "proficiency in the language opens more opportunities"; "it is possible to earn more, spend less effort"; and, "it is difficult to study here". 26.5% have never wanted to work as teachers for low pay-rates, lack of respect from the state and, consequently, from its citizens, and the necessity for working long hours.

## Conclusion

The sampling shows that the majority of gifted students are willing to expand their opportunities for development and self-development. They are also not only interested in subject preparation, but also in extracurricular activities allowing them to reveal their creative abilities alongside their academic ones. We consider their proposals of making academic and extracurricular processes more active instead of only consuming what is offered to them to be an indicator of their giftedness. The majority of high-achievers point out to sloth and inertia as the main factors which have a negative effect on their studies, so it is very important to involve them in various additional activities which will allow them to maximize their potential.

We are convinced about the necessity to develop a network of pre-university educational institutions, such as a Physics and Mathematics school at NSU, as they are not only one of the means of identifying gifted students, but they are also a kind of adaptive platform for the students from other parts of Russia, Central Asia and Kazakhstan which allows them to integrate into the new cultural and educational environment in the shortest possible time and with less effort and losses. In addition, studying at such institutions has a significant impact on the feeling of belonging to a certain group of people which can compensate to some extent for the loss of ethnic identity that migrant-students experience, at least to begin with.

It is also of importance that all the successive elements of the sequence "school-university-professional activities" exist in close collaboration. In Novosibirsk, there are three pedagogical colleges conducting initial teachers' preparation, but none of the NSPU students mention this fact either as a factor influencing their choice of university or contributing to their professional development. So we can assume that there is no system of linking between them and the university, at least at the Departments of Foreign Languages.

Meanwhile, NSPU shows a flair for innovation and successful application which has an impact on students' awareness of their giftedness as well as an increase in their motivation to work as teachers.

The problem of the "brain drain" confirms that the intellectual and creative potential of such students is not always used effectively as there are not enough favourable conditions for their abilities to be utilized. Sometimes – for various reasons like "I would like to leave for somewhere warmer" or " I think I will go abroad in search of better life and for self-improvement" – migrant-students consider the Siberian universities as a transit point on their way to other parts of Russia or even further abroad. So organizing the necessary measures for their retention in Siberia is a task for the whole region.

Assessing the universities' work with gifted migrant-students, we assume it will best meet the expectation and needs of these students only if there exists: a collaborative link between "school-university-professional activities", special pedagogical flair for innovation, and individual and differential approaches for this group of students, who might become, due to their distinctive features, either a problem or a powerful intellectual potential strengthening the Siberian region.

## References

Dorozhkin, Y. N., & Mazitova, L. T. (2007). Problems of social adaptation of foreign students. *Sociological research, Moscow, 3*, 73–77.

Dyuzhakova, M. V. (2008). The problems and the development of teacher preparation in terms of migration process (in Voronezh region). *The world of education – the education in the world, Moscow, 4*, 208–219.

Konstantinovsky, D. L. (2010). Inequality in education: the Russian situation. *Monitoring of public opinion, 5, September-October*, 40–65.

Kulemzina, A. (2009). To a teacher about gifted children (psychologist's point of view). *Public education, 2*, 236–246.

Margolis, A. A., & Rubtsov, V. V. (2011). State policy in the field of the education of the gifted students. *Psychological science and education, 4*, 5–14.

Reynolds, G. (2008). *The impacts and experiences of migrant children in UK secondary schools. Working Paper No 47*. University of Sussex, Sussex Centre for Migration Research.

Saksonova, L. P. (2010). Transformation of the content of higher technological education in accordance with the principle of conformity to cultural environment and professional competence of the students. *Education and society, 1*, 23–28.

Vasilenko, D. V. (2002). Psychological adaptation of migrant-students. *Humanities, SCSTU, Stavropol, 10.*

Verma, G. K., Zec, P., & Skinner, G. (1994). *The ethnic crucible: Harmony and hostility in multi-ethnic schools.* London: Falmer Press.

Yurieva, L. A. (2009). Improving psychological readiness of migrant-students for teaching. *The world of education – the education in the world, Moscow, 4,* 165–170.

# Attitude toward Honours Education

## An Explorative Survey Research at the Hanze University of Applied Sciences

*Judith Volker*

## Abstract

This study aims at identifying the attitudes of students at the School of Social Studies of the Hanze University of Applied Sciences in the city of Groningen, the Netherlands, regarding excellence in higher education. Based on literature, a survey was designed which was answered by 100 of the 1918 full-time students at the School of Social Studies. About 20% of the respondents participate or have plans to participate in an honours programme. The most important reason for participation is to get a better chance in the employment market. Already finding enough challenge in the regular education programme counts as the most important reason for not participating. The attitude toward honours programmes isn't related to whether a student has concrete plans to participate in a certain programme. Only the student's age is related to the attitude towards excellence in higher education.

## Introduction

All over the world, the stimulation of talent is a trending topic in government policy-making in the educational sphere. In the Netherlands, the government and business have the ambition to be included in the top five world knowledge economies. The aim is that, by the year 2014, ten percent of all higher education students will be participating in a programme that promotes student excellence. A culture of challenge, performance and capacity has to be established by 2025 (Ministry of Education, 2011).

From these goals, the opinion of the Dutch government and business on excellence in education is clear, but what do students think of excellence and exceeding? How can their attitude towards specially designed curricula and other initiatives for talent development be described? The aim of this paper is to investigate how students appreciate the opportunity to exceed in education by participating in honours programmes.

## Theoretical Background

There are few studies that investigate the difference between honours and non-honours students and the reasons why students decide to participate in an honours programme or not (Rinn, & Plucker, 2004). One reason is probably because there is no such thing as 'the honours student' (Laycock, 1984). Honours students differ from non-honours students because of their active attitude inside and outside the classroom (Wolfensberger, Pilot, Van der Vaart, van Eijl, & Tromp, 2004), and the way they appreciate the quality of teachers, fellow students and courses (Wolfensberger, 2004). High standards are valued, as are asking questions and debate (Wolfensberger et al., 2004). According to Astin (1999), honours students have more self-esteem and they aspire to achieve diplomas and degrees more than regular students. Rinn (2004; in Rinn, 2005) states that there is a significant difference between honours and non-honours students in grades, academic self-concept and career aspirations.

Looking at the differences above, several reasons could be deduced as to why certain students feel the need to participate in a challenging programme on top or instead of their regular schooling and why certain students don't feel that need. Freedom, a stimulating learning context, the opportunity to ask questions and kind and inspiring teachers, inside and outside the educational context, are important motives to participate in honours education (Wolfensberger, 2004). In further literature, the concept of engagement is used to describe the quality of effort and involvement in productive learning activities (Kuh, 2009). Engagement in educational activities gives a positive effect on study success, student achievement (Feldman & Matjasko, 2005; Skinner, Zimmer-Gembeck, & Connel, 1998), the extent of expectations of academic possibilities (Skinner et al., 1998) and final grades (Connell, Spencer, & Aber, 1994). Engagement also reduces the number of drop-outs (Alexander, Entwisle & Horsey, 1997). The possible stereotypical way of thinking about honours students and the supposed elite image of excellence education were researched by McClung and Stevenson (1988). They concluded that 12.5% of the examined students saw this as a reason for not participating in an honours programme.

## Methods

The research has been carried out at the School of Social Studies of the Hanze University of Applied Sciences in the city of Groningen, the Netherlands.

At this school, students can participate in one of the three different bachelor studies: Social Work & Social Pedagogics, Social Work & Social Services, and Applied Psychology. These courses of study have one thing in common; the exploration of human actions. Looking at the attendance of students in honours programmes, only 1.1% of all fulltime students at the School of Social Studies (N=1918) participates in a certain programme. When differentiating between courses, more students of Applied Psychology join an honours programme than students from the other two areas of study.

For this research, all fulltime students were asked to answer a survey. Only 100 students responded (5.2%). This research group was unequally distributed regarding participation in honours programmes, gender and education.

The research was performed by using a digital survey containing 49 opinion items on a five-point scale and background variables (gender, age, educational programme, year of study, average grade, earlier schooling, average grade at the final exams and activities besides school). Of all items, 33 were based on the instrument used in the research of Platform Béta Techniek, YoungWorks and Motivaction (2011). In this study, an insight is shown into the opinion of 1,337 students from 12 to 25 years towards exceeding in education. This resulted in the Excellence Model; a division into four categories of students regarding their attitude toward exceeding in education. Factors that are of great influence on excellence in youngsters are included and the model offers practical methods for stimulating excellence by different actors. The other 16 items of the digital survey were based on relevant literature.

## Conclusion and Discussion

Overall, the most important reason for students participating in honours programmes is to get a better chance in the employment market. Belonging to a group of excellent students and a challenging social environment is apparently reckoned as not that important. These findings do not match with the literature, however Wolfensberger (2004) states that a challenging learning environment, intrinsic motivation and being part of a community of honours students counts as reasons to attend instead of a better job perspective. An explanation for this can be found in the focus of the information that students receive about excellence programmes from their teachers or school. The career perspective can be used to persuade students to attend. In times of economic crisis and uncertainty, students need to discern themselves from fellow students. An honours programme offers the opportunity to acquire skills and useful contacts that are valued and asked for in the real world.

Finding enough challenge in regular education counts as the most important reason to refuse participation. Honours education offers challenge and intensification, but apparently students already have their hands full in attending the regular programme. Is there still a need for honours, then? A university of applied sciences has a rich and varied inflow of student preliminary studies, from higher education to secondary vocational and academic education. Honours programmes offer the opportunity to serve the students at their own level. Excellence education can be seen as a chance to make the study more fitting for each individual student.

Looking at the attitude toward honours programmes, this research shows that it is not related to whether a student has concrete plans for participating in certain programmes. There is also no difference in attitude between the sexes. Only the student's age is related to the attitude towards excellence in higher education. When a student is older or attends a higher year of schooling, he or she possesses a brighter view of the future than do younger students. The older age-group uses little less the opportunity to participate in a programme build on opportunity and intensification.

Finally, cluster analysis showed a weak differentiated difference between groups with a homogeneous score on the six scales of The Excellence Model (Platform Béta Techniek, YoungWorks & Motivaction, 2011). The four categories of students could not be distinguished within the response group. A possible reason for this is the limited size of the response group in comparison to the random sample of The Excellence Model.

## Future Recommendations

Bearing in mind the stated goal of the Dutch government and business for the year 2014, this research stresses the need for investigating the attitude of students toward honours. To get an insight in the attitude of students, this research could be repeated with a representative sample of different schools of the Hanze University of Applied Sciences. It is possible that a division into categories of students regarding their attitude toward honours programmes and exceeding in education could be made in order to get a clearer profile of the Hanze University student. With that knowledge in mind, policy and educational programmes could be adjusted to the needs of the student and the 2014 goal of the Dutch government and business – ten percent of all higher education students participating in a programme that promotes excellence – would come a little bit closer.

# References

Alexander, K. L., Entwisle, D. R., & Horsey, C. S. (1997). From first grade forward: Early foundations of high school dropout. *Sociology of Education, 70*, 87–107.

Astin, A. W. (1999). Student involvement: A developmental theory for higher education. *Journal of College Student Development, 40* (5), 518–529.

Connell, J. P., Spencer, M. B., & Aber, J. L. (1994). Educational risk and resilience in African-American youth: Context, self, action and outcomes in school. *Child Development, 65*, 493–506.

Feldman, A. F., & Matjasko, J. L. (2005). The role of school-based extracurricular activities in adolescent development: A comprehensive review and future directions. *Review of Educational Research, 75*(2), 159–210.

Kuh, G.D. (2009). The national survey of student engagement: Conceptual and empirical foundations. *New Directions for Institutional Research, 2009*(141), 5–20.

Laycock, F. (1984). Bright students and their adjustment to college. *Journal for the Education of the Gifted, 8*, 83–92.

McClung, J. J., & Stevenson, J. L. (1988). What do students say? Benefits of participating in honours, a survey of honours students. *Forum for Honours, 18*(3), 9–21.

Ministry of Education (2011). *Kwaliteit in verscheidenheid. Strategische Agenda Hoger Onderwijs, Onderzoek en Wetenschap.* The Hague, the Netherlands: Ministry of Education.

Platform Béta Techniek, YoungWorks, & Motivaction (2011). *Het Excellentiemodel. Jongeren over uitblinken.* Amsterdam, the Netherlands: YoungWorks.

Rinn, A. N. (2004). Effects of perceived programmatic selectivity on the academic achievement, academic self-concepts, and aspirations of gifted college students (Doctoral dissertation, Indiana University, 2004). *Dissertation Abstracts International, 65*, 1665.

Rinn, A. N. (2005). Trends among honours college students: An analysis by year in school. *The Journal of Secondary Gifted Education, XVI*(4), 157–167.

Rinn, A. N., & Plucker, J. A. (2004). We recruit them, but then what? The educational and psychological experiences of academically talented undergraduates. *Gifted Child Quarterly, 48*, 54–67.

Skinner, E. A., Zimmer-Gembeck, M. J., & Connel, J. P. (1998). Individual differences and the development of perceived control. *Monographs of the Society for Research in Child Development, 63*(2–3).

Wolfensberger, M. V. C. (2004). Qualities honors students look for in faculties and courses. *Journal of the National Collegiate Honors Council - Online Archive.* Paper 172.

Wolfensberger, M. V. C., Pilot, A., Vaart, R. J. van der, Eijl, P. J. van, & Tromp, S. (2004). *Studenten in honours programmes: Hun kenmerken en concepties van universitair onderwijs. Een pilotstudie.* Paper presented on the Education Research Days June 2004, Utrecht, the Netherlands, University of Utrecht.

# Excellent Students

## They Don't Wait until Tomorrow, But Do Their Study Duties Now

*Lieke Woelders, Marije Nije Bijvank, Tamara van Batenburg-Eddes,
Bjorn de Koning, Geertje Tonnaer, Carien Verweij and Jelle Jolles*

## Abstract

Recent insights from the neurosciences and developmental neuropsychology
provide a good starting point for explaining the susceptibility to (developmental) change during late adolescence. Especially brain regions that are
important for the adaptation to a changing environment and for learning
continue to develop into adulthood. These are the regions which underly the
so-called executive functions. The purpose of this study is to identify the relation between particular executive functions and students' study progress in
higher education. Results of the current study (n = 301) show that the more
Attention, Self-control and Self-monitoring and less Procrastination students
demonstrate, the more study credits they obtain. Supporting and stimulating
executive functions among late adolescents may foster better study performance. It is expected that such educational intervention might contribute to
evoking excellence in more students in the domain of higher education and
reduce the number of students who underperform or even drop out.

## Introduction

In past years, the lack of higher education students' motivation to learn has
become a concern for teachers and policy-makers (HBO-raad, 2011). Teachers
expect students to take responsibility, to be motivated, to be good planners,
and to have a pro-active attitude. These expectations of students are in line
with the theory of social constructivism that has been the foundation of
education since the end of the twentieth century. Within this constructivist
perspective, students are expected to use their freedom to be 'the director of
their own learning process' (Slavin, 2006).

In practice, however, it seems that many students often do not know how
to cope with the freedom which they experience in higher education. Too

many students hand in papers too late, do not have the study attitude which their teachers expect from them, are more interested in their peers than in their teachers or study material, have a lack of engagement, and have trouble with study-planning, decision-making and so on. Unfortunately, it is not only the lack of such characteristics in many students that are a concern, but also their their disappointing academic achievements. In the Netherlands, 30% of the students in universities of applied sciences drop out after the first year. Only 70% of the students appear to have graduated after 8 years (HBO-raad, 2010). Besides these concerns about the students who are at risk for underperformance and drop-out, society has a growing interest in those at the upper end of the spectrum: excellent students. Recently, the Dutch government invested heavily in the development of programmes for excellent students (Sirius Programma, 2013). These students (often) hand in their papers on time, do not have trouble with planning and decision-making, and mostly outshine others in their study achievements. Interestingly, circumstantial evidence shows that the labels 'at-risk' and 'excellent' may apply only for a limited period: students who do not excel in their first year of studies can become excellent students in their graduation phase, for example.

Recent insights from the neurosciences and developmental neuropsychology provide a good starting point for explaining the susceptibility to (developmental) change during late adolescence. This applies to the age period of 18–25 years (Amodio & Frith, 2006; Blakemore & Frith, 2005; Zimmerman, 2000). These insights contradict earlier assumptions that the brain's plasticity is limited to childhood, and apply to late adolescents who enter the study programme in higher education at age 17–18. New findings imply that the brain matures up until well into the third decade of life. Particular areas in the brain appear to be characterized by structural changes after age 25. Accordingly, the brain of late adolescents is still maturing. Individual differences exist in the trajectory of adolescents' brain development, however Longitudinal studies have shown sex differences in the trajectory of brain development, with females reaching peak values of brain volumes earlier than males (Lenrood & Giedd, 2010).

Especially brain regions that are important for the adaptation to a changing environment and for learning continue to develop into adulthood (Amodio & Frith, 2006; Blakemore & Frith, 2005; Zimmerman, 2000).These are the regions which underly the so-called executive functions. Executive functions (EF) is an umbrella term that refers to cognitive abilities needed to control, plan and coordinate our thoughts and behaviour. Notable are planning, attentional functions, self-evaluation and self-regulation as well as social monitoring (Van der Elst, Ouwehand, Van der Werf, Kuyper, Lee & Jolles, 2011). The executive functions are important for educational performance (Alexander & Winne, 2006; Hein & Singer, 2008; Zimmerman, 2000, 2001).

EF are needed to make complex 'well considered' decisions. It has been suggested that measures of EF may allow for a better prediction of study performance than more general cognitive indices, such as IQ (Best, Miller, & Jones, 2009). Thus, knowledge of how the brain develops and learns could have a profound impact on education (Ansari & Coch, 2006; Blakemore & Frith, 2005). Some even argue that aims of education for adolescents should include strengthening EF (Hinton, Miyamoto & Della-Chiesa, 2008). Therefore, it is important to study the implications of these insights about brain development on education. Up until now, how the EF are related to study progress, and whether this relation is different for female and male students, has been largely unexplored.

The purpose of this study is to identify the relation between particular EF and students' study progress in higher education. Primarily, the focus is on attention, self-monitoring and self-control, and the procrastination of study activities. We hypothesize that students who are characterized by higher scores on these EF will have a higher number of study credits after the first year. Furthermore, we hypothesize that these relations are stronger for female than for male students, given the recent findings that – speaking in terms of group means – the female brain matures several years earlier than that of the male. The study involves a large-scale survey in a university of applied sciences. EF were measured by self-evaluation and thus reflects a subjective judgment.

## Method

### Participants

Data were derived from the 'Hospitality, Brains & Learning' study. This is a large-scale study performed by the Hospitality Business School (HBS) at Saxion University of Applied Sciences in cooperation with the Centre for Brain & Learning within the LEARN! Research Institute at VU University, Amsterdam. The study was set up according to a longitudinal design and aims to gain insight in to the determinants of adolescents' study careers. The current paper gives the findings of the first wave: a total of 301 student who entered the Dutch stream in 2010–2011. The mean age of the participants was 19.4 years (SD = 1.8). There were more female participants (72%) than male.

*Instruments and Procedure*

Students gave a self-report on three aspects of executive functioning in a questionnaire. The EF which were measured were scored on a 5-point Likert scale: a) Attention, b) Self-control and Self-monitoring (Van der Elst et al., 2011), and c) Procrastination (Bembenutty & Karabenick, 1998). Table 1 shows the descriptive statistics. The internal consistency ranged from α=.59 (Self-control and Self-monitoring), α=.66 (Procrastination) to α=.71 (Attention). Additionally, the outcome variable for excellence in education was measured by first year's individual study progress (described in terms of European Study Transfer Credits achieved on the first attempt).

*Statistical Analysis*

In order to investigate whether the three aspects of EF predict study progress, separate regression-analyses were performed for Self-control and Self-monitoring, Attention, and Procrastination. In a second step, sex was included as a dummy-variable to investigate whether these relations were different for female and male students.

*Table 1:    Descriptive statistics of EF and study progress*

| EF Variable | Mean | SD | Range |
|---|---|---|---|
| Attention | 2.91 | .7 | 1–5 |
| Self-control & Self-monitoring | 3.30 | .7 | 1–5 |
| Procrastination | 11.00 | 2.7 | 4–16 |
| Study credits | 39.01 | 13.2 | 0–60 |

## Results

Table 2 shows the results of separate regression-analyses for students' study progress. Attention and Self-control and Self-monitoring appear to be significantly associated with the amount of study credits obtained. The better students were able to hold their attention and control their thoughts and behaviour, the more study credits they obtained. Furthermore, a high level of procrastination contributed negatively to study progress. Regarding their study duties, the more students procrastinated, the less study credits they ob-

tained. The inclusion of the dummy variable of sex did not result in an interaction effect for Procrastination, Self-control and Self-monitoring. However,
an interaction effect was found for Attention. Female students who are better
at holding their attention obtained more study credits than male students who
are better at holding their attention. Female students who increased one point
on the 5-point Likert scale for Attention obtained five more study credits.

*Table 2:*    *Results of separate regression-analyses to predict students' obtained
study credits after the first year*

| Variable | B | SE (B) | ß | t | Sig. (p) |
|---|---|---|---|---|---|
| Sex | .62 | 1.88 | .02 | .41 | .74 |
| Attention | 3.72 | 1.17 | .19 | 3.33 | .00 |
| Self-control & Self-monitoring | 3.12 | 1.20 | .16 | 2.59 | .01 |
| Procrastination | -.82 | .30 | -.17 | -2.75 | .01 |
| Attention*Sex | 5.59 | 2.70 | .58 | 2.07 | .04 |

## Discussion

This study shows that the more Attention, Self-control and Self-monitoring
and less Procrastination students show, the more study credits they obtain in
the first year. These conclusions support the expectation that EF relate to study
progress. Identifying the impact of EF on study progress helps us not only to
identify at-risk students, but also to identify (potential) excellent students.
The observed individual differences in EF suggest that these functions are still
maturing during late adolescence. A recent fMRI-study from Veroude and
colleagues (2013) confirmed this hypothesis. In this study, functional brain
differences in late adolescents and young adults were investigated. Results
showed that late adolescents and young adults differ in their neural basis of
cognitive control. This suggests that the neuropsychological functions – especially on the domain of executive functioning – develop well beyond the age
of 18 and further in young adulthood.

Together, these findings show the importance of investigating the level
of EF among first-year students. They imply that interventions focusing on
training EF might be promising in making learning at this stage of students'
lives more rewarding; this can lead to 'personal growth' which is characterized by improved skills in planning, self-evaluation and self-regulation. This,
in turn, will give the student more opportunities for finding efficient routes

through study, more motivation to perform, and more insight into the many factors that potentially have a negative influence on academic performance. We propose that experimental programmes directed at 'growth in higher cognitive functioning and EF' are set up and evaluated in the setting of higher education. Supporting and stimulating EF among late adolescents may foster better study performance. It is expected that such educational intervention might contribute to evoking excellence in more students in the domain of higher education and thus reduce the number of students who underperform or even drop out. Such interventions should be planned and evaluated in an evidence-based manner in order to provide as much profit as possible.

## References

Alexander, P. A., & Winne, P. H. (2006). *Handbook of educational psychology* (Second edition). Mahwah, N. J.: Lawrence Erlbaum Associates and Division 15 of the American Psychology Association

Amodio, D. M., & Frith, C. D. (2006). Meeting of minds: the medial frontal cortex and social cognition. *Nature Reviews Neuroscience, 7*, 268–277.

Ansari, D., & Coch, D. (2006). Bridges over troubled waters: education and cognitive neurosciences. *Trends in Cognitive Sciences, 10*, 146–151.

Bembenutty, H., & Karabenick, S. A. (1998). Academic delay of gratification. *Learning and Individual Differences, 10*, 329–346.

Best, J. R., Miller, P. H., & Jones, L. L. (2009). Executive functions after age 5: Changes and correlates. *Developmental Review, 29*, 180–200.

Blakemore, S.-J., & Frith, U. (2005). *The learning brain: lessons for education.* Oxford, UK: Blackwell Publishing.

Elst, W. van der, Ouwehand, C., Werf, G. van der, Kuyper, H., Lee, N., & Jolles, J. (2011). The Amsterdam Executive Function Inventory (AEFI): psychometric properties and demographically-corrected normative data for adolescents aged between 15 and 18 years. *Journal of Clinical and Experimental Neuropsychology, 33*, 1–12.

HBO-raad (2010). *Feiten en cijfers. Afgestudeerden en uitvallers in het hoger beroepsonderwijs.* Den Haag.

HBO-raad (2011). *Kwaliteit als opdracht.* Den Haag.

Hein, G., & Singer, T. (2008).*Understanding others: empathy and cognitive perspective Taking in the human brain.* Inaugural Herzliya Symposium on Personality and Social Psychology: pro-social Motives, Emotions, and Behavior, Herzliya, Israel.

Hinton, C., Miyamoto, K., & Della-Chiesa, B. (2008). Brain Research, Learning and Emotions: implications for education research, policy and practice. *European Journal of Education, 43,* 87–103.

Lenrood, R. K., & Giedd, J. N. (2010). Sex differences in the adolescent brain. *Brain and Cognition, 72,* 46–55.

Sirius programma (2013): *Strategie en acties 2012–2014.* (Online) www.sirius programma.nl.

Slavin, R. E. (2006). Educational Psychology. Theory and Practice (8th ed.). Needham Heights, MA: Allyn and Bacon.

Veroude, K., Jolles, J., Croiset, G., & Krabbendam, L. (2013). Changes in neural mechanisms of cognitive control during the transition from late adolescence to young adulthood. *Developmental Cognitive Neuroscience, 5,* 63–70.

Zimmerman, B. J. (2000). *Attaining Self-Regulation: a social cognitive perspective.* In M. Boekaerts, P. Pintrich, & M. Zeidner (Eds.), Handbook of self-regulation. San Diego, CA: Academic Press.

Zimmerman, B. J. (2001). Theories of self-regulated learning and academic achievement: An overview and analysis. In B. J. Zimmerman & D. H. Schunk (Eds.), *Self-regulated learning and academic achievement: Theoretical perspectives* (pp. 1–37). Mahwah, NJ: Lawrence Erlbaum Associates.

# Implementation of the Reflective Professional Profile in Saxion Honours Programmes

## Current Position, Expectations and Examples

*Simone van der Donk and Mark Gellevij*

## Abstract

The Saxion honours programmes steering committee has formulated an honours student profile, called the Reflective Professional (RP), which is intended to describe the competences honours students should have obtained when completing their honours programme (HP). The (six) RP competences are described in rather general or abstract terms to give the 12 Saxion honours programmes the opportunity to fill in these competences according to the vision and content of their own unique honours programme. In this study, questionnaires for both honours teachers and students are used to examine honours students' and teachers':

- impressions of the meaning of the RP competences
- recognition of these competences in their HP
- possibilities for improved implementation of the RP competences in their HP
- rating of the importance of the RP competences for their specific HP profile.

The outcomes of this study are intended to contribute to the further development of the Saxion and other honours programmes.

## Introduction

At Saxion University of Applied Sciences, 12 honours programmes (HPs) are in progress. With the start of these HPs, a research group was formed to support and evaluate the (further) development of the HPs by studying, among other things, the outcomes of the HPs in light of the proposed Reflective Professional (RP) profile. The Saxion honours programmes steering committee has formulated an honours student profile intended to describe the competences that honours student should have obtained when completing their honours programme. This profile is called the Reflective Professional (RP) (Van Dijk, 2011). The (six) RP competences are described in rather general or abstract terms to give the 12 Saxion honours programmes the opportunity to fill in these competences according to the specific vision and content of their own unique honours programme. The programme committee defined the RP as applying to someone who:

- is a cross-border professional
- is professionally inspiring
- is a professional learner that is socially aware
- has methodological quality and a scientific attitude
- has excellent reflective power
- develops a differentiated profile.

In addition to these competence 'labels', criteria are defined for each competence identifying more specific behaviour that is expected to illustrate the acquisition of that competence. The Saxion honours programme has taken various measures to inform the developers of the honours programmes about the RP profile. In this study, the research group examined to the extent to which and how the RP profile actually has been implemented in the HPs, and how participants in the HPs experience the (importance of the) RP competences (Gellevij, Banis-den Hertog, Van der Donk, 't Mannetje, & Truijen, 2013).

## Methods

In this study, almost identical questionnaires were used to examine honours students' and honours teachers':

1. impressions of the meaning of the RP competences
2. recognition of these competences in their own HP
3. possibilities for how to improve implementation of the RP competence in their HP
4. rating of the importance of the RP competences for their specific HP profile

A series of open and closed questions was developed for each of the six RP competences. Students' and teachers' impressions of the meaning of an RP competence were measured by asking them to give their own description of an RP competence, based solely on its 'label'. Then the definition (based on the RP competence criteria) was presented and respondents were asked to rate, on a five-point scale, to what extent their own description deviated from this definition. The next question measured to what extent, based on the given RP definition, they recognize learning or training measures in their HP for obtaining that competence, on a five-point scale. In case the rating is on the (very) positive extreme, they were asked to 'prove' this by giving an example. In the next question, they were asked how the RP competences could be (further) implemented in their HP programme. Finally, they rated the importance of the mentioned RP competences for their HP profile on a five-point scale. The questionnaires were sent to all participating honours teachers (about 60) and students (about 150).

## Results

105 (87%) students and 29 (63%) teachers responded on the questionnaire. Because of the response of honours teachers in combination with the number of HPs (29 divided over 12 HPs), it was decided, in agreement with the steering committee, to describe and report only the responses of the students to avoid misinterpretation of the teachers' responses.

The results of the students' questionnaire showed that students recognize their understanding of the meaning of the RP competences in the given definitions of these competences. To measure whether their understanding of the RP competences really matches with the competences of their HP, the students' definitions were analysed. The definitions of the competences were separated into elements (Table 1). How many of these elements were described in the students' definitions was counted. This analysis showed that students were only to a very limited extent able to come up with a definition that matched the described definitions of the competences of their HP.

The second question was: *To what extent do you learn to work on the RP competences?* Students could answer this question on a five-point scale (Not or hardly – very much). The answer that was given most was 'much' / 'very much'. This shows that students agree that they do learn to work on the competences of their HP.

*Table 1:*   *Students' outcomes on coded elements for the competence 'exceeding bounds with respect to subject matter', for each HP.*

**Competence: 'exceeding bounds with respect to subject matter'**

Definition: Working in a way characterized as 'exceeding bounds with respect to subject matter' means the ability to use knowledge (specialist and/or broad knowledge with regard to subject matter from your own and other disciplines) creatively for new solutions in complex systems and issues from professional practice with an international orientation.

| Coded Element: | ABO (n=8) | ABR (n=15) | AMA (n=5) | APO (n=18) | LA&S (n=29) | LED (n=4) | MIM (n=8) | TFNL (n=7) | Total (n=91) |
|---|---|---|---|---|---|---|---|---|---|
| Specialist knowledge | 2 | 8 | 4 | 9 | 6 | | 2 | 2 | 33 |
| Other disciplines | 2 | 5 | | 7 | 11 | 1 | 1 | 2 | 29 |
| Broad knowledge | 2 | 4 | 1 | 3 | 4 | | | 2 | 16 |
| creative | | | | | | | | | 0 |
| solutions | 1 | 1 | | | | | | | 2 |
| Professional practice | 1 | | | 3 | | 1 | | 1 | 6 |
| International orientation | | | | | | | | 1 | 1 |
| other | | 2 | | 2 | 4 | 1 | 2 | 1 | 12 |
| no answer | 1 | 1 | | 1 | 1 | | | 1 | 5 |
| Not specific enough | 2 | 2 | 1 | 3 | 5 | 1 | 5 | | 19 |

Answers to the following question showed that students consider the RP competences as important, based on a five-point scale from 'not important at all' to 'very important'. The competences – 'professional learner that is socially aware' and 'excellent reflective power' were considered to be very important.

To be able to improve the implementation of the RP profile, students were asked to give suggestions on how working on the RP competences could be encouraged. Because these suggestion were specifically focused on each HP, the outcomes were described in the independent reports on the HPs. The HP-specific suggestions which were made could not be generalized into general/overall HP suggestions.

## Conclusion and Discussion

The outcomes of the questionnaires give insight in the actual state of the developed honours programmes regarding the implementation of the reflective professional profile. Based on these outcomes, it could be concluded that:

- the majority of students have a general view of the competences
- students' definitions are far from complete in comparison to the detailed/ given definitions
- students sometimes (but not always), learn to work demonstrating the characteristics of the RP competences, but there are large differences between the HPs
- Students consider the RP competences important for their honours profile.

The qualitative data about the concrete opportunities to improve the programmes are described for each HP separately. In addition to these reports, interviews were organized with the HP directors. The examples and suggestions that teachers and students gave were discussed and translated into opportunities for improving their programmes, in order to encourage the directors to bring about further development.

An interesting point of discussion is whether it will be possible for the HPs – with their unique and varied main focal points, specific content, and diverse characteristics – to meet all the six competences of the RP profile in their curriculum. To examine this, the research group is continuing its research on the Reflective Professional profile. In June 2013, they will measure each competence by using standardized questionnaires. The outcomes of these questionnaires will then be correlated with the students' satisfaction about, and learning perception of, their HP. A presentation on the outcomes of this study was accepted for presentation at the NCHC conference 2013 in New Orleans.

## References

Dijk, T. van (2011). *The Reflective Professional.* Enschede/Deventer: Saxion. http://buitengewoon.saxion.nl/custom/page/page_block/111013-richtlijnen-rp-gb-buitengewoon-def-1.pdf

Gellevij, M., Banis-den Hertog, J., Donk, S. van der, Mannetje, J. 't, & Truijen, K. (2013). *Uitkomsten Onderzoek studenten Saxion Honours Programmes. Buitengewoon deel 4.* Enschede: Saxion Hogeschool. http://issuu.com/saxion-buitengewoon/docs/excelleren_4_web/41

# Evoking Excellence[1]

*Thom de Graaf*

Allow me to start by saying that I feel honoured that the organizer of this congress, Marca Wolfensberger, professor at the Hanze University of Applied Sciences, has asked me to contribute to a congress with such an intriguing title as 'Evoking Excellence in Higher Education and Beyond'. I have to say that I not only felt honoured, for I felt somewhat challenged as well. Especially because of those last two words '... and beyond'. Saying something about excellence in higher education is a task that I dare do. But the words '... and beyond' evoked a feeling of 'to boldly go where no-one has gone before' inside me.

The title of this congress implies that excellence in higher education is something that, when realized, could have – or even should have – effects outside of the actual education process. To put it in other words: excellence in education contributes to excellence in society. I agree completely with such a statement because excellence should prove itself especially after schooling has taken place, meaning in society. Without this understanding, excellence in education would be a fruitless exercise in glorifying oneself. For excellence may not be constructed out of vanity. "Look at us being great!" I know that from my past experience in politics all too well. Excellence, meaning rising above, should not only serve to bring honour and glory to the students and to the establishment that wishes to 'score' with its students. From that perspective, I would like to go into how universities of applied science, in my opinion, should handle this theme.

You know better than I do that education is the biggest motor for emancipation known to society. Allow me to limit myself to discussing only higher education at this moment, to prevent myself from giving a lecture on history.

Until well after the beginning of the 19th century, participation in higher education was restricted to a 'happy few': nobility, clergy and a handful of wealthy citizens. Slowly that changed and, after the Second World War, progressively larger groups of people obtained access to higher education. To speak of it very roughly, in the 60s it started with what was then called the

---

1   Written version of the speech delivered by Thom de Graaf, president of the Board of the Universities of Applied Sciences (Vereniging Hogescholen, voorheen HBO-raad) at the international conference "Evoking Excellence in Higher Education and Beyond" 5 October 2012.

'working class'. Around the 70s, women followed and did so with so much success that more than 50% of students following higher education at the moment are of the truly stronger sex. And, by the end of the last century, more and more persons with an immigrant background started enrolling into higher education. For this group, also, the motor for emancipation is running at high speed: even if your parents have not gone through a form of higher education, you are truly welcome to attend a university of applied science.

Because of their participation in higher education, these groups of people got chances to develop themselves, to outgrow their backgrounds, and to escape the traditional patterns society pushed on them. That, by itself, is already good. But our society as a whole also leaps forward because of higher education. Having more people that have completed a form of higher education means that there are more talented people, more non-conformist thinkers and – last but not least – having more people that have completed a form of higher education also means more economic growth. This is because those who who are in this position are capable of thinking in an innovative way, walking up new paths, obtaining knowledge and applying this knowledge. And, of course, they are good for economic growth because more highly educated people simply earn more money and, therefore, spend more as well.

This development is not a phenomenon restricted to the Netherlands. 'Widening participation' is happening at a global level. The question is, of course, where the boundaries lie. Is the Lisbon strategy's goal of wanting 50% of the population to have finished a form of higher education obtainable and desirable? Are there enough jobs to make that happen and won't there be a serious shortage in other types of worker? The enormous growth in the Netherlands brought about problems that can be expected when institutes have to grow by leaps and bounds, even though these institutes were geared towards educating small groups of students only due to the elite character of the institute's structure and method of working. And that large growth should not be underestimated by us! Allow me to illustrate this by using an example from the western part of the country. In 2000, the University of Applied Science of Amsterdam (HvA), at that time the biggest university of applied science of the Netherlands, had 20.000 students. In 2010 that same university of applied science was still the largest one in the Netherlands, but by then had 42.000 students. In less than 10 years, the Hva has doubled in size and the number of students has continued to increase since then. And that goes for many other universities of applied science, too. The situation at the Hanze University of Applied Sciences, for example, will be similar to that of the University of Applied Science of Amsterdam.

Apart from that, I would like to stress that this also proves wrong those who continuously harp on the idea that the growth of the universities of applied science stems from the urge of the boards of these schools to expand: that they are supposedly out to merge in order to run institutions that become progressively bigger. It is true that, between 2000 and 2010, the HvA merged with another university of applied science in Amsterdam (the HES Amsterdam), but that school had a 'mere' 4.000 students. Well over 60% of the growth of the HvA was caused by the enrollment of extra students and was not caused by processes of fusion.

This is partly autonomous growth: the population growth that has been taking place since the 60s and 70s can also be found reflected in higher education. Nevertheless, by far the most important cause for the growth of the universities of applied science is the successful striving of government, politics and society as a whole to continuously increase participation in higher education. For that purpose, we have settled on the objective that, by 2020, half of the European population has to have completed a form of higher education.

The developments that had been started to help realize this objective belong to the most successful policy within the public sector – obviously in collaboration with our partners in the business community – that has ever been developed.

The successful policy that is aimed at continuously increasing participation in higher education has its drawbacks, however I already mentioned possible shortages in other parts of the job market.

Universities of applied science and research universities have been forced to be preoccupied, perhaps too much, with dealing with the enormous growth which has resulted. Accommodation, IT, more high-quality employees, keeping the quality of the education high, adjusting educational methods for massive education participation, students that are fully justified in demanding value for their money, adapting organization and management – these are all issues that have been on top of the agenda during recent years. And yes, sometimes all at the same time.

In addition, the increase in funds, the means universities of applied science and research universities have at their disposal, did not increase in parallel with the growth of these institutions. For a long time, to put it optimistically, we had to do more with the same. In recent years that trend has been warped: universities of applied science now have to do even more with less. This is not me complaining for I am only stating a fact.

What does that development have to do with excellent education? Well, given the large number of students enrolling into a form of higher education and the adjustments to the system which therefore had to be made, we simply had insufficient time to be concerned with the differences between students. Only during the past five years or so have the tables begun to turn on that point. The fastest growth in higher education now lies behind us; the curve is flattening. The biggest adjustments that were necessary to handle the large groups of students enrolling have been made. We can and should now shift our attention from quantity to quality. This is necessary because the quality lagged behind while the quantity leaped forward. Because of this, many universities of applied science now have a policy stating their wish to not grow any further.

Because of the massive number of students, we have also become more and more conscious of the fact that, even though all students are equal, they don't all share the same backgrounds and talents. The bigger a group is, the more diversity there will be and this applies to groups in higher education as well. The diversity in the group of enrolling students is one of the points for which attention is requested in 'Kwaliteit als opdracht' ('Quality as Assignment'), the strategic plan that the board of the universities of applied science (HBO-raad) brought out in 2009. The Veerman commission, in its advice from 2010, 'Differentiëren in drievoud' ('Differentiation in triplicate'), had looked in depth at differences in level, interests and talents between students. One of the commission's recommendations was to "Pay more attention to education, take into account the learning styles and backgrounds of the students, make education programmes more flexible and organise the education in a better way".

And, even though little is said here to about the excellent student, that is nevertheless one of the most important developments of recent years: that, within the large mass of students brought about by the successful implementation of the aim to increase the number of those participating in higher education, attention should also be given to the differences between individual students. During recent years, in other words, a 'silent revolution' has been taking place in higher education, including universities of applied science, that I would like to describe as from 'one-size-fits-all' to (as much as possible) 'custom made'. Step by step. Group by group.

So far, while designing this custom-made education, relatively more attention has gone to the group measured by using dropout rates; that is, the least successful at the universities of applied science. This group consists of the students that had first finished senior vocational education (Mbo) and, on average, represented 20% of the first year students at universities of higher education. Then, there are those with a higher general secondary education (Havo) diploma, representing 70% of first year students at universities of applied science. Finally, a small 10% of the students at a university of applied science entered their higher education with a pre-university education (Vwo) diploma or another form of preparatory training.

In other words, we have paid much more attention to students with arrears and low levels of preparatory education and have invested a great deal to get rid of the arrears, but we have paid little attention to students who could use extra challenge. Perhaps that is very Dutch. For a long time, talking about excellence was too much of a taboo. But, let me be clear on this point as well: within our current way of bearing the costs within higher education, attention to diversity between groups of students is limited and more attention to one group should not interfere with other interests.

The group of students that is capable of more and wants more also needs our attention. This group needs our attention more than before. In the mean-time, much is happening in that area, but more can be done to turn our most excellent students into our showpieces.

With that goal in mind, the Sirius programme began in 2008. A study carried out in 2010 and 2011 by Marca Wolfensberger and her team, by order of the board of the universities of applied sciences (HBO-raad), found that, in the academic year 2009–2010, 10 out of the 40 Dutch universities of applied science were in one way or another involved with an excellence programme.

The report of this study was named 'Leren excelleren' ('Learning to excel') It can be found as a pdf on the website of the board of the universities of ap-plied science (HBO-raad) and also as a booklet that can be ordered from the same board. I recommend reading this report because it gives a good over-view of what has already been accomplished and it also informs us of which challenges we will be facing if we want to achieve more.

As already said, the report states that, in the academic year 2009–2010, a quarter of Dutch universities of applied science were offered an excellence or honours programme. That sounds good, but the painful truth is that less than a quarter of one percent of students at universities of applied science have participated in one of these programmes. And that is too little. For compari-son: at that same moment, approximately 3.5% of research university students were involved in an excellence programme, this percentage being more than ten times larger. And, even though the number of students at a university of applied science participating in an excellence programme has increased during the academic year 2012–2013, the same applies to those at research universities. This means that the universities of applied science are behind in this matter. I believe that this difference should be eliminated. But I am not going to give an objective in the form of numbers or something comparable to that. That task does not belong to me in my role of president of the board of the universities of applied science (HBO-raad). However, I will give you my opinion. And that is, more specifically, that I believe universities of applied science will be acting in their own interest when they pay more attention to, and therefore are investing in, excellent education. Why?

Firstly, because the goal most of the existing excellence programmes have is educating their students to become excellent professionals in their future field of work. Those already working regularly mention that not only well educated professionals are needed but, also, excellent workers. It makes sense, therefore, that many more universities of applied science should offer honours programmes or another kind of programme meant for students who are capable of taking an extra step. And in that lies the obvious importance of those two words '... and beyond' that I referred to at the beginning. Offering excellent students the chance, through special programmes, to develop themselves into excellent future workers is not something universities of applied science do only to make themselves seem better: it is also granting a wish coming from the work field itself. More differentiation is being asked for, more differentiation that we can offer! But, in my opinion, that is not the only goal that should be aimed for when offering excellence programmes. Education, especially higher education, next to imparting knowledge, competence and skills that a student will need in order to become a successful worker – because that is their task – also has a responsibility in terms of the general formation of its students. At present, this is often referred to as 'Bildung'. But you could also simply call it personal development or development of values, independence, creativity and a sense of responsibility. In this too, students who can do more and want more can be challenged further. Challenging students to get the best out of themselves requires a willingness to make distinctions! And, in my opinion, there is even a third reason (or opportunity) why universities of applied science should offer excellence programmes. And that is practically-oriented research, an area that is being manifested more and more by the universities of applied science and, according to the legislator, belongs to the main tasks of these schools. What makes more sense than using excellent students for this research? But, in order to do that, you would of course have to know who the excellent students are. And then it is smart to offer them an education course that also prepares them specifically for practically-oriented research: a course that will challenge them more, ask more of them compared to other students but also offers them interesting and challenging extras: an excellence course that is not only 'more' but which is also 'different'.

The question facing us now, of course, is – is all of this sound? Is it possible to pay extra attention to such a small group of students? And who has to pay for this? All such questions are fully justified. Excellence and honours programmes are, after all, essentially different from excellent education in general. All of the education that a university of applied science offers has to be excellent; that is part of its fundamental role. Furthermore, the education for the averagely talented and especially the education that is meant to prevent the less achieving students from drowning or to help them switch to a more suitable study course, has to be excellent. This is more than obvious.

Excellence programmes are all about offering more for the most talented students. When we are talking about excellence programmes or the stimulation of talent in higher education, we are already aiming at the students with a more than average intellectual ability. In relation to this target group, in addition to what has already been said, it has been found in the Sirius programme that character traits such as creativity, determination and 'wisdom' were playing an important role in respect to the target group for honours programmes. Excellence programmes are, therefore, aimed at a very specific group of students: having an above average intelligence, creative, and blessed with a substantial amount of determination, curiosity and stability. And that is, by definition, a minority. That can never be more than 10% and probably 5% is more likely. Is that a small group? If my estimation is correct – that we are dealing with somewhere between 5 and 10 percent of our students – then this might amount to somewhere between 25 and 30 thousand students. That does not sound very small. In the Netherlands, we have quite a few universities of applied science of approximately that size.

Let's conduct a thought experiment for a moment. Imagine that it appears that we have been paying too little attention to a group of 20 to 25 thousand students that find themselves at the bottom of the ranking, to put it like that. And imagine now that those students, because of this lack of attention, were to drop out because the amount of talent that they possess is just a little less than that needed to be able to complete a study at a university of applied science with ease. What would happen then? I suspect that there would be much protest because 5% would then suddenly appear to be a large amount. Isn't it, then, just as logical to demand that we invest enough time, money and attention in those capable of more and who want more? Indeed, you could say: those young men and women could save themselves. And that is probably true: they won't drop out quickly. But isn't it wasting talent not to challenge them to reach their full potential? And wouldn't that be a pity for those students, for the universities of applied science, and for society?

And for those who are still not convinced, I have a further argument. Research has shown that excellence programmes exude an effect on regular education. It turns out that the experiences these institutions have gained within their excellence programmes – relating to organization, content and curriculum – can be used to raise the quality of all the education offered by an institution.

In addition to this, the culture within an institution also changes when a significant group of students is participating in an excellence programme. A more ambitious study culture will emerge because the excellent students will influence the rest of the student population with their enthusiasm and ambition. In other words, honours courses can be used as a laboratory for reformation and as a lever for the quality of education provided by the university of applied science as a whole.

In the past 20 years, universities of applied science have developed themselves into big, self-aware and especially multi-sectored educational institutions, with a very diverse population of students. This development has not always been smooth and, because of the growth spurts the institutions have had to go through, the focus for a long time had been on accommodating to that increasing size. The quality of education has not necessarily suffered because of that, even though there were, of course some regrettable incidents. However, past years have been characterized with a certain degree of the 'one size fits all' approach. We were ready for an increase in quality. We wanted to raise the bar and offer more personal education. It is justified that universities of applied science are being asked to adjust their education to the diversity of its new students. That much attention goes out to students that have more difficulty reaching the finishing line is understandable. But the group that needs to be challenged more is not a marginal one and the students, universities of applied science and the corresponding fields of work benefit when we not only turn out average, 'normal' graduates, but also turn out excellent beginner workers. Paying attention to that does good to all those involved. It is part of the process of improving the quality of education and study in such a way to make it easier to complete. The other aspects of this process of improvement are making education more diverse and stressing the distinctive features about which we, as a sector, make agreements on objectives with the minister of state.

It gives me much pleasure to be able to say that 5 out of the 40 universities of applied science have chosen to offer honours education as performance indicator of quality education. The Hanze University of Applied Sciences is one of those five universities of applied science. That is good and fits in well with the predicate 'excellent' that the Hanze University of Applied Sciences had recently received because of the school's presentation suggestions.

# Engineering Honours Programme

## A Different Approach

*Peter van Kollenburg, Diviyia Kanagalingam, Deep Raj Khadka
and Michael Kruger*

## Abstract

In September 2009, the department of Engineering of Fontys University of
Applied Sciences in the Netherlands started a pilot honours programme for
excellent engineering students called PRogramme OUtstanding Development
(PROUD). The aim of this programme is to give those engineering students,
who have the ambition, the opportunity to work on extra profession-related
challenges in their study.

The department started PROUD-related research together with engaged
engineering students who really want to improve the engineering education.
In 2008, engineering students carried out this research among their fellow
students, lecturers, other institutes and industry (Van Kollenburg & De Waal,
2011). This resulted in an honours programme proposal for the department
of Electronic and Electrical (E&E) engineering that, compared to other programmes (Van Eijl et al., 2003), had a quite different approach.

In the PROUD programme, students are stimulated to personally shape
their educational careers and to explicitly work on developing their own competences. The PROUD programme starts after the first year and extends to
at least 3 semesters in the following years. The student works on building an
excellent portfolio at the university as well as in industry. During this period,
the PROUD student will carry out extracurricular work in industry for at
least one day a week.

Each year, about 20 students apply for a place in PROUD but thus far only
about 3–4 pass the interviews. As it has turned out, students, the university
and industry are all eager to participate in the PROUD programme.

## PROUD Development Process

Honours programmes at universities are usually broad and the same for all
students. Universities mostly choose minors for honours and, in these minors,
students collaborate in an interdisciplinary manner at a subject related to so-

cietal problems e.g. sustainable energy, C2C, pollution, traffic control (Van Kollenburg & De Waal, 2011). This kind of honours programmes is available at our university but, before introducing an honours programme in our Engineering department, we decided to start a work group to investigate the wants and needs of our engineering students regarding an honour programme.

Five engineering students and two lecturers started research on this topic of excellence and produced a recommendation for the management of our department. The first inquiry was started to find what engineering students would like the 'specification' of the honours programme to be. The result was that 45% of Fontys first year engineering students (N=75) wanted to participate in an honours programme (Van Kollenburg & De Waal, 2011). If these first year students could choose, then 60% wanted to become an outstanding engineer. This was in contradiction to 28% of first year students who would opt for a more academic education: more courses and more theoretical background which is also a very good option (Cowdroy, 2008). The PROUD development team was astonished about the specification list of the engineering students. All respondents agreed that an honours programme is only serious if it includes extracurricular effort for the student: it should be additional study/work on top of the whole engineering programme. The students in general disapproved of the thought that one could be excellent just by having a specific honours minor instead of regular minor, as is the idea of our university management (see Fig. 1). "If one is excellent then the student should have (spare) time to do extra work/study" was a point of view which was often voiced.

So now the question arose: "what should the honours student do in this extracurricular time?" The inquiries showed that 80% of our students had a part-time job alongside their studies. So it is obvious what students did in their spare time: work and earning money. If students joined our engineering honours programme, and this programme required spare time from the participating students, then it would conflict with the part-time jobs they already have. And, indeed, it turned out that students would apply only for our honour opportunity if they got paid for this extracurricular work. Combining this with the students' indication of getting more engineering experience, it was obvious that the department had to look for ways of collaborating closely with industry so that "becoming experienced" and "getting paid" went well together.

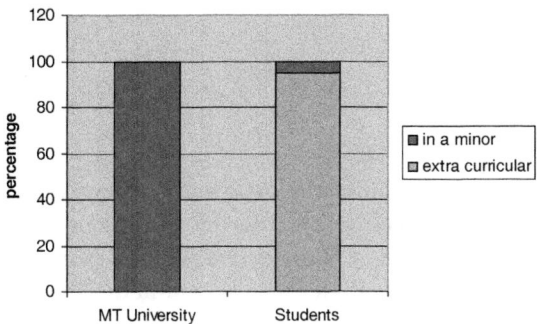

*Figure 1:* *Honours curricula seen by Fontys Management and engineering*
*students*

All over the world, practical training in companies has been recognized for many years as a major component of the education of engineering students. This is especially important for engineering graduates wishing to compete in a global labour market. At present, employers highly value new engineers with practical training, as a way to guaranteeing that they have competences in engineering skills, team working, communication abilities, leadership and so on. It is in this context that some people have asked for the inclusion of compulsory work placements in engineering study programmes (Magdaleno & Domínguez, 2010). Our honours programme translates this into a voluntary extra-work experience for honours students besides traineeship and thesis work. These students broaden their engineering horizons in selected companies. In this interaction with industry, they work to solve real-world engineering problems at an increasing level of complexity. This resulted in an honours programme proposal for the department of Electronic and Electrical (E&E) engineering that, compared to other programmes (Van Eijl et al., 2003), had a quite different approach.

## PROUD Realization

In the PROUD programme, students are stimulated to shape their educational career and to explicitly work on developing their own competences. Six profile points are defined and, in industry, the student will work on the first five:

1. Passion
2. Ambition
3. Professional skills
4. Innovative skills
5. International orientation
6. Leadership.

Becoming aware of these skills and the ability to express this to others is essential for participant PROUD students. Fontys Engineering offers the PROUD student different ways to work on point 3 (Professional skills) and point 6 (Leadership) at the university. Therefore, students have to fulfil the following assignments:

1. Workshops and/or guest lectures given for other students.
2. The technical support of fellow students in projects (semester 3–4) or practical assignments or help in study (the student as a role model for fellow students).
3. Introduction and guidance of a second year project based on the company-gained experience and skills. The PROUD student reflects on how he/she professionally supervised and assessed the second year project group in the role of departmental or group leader.
4. Contribution to the Engineering's Promotion Team (Product Relations, think tank, advisory committee) or work in a student council.
5. The contribution and critically evaluation/comments of the E&E curriculum.

During their PROUD honours time, students are guided by a university coach and a coach from industry. Together, each semester they approve the students' proposed learning goals and agree on improving competence goals. PROUD members also get access to the dedicated PROUD programme advisory committee to discuss these goals.

## First PROUD Results

Each year, about 45 national E&E engineering students start the second year of their study as well as another 50 students from our international E&E department. These are the target groups for the PROUD programme. The first step is an introduction to the PROUD honours programme, nowadays given by participating students. Besides this, posters are used to inform the first year students. In the first year, about 20 students were interested but only 11 students applied for a place in PROUD by sending in their application letter and CV. Two members of the PROUD committee interviewed these 11 students. In this first round, only three students passed. All the other students were rejected, a decision based on:

1. poor motivation
2. study results too low
3. insufficient time available for extracurricular activities.

In table 1, an overview is shown of the accepted students in the PROUD route so far:

*Table 1: Number of students accepted in PROUD*

| Year | Interested students | Applied | Accepted |
|------|---------------------|---------|----------|
| 2009/2010 | 20 | 11 | |
| Autumn | | | 3 |
| Spring | | | 2 |
| 2010/2011 | 24 | 6 | |
| Autumn | | | 2 |
| Spring | | | 3 |
| 2011/2012 | 32 | 13 | |
| Autumn | | | 5 |
| Spring | | | 7 |
| 2012/2013 NL | 23 | 7 | 3 |
| Autumn EE | 17 | 14 | 6 |
| Spring | | | |
| Total | 116 | 50 | 31 |

During the first two years, only one student has left PROUD. All the other students participating in PROUD are highly motivated and show eagerness in their situation in the company. They show real progress in their practical engineering skills. Additionally, all students learn new technologies used in their companies. PROUD students bring these new technologies into project work for the other students they manage at the university in cooperation with their companies. Due to this the university is able to rapidly introduce these new technologies into their curriculum.

## Conclusions and Recommendations

It turns out that engineering students, industry and university are eager to participate in this Electric and Electronic PROUD programme. For students, the main advantages are that they gain:

- University and educational experience that is challenging and honours their ambitions. They are able to contribute substantially to the development of the curriculum and the introduction of innovative technologies.
- A reasonably well-paid job besides their studies which contributes to their professional education. In particular, they work on professional and innovative skills, international orientation and leadership.
- An excellent portfolio and PROUD designations (honours certificate) on their transcripts to show to advantage when applying for jobs.

Practice proves that many students apply but only few students pass the intake process. Motivation, study results and insufficient time available for extracurricular activities prove to be a serious threshold.

From the first experience with the PROUD programme, we can conclude that the selection criteria are not yet sufficiently specific, measurable, and unbiased. Sometimes students are refused participation but this is not based on sufficiently hard criteria. Improving the selection criteria and the intake process is therefore recommended. For participating companies, the advantage is that they:

- Have an excellent opportunity for pre-selecting future employees.
- Have a highly motivated junior employee doing a job.
- Can contribute to the practical training of students and introduce the student in the company's way of working in product development and design methods.
- Can maintain contacts with educational institutes.

The first experiences with PROUD shows that participating companies in general are very enthusiastic about the excellence programme. A drawback is that students often demand high flexibility in working hours (working in the evening hours or on Saturday, for instance). Not all companies can fulfil this demand and students, therefore, choose another company. This sometimes leads to disappointment on the part of the company management.

Another practical problem of the PROUD scheme is that in the company a workplace (desk, computer etc.) has to be allocated, which is then only used one day a week! A further point of attention is the in-company learning path for the student. When PROUD students enter a company, they have just finished their first year at university. By the end of the programme, they are third/fourth year students. Though the first participating students have been doing a variety of in-company activities, the learning path is not explicitly specified and is more or less ad hoc.

We recommend that the learning path in the company is explicitly planned and documented from the beginning and updated every semester. For the university the advantages are that:

- Challenging educational activities are provided for excellent students.
- It keeps in touch with innovations in industry as well as an easy route to implementation by means of the contribution of PROUD students in curriculum development and in the coaching of other students.
- It maintains contacts with industry in the region with the goal of staying up to date and stimulating the participation of industry in the curriculum.
- Highly motivated students contribute to all kind of PR-activities.
- The PROUD honours programme is used in PR presentations of the university. It shows in practice that parents consider the excellence programme an important extra possibility for the education of their child.
- Interaction within their learning environment with equally motivated and successful engineering students is provided. (The LinkedIn group "PROUD members of Fontys Engineering" has been setup to facilitate this interaction.)
- Students contribute to the Fontys Engineering community through their extracurricular activities and, more specifically, to the PROUD community through team-building within this group by organising (informal) meetings, get-togethers and presentations with other PROUD student members, thus increasing team-building for PROUD group members.

Until now, PROUD students have been asked to contribute to curriculum development and PR activities on a more or less ad hoc basis. We recommend that the E&E Department integrates the contribution of PROUD students in a more structured way.

Overall, PROUD is a very special honours programme of the Fontys Department of Electrical and Electronic Engineering which has had appreciable results for all participating members.

## References

Cowdroy, R. (2008). *Beyond excellence achieving brilliance in engineering educa-tion.* Quality Assessment, Employability and Innovation – SEFI Annual Conference, 2008, Aalborg, Denmark.

Eijl, P. J. van, Wolfensberger, M. V. C., Cadée, M., Siesling, S., Schreve-Brinkman, E. J., Beer, W. M., Faber, G., & Pilot, A. (2003). *Plusprogramma's als proeftuin.* Mededeling nr. 69 van het IVLOS. Universiteit Utrecht, Utrecht, the Netherlands.

Kollenburg, P. van, & Waal, A. de (2011). *Engineering honours programme. A different approach.* Global Engineering Recognition, Sustainability and Mobility – 1st World EE Flash Week – SEFI Annual Conference 2011, Lisbon, Portugal.

Magdaleno J., & Domínguez U. (2010). *Industrial training in engineering education in Europe.* Joint International IGIP – SEFI Annual Conference 2010, Trnava, Slovakia.

# Excellence and Citizenship in Honours Education

*Joseph Lewandowski*

The motto of The Honours College at my home institution, The University of Central Missouri, is: 'Education for Excellence'. But 'excellence' in what sense and to what end, precisely?

I should like to consider the theoretical and practical significance of that motto and the question it begs for honours students and the global world in which they live. For when it succeeds, the power of an honours education does not simply reside in the intellectual and material accomplishment of individuals – it does not, that is to say, simply produce better-educated and more prosperous individuals. More profoundly, the force of an honours education lies in its potential to foster cooperative habits of critical inquiry and action essential to a democratic way of life.

Such a force is especially crucial in today's globalized world, where populaces are increasingly controlled – and even dominated – by the long reach of what I have elsewhere characterized as 'global elites' (Lewandowski, 2009). Put somewhat differently, excellence in honours education can, at its best, cultivate precisely the kind of citizenship needed to critique and bring under democratic control today's global elites. Thus, it must be emphasized that my thoughts about the connection between honours education and elitism runs counter to the standard skeptical view. Indeed, it is not honours education that risks the production of elites; on the contrary, it is honours education that can produce the kinds of citizens best able to tame the power of global elites in democratic societies.

Most generally, my sense is that what education for excellence entails is the cultivation of a form of citizenship that is a necessary precondition for democratic co-existence in today's global world. I call that form 'reflexive citizenship'. 'Reflexivity' is a form of practical reason in which human agents make explicit, normatively optimize, and alter the conditions that enable and limit thought and action. 'Citizenship' is a term I use here in a loosely sociological sense to describe individuals who are joined together by virtue of shared commitments to associational practices anchored in mutual recognition and social cooperation. Citizenship, that is to say, is about embedding individuality in sociality.

I want to begin simply by stressing the uniquely social dimensions of any educational form that lays claim to 'excellence'. Indeed, among a variety of factors, what makes an honours education excellent is the understanding that the realization of individual student achievements is only part of the educational experience. For to achieve excellence in honours education we must grasp and enhance the ways in which the educational process is a profoundly *so-cial* undertaking. In a genuinely excellent honours classroom, lecture hall, or laboratory, students don't simply learn about facts, theories and ideas. Rather, the educational experience itself is a highly engaged form of reflexive social cooperation. Students learn *alongside* and *from* and *with* others. In so doing, they begin to cultivate shared ways of interacting that far exceed particular educational contexts and have profound ramifications for the production of a democratic way of life.

More specifically, excellence in honours education is, or so I want to suggest here, about cultivating habits of engaged inquiry, such as perspective-taking, deliberation, and experimentation, that are crucial to the maintenance of a vibrant democratic culture. Let me briefly examine and make explicit the relevance of each of these in turn.

It is not hard to see how honours education demands achieving proficiency in the art of perspective-taking. Most generally, in that learning process, understanding a fact, theory or idea invariably involves taking up the perspectives and contexts of others. For knowledge – like truth – does not descend from the heavens. Instead, knowledge and truth are, to borrow a phrase from Foucault (1980), things of this world – they are produced by and the (re)producers of material life-worlds. In learning to take various points of view that are not their own, honours students necessarily learn how to stand outside themselves and inhabit, if only partially, what counts as knowledge and truth in the worldviews of others.

Of course, it hardly needs to be added that this kind of multi-perspectival competency is crucial in a globalized world. Indeed, in acquiring the highly reflexive habit of multi-perspectival inquiry, students enlarge the range of their own intellectual and moral horizons, come to a deeper understanding of the intellectual and moral horizons of others, and gain an awareness of the complexities of the contexts in which all human perspectives are embedded.

Put somewhat differently, multi-perspectival inquiry enhances honours students' capacities for mutual recognition and empathy as diverse members of pluralistic and overlapping associations and communities. In this regard, the epistemic virtues of perspective-taking and the ethical virtues of empathetic agency become practically intertwined in the honours educational experience.

Of course there is much more to the story about what one learns in an honours educational experience. Perspective-taking is necessary, but not sufficient. Honours students must learn how to evaluate and scrutinize what they come to understand and empathize with in the process of adopting the perspectives of others. Honours students must learn, that is to say, how to deliberate with others about *what counts* as knowledge and truth.

Deliberation is simply another word for the open-ended give and take of reasons among individuals. It is dialogue governed by argumentation and justification. Learning to deliberate is learning how to talk and listen to others in *critical* but non-coercive ways – ways that recognize and respect but also challenge others to explain and give reasons for the points of view they hold.

Acquiring deliberative ways of thinking and interacting is a necessary condition not merely for the rational critique of individual perspectives. It is also decisive for the *peaceful* transformation of society, and thus indispensable as a mechanism of non-violent change in a democracy. In the US context, one thinks especially of the deliberative power of dialogue that was unleashed during the Civil Rights Movement – where arguments about judging human beings by the 'content of character' rather than the 'color of skin' made explicit what the philosopher Jürgen Habermas has rightly called, 'the unforced force of the better argument' (1998).

Now, to be sure, deliberations can and do become rigid, stagnate, or suffer from a dearth of imaginative reasoning and argumentation. It is precisely for that reason that excellence in an honours education must also characteristically stress the importance of experimentation. Experimentation in the broadest sense should be understood simply as creativity vis-à-vis constraints. When honours students learn to experiment – with a hypothesis or a chemical compound or a piece of clay – they learn how to innovate within a given set of parameters. In the sciences, such parameters are known as methods; in the arts, they typically take the form of genres.

Yet, experimentation also entails the improvisational ability to 'think outside the box' – and, indeed, the courage to create new constraints and better structures. It would not be an exaggeration to say that this ability, along with the ability to pursue creativity within constraints, is crucial not only for excellence in an honours education but also for the cultivation of the reflexive use of reason and a democratic culture. For, in many ways, democracy itself is an ongoing experiment in how to achieve maximum freedoms within minimally shared constraints. Indeed, the flourishing of a democratic way of life depends in part upon cultivating a community of reflexive citizens.

In one way or another, the attempt to develop an adequate account of reflexivity has been central to my work for the past decade or so. Inspired and yet critical of the work of Pierre Bourdieu, early on in my research and teaching in the philosophy of social science I argued for a hermeneutical sense of reflexivity. Interpretation, to put the matter bluntly, is about making explicit the situatedness of beliefs, norms and practices – what I call 'thematizing embeddedness' (Lewandowski, 2000, 2001).

As a matter of reflexive practice, interpretation is always multi-layered and multi-contextual. In fact, thematizing embeddedness requires that individuals adopt a highly reflexive observer-participant stance toward their perspectives, the perspectives of others, and the contexts in which all those perspectives are situated. In this way, reflexively thematizing embeddedness can serve to make the mundane exotic and the exotic mundane in ways that produce disruptive insights into the taken-for-granted character of particular perspectives and the complex contexts that inform (and sometimes deform) those perspectives and contexts. Reflexivity is thus not merely of epistemic value; it also, as Pierre Bourdieu maintains, 'makes possible a more responsible politics' (Bourdieu & Wacquant, 1992). And indeed, it is difficult to imagine a greater task facing higher education today. For the practice of a democratically responsible politics depends in no small way upon agents who reflexively make explicit the perspectives, contexts and material conditions in which they and others are embedded.

Hence, in my own honours courses and in my research, I have persistently explored – and continue to explore – this *critical* power of reflexivity. I have examined the uses of reflexivity in a wide range of empirically based discussions, including that of globalization, democratization, urban cultures, social capital formation, and even boxing. In studying how embeddedness is reflexively thematized in such processes, locations and practices, I have sought to demonstrate to my students how human beings do not merely interpret the world in which they live, but also continually critique and transform it as reflexive citizens.

Now, to be sure, reflexive citizenship can – and often must – be an improvisational kind of practice. For there are unique periods and contexts of human history when entirely new sets of constraints must be fashioned – when the boat needs to be rebuilt at sea, as the saying goes. In fact, in the present context one hardly needs look further than the revolutions and transitions to post-socialism in the 'New Europe' or, indeed, the ongoing economic, political, and social challenges facing the European Union (E.U.). For, while it might rightly be said that revolutions, be they political or economical, aim to deconstruct existing constraints, successful transitions typically demand the improvised creation of and joint adherence to new constraints.

In a profound way, developing the constraints that constitute the E.U. stands as an exemplary adventure in the practice of reflexive citizenship. Forming integrated democracies and market economies *across* borders – both physically and culturally – entails thematizing embededdness in ways that not only transform existing contexts of constraints but also foster the emergence of entirely new ones. And inhabiting and appropriating such innovative contexts in turn depends upon a highly reflexive citizenry – a kind of citizenry that can and should be uniquely cultivated in honours educational settings.

For, creating integrated transnational democratic institutions and market economies, however complex and contested, is at its core a reflexive constraint-making endeavour or series of endeavours. Integrated transnational markets and democracies must be constrained enough to enable efficiency and fairness, yet loose enough to ensure a maximum amount of liberty and innovation. In composing integrated transnational market-based democracies, the reflexive use of reason aims to design and engender a kind of embeddedness in which continued reflexive orientations towards constraints is possible.

In closing, let me briefly summarize my reflections. The power of an honours educational experience is disclosed most fully in the acquisition of a constellation of cooperative habits that are not merely compatible with a democratic way of life but – more fundamentally – normative preconditions for such a life. Put differently, pursuing excellence in honours education is not about producing elites but rather about cultivating the kind of reflexive citizens intellectually and socially equipped to criticize and transform a global world all too often unduly influenced by the extra-democratic forces and interests of elites.

Indeed, taken together, perspective-taking, deliberation and experimentation constitute highly engaged forms of reflexive social cooperation and critique. Once honed and put into everyday practice, such habits are not simply instruments or tools of inquiry or ends in themselves but, rather, collective ways of thinking, engaging in and peacefully transforming the world. That is no small task, to be sure. But if I am right about the democratic potential inherent in the achievement of excellence in honours educational settings, then there is some reason to hope that the honours students of today's globalized world will be suitably prepared to meet the challenge.

# References

Bourdieu, P., & Wacquant, L. (1992). *An Invitation to Reflexive Sociology*. Chicago: University of Chicago Press.

Foucault, M. (1980). *Power/Knowledge: Selected Interviews and Other Writings, 1972–1977*. New York: Vintage.

Habermas, J. (1998). *Between Facts and Norms: Contributions to a Discourse Theory of Law and Democracy.* Cambridge, MA: MIT Press.

Lewandowski, J. (2000). Thematizing Embeddedness: Reflexive Sociology as Interpretation. *Philosophy of the Social Sciences,* 30 (1), 49–66.

Lewandowski, J. (2001). *Interpreting Culture: Rethinking Method and Truth in Social Theory.* Lincoln, NE: Nebraska University Press.

Lewandowski, J. (2009). Elites without Borders: Reflections on Globalization, Stratification, and Social Distrust. In J. Lewandowski and M. Znoj (Eds.), *Trust and Transitions: Social Capital in a Changing World* (105–121). Newcastle: Cambridge Scholars Press.

# Research on the Effectiveness of the Online Honours Course

*Ingrid Schutte and Carolyn Oxenford*

## Introduction

A team from the USA and the Netherlands were selected as Fellows of the SUNY Institute for Collaborative Online International Learning (COIL) to develop an interdisciplinary honours course on global awareness. Students from the Netherlands and the United States experienced working together across cultures as they explored global themes together.

Part of the project is a case study focusing on effects on students with regard to aspects of global citizenship. In this article, we present the development and design of this research and reflect on the challenges involved with this international cooperative venture.

## Development of the Research

The effectiveness of the course will be measured with specific attention to possible gains in students' social responsibility and civic engagement (as part of a doctoral research project). An underlying principle of the project is that honours programmes should prepare students not only to contribute to the market and knowledge economy, but also for social responsibility in the globalised world. The aim of the case study is to determine whether this course provides progress in these respects.

Developing this research in an international setting (USA and the Netherlands) revealed several issues that reflect the differences in culture and tradition between the USA and the Netherlands. For example, the IRB (Institutional Review Board) at the US university requires a very careful documentation of research procedures and submission of all the instruments, letters, and methods beforehand to get permission for the research. In addition, students' permission is needed in order to release the products of their work. At this university, teachers conduct research on their own courses and students, whereas, in this project, teachers and researchers cooperate on the research part. Finally, the course itself will be slightly different at each university, due to different course requirements at the respective university.

## Methods and Instruments

Literature research, combining knowledge of characteristics, underlying concepts and pedagogical practices with regard to global citizenship education and service learning, with possible characteristics of gifted higher education students (based on e.g. Davies, Evans, & Reid, 2005; Nussbaum, 1997; Andreotti, & De Souza, 2008; Terry, & Bohnenberger, 2003) has taken place. This led to a conceptual model with associated design principles and teacher guidelines for an honours course aiming at social responsibility in the globalized world. Four main elements of the model are:

1.  Knowledge and understanding. Examples of design principles are: *choose one global issue to be the central theme of the* course *challenge the students to investigate the emergence of a problem or issue (historical dimension) in order to be able to find possible solutions for the future.*
2.  Skills and attitude. An example of a design principle is: *provide contact and interaction with people varying in socio-economic and cultural backgrounds, who are different from the students in life changes, experiences and world views.*
3.  Critical reflection. An example of a design principle is: *expose learners to different perspectives and invite them to engage with the possibilities and limitations of each of them in order to promote more accountable reasoning.*
4.  Take action. An example of a design principle is: *incorporate at least 15–20 hours of community practice (service learning) in the course.*

Possible effects of the course on the development of the students are measured with mixed methods – both qualitative and quantitative – each focusing on a different aspect of social/global involvement. The research questions include:

•   *Do both groups of students register levels of change on the Ethical Sensitivity Scale Questionnaire (ESSQ) and the Intercultural Sensitivity Scale Questionnaire (ICSSQ) between the beginning and end of the course?* Aspects of moral development and growth of intercultural competences will be assessed pre- and post-test by the ESSQ (Tirri, & Nokelainen, 2011) and ICSSQ (Holm, Nokelainen & Tirri, 2009). The comparison with a control group will make stronger statements possible on the possible relationship between participation and learning outcomes. We expect that students who complete the course will show gains in their intercultural competencies as well as gains in their moral sensitivity compared to the control group. Moral sensitivity, because of the contact with people in other life situations provided by the course, could be morally transformative (Strain, 2005).

- *When completing their assignments – do both groups of students explain what they are observing in terms of how the process of globalization has influenced contemporary events? – do both groups of students critically reflect on values and on mainstream a 'Western' perspective?*

Knowledge and understanding of the historical and social context of the (main) global issue of the course and critical reflection on values and dispositions will be examined by content analyses of students' Blogs and final assignment.

- *At the end of the course, do students state that they are willing to make a contribution to achieving a more just world?* Motivation and seeing possibilities for making (a small) contribution to achieving a more just world will be assessed by interviews or questionnaires asking students to reflect on their learning process and their thoughts on possible social involvement in the future. This measurement will also provide additional information on the effectiveness of the course from the point of view of the students who participated.
- *How did the course, as implemented, differ from the conceptual model?* Possible differences between conceptual model and the actual course in relation to to the measured development of students in the different aspects of social responsibility in the globalized world, might give some insight into possible improvements of both the course and the model (inductive method).

## In Summary

Honours programmes should also prepare students for social responsibility in the globalised world. This course aims at preparing undergraduate honours students in such a way. Research on the effects of the course on students with regard to aspects of global citizenship might add to knowledge on how to evoke excellence in this respect.

## Acknowledgement

'The global village' was initiated in conjunction with an NEH grant received by Collaborative Online Learning (COIL) at the State University of New York (SUNY) Global Center, administrative support and funding from Marymount University (USA) and Hanze UAS (NL) and its Research Center Talent Development in Higher Education and Society.

## References

Andreotti, V., & de Souza, L.M.T.M. (2008). Global learning in the 'knowledge society'. Four tools for discussion. *ZEP, 31*(1), 7–11.

Davies, I., Evans, M., & Reid, A. (2005). Globalising citizenship education? A critique of 'global education' and 'citizenship education'. *British Journal of Educational Studies, 53*(1), 66–89.

Holm, K., Nokelainen, P., & Tirri, K. (2009). Relationship of gender and academic achievement to Finnish students' intercultural sensitivity. *High Ability Studies, 20*(2), 187–200.

Nussbaum, M.C. (1997). Cultivating humanity. Cambridge: Harvard University Press.

Strain, C.R. (2005). Pedagogy and Practice: Service-learning and students' moral development. *New directions of teaching and learning, 103,* 61–71.

Terry, A. W., & Bohnenberger, J. E. (2003). Service learning: Fostering a cycle of caring in our gifted youth. *Journal of Secondary Gifted Education, 15*(1), 23–32.

Tirri, K., & Nokelainen, P. (2011). *Identifying and measuring multiple intelligences and moral sensitivities in education.* Rotterdam: Sense Publishers.

# Moral Education for High-Ability Students

*Kirsi Tirri*

## Introduction

According to Bebeau, Rest, & Narvaez (1999), morality is built upon four basic component processes. These processes include moral sensitivity, moral judgment, moral motivation and moral character. In this article, the emphasis is on ethical sensitivity which is the component that has been studied least (Tirri, 2011). High-ability students reflect on moral issues within a broader ethical framework than previously presented. A new moral orientation – an 'ethic of empowerment' – is put forward, which describes scientists' beliefs and values in the context of an academic work ethic. An ethic of empowerment describes values and beliefs related to academic motivation, self-image, and academic work culture (Koro-Ljungberg, & Tirri, 2002). The conceptualizations and understandings of scientists' work ethics must go beyond justice and care-oriented reasoning. Gifted, creative scientists need an ethic of empowerment that is built on their own inner drive to excel and create new things. The hacker work ethic presented in this article includes many aspects that suit gifted and creative minds. Moreover, the hacker ethic is introduced as an ethic that can help scientists to combine ethics with excellence.

## What is the Hacker Ethic?

Combining excellence with ethics relates to ethical models developed in the academic context, such as Pekka Himanen's theoretical approach to the hacker ethic. In his work, Himanen (2001) introduced a new kind of ethic, "the hacker work ethic", that has replaced the dominance of the Protestant work ethic with a passionate attitude and relationship to one's work. He used the word 'hackers' to refer to people who did their work because of intrinsic interest, excitement, and joy, whereas the Protestant work ethic emphasized work as a duty and a calling. Successful scientists resemble hackers with their strong inner drive to excel (Tirri, & Campbell, 2002; Koro-Ljungberg, & Tirri, 2002).

In Himanen's study, hackers wanted to realize their passion together with others, and they wanted to create something valuable for the community and be recognized for that by their peers. A passionate attitude towards work, a desire to learn more about subjects and phenomena, was not an attitude found only among computer hackers, but also among research scientists. Himanen (2001, p. 9) identified the monastery as the historical precursor to the Protestant ethic. For the hacker work ethic, the academic community was the precursor. Historically, the academic community has always defended a person's freedom to organize his/her work schedule. Hackers did not organize their lives in terms of routined and continuously optimized workdays, but in terms of a dynamic flow between creative work and life's other passions. Scientists working within the academy were occasionally free to organize their days according to a flow between creative work and other passions, but equally as often, scientists were committed to rigid schedules, timelines, and assigned tasks (Koro-Ljungberg, & Tirri, 2002).

According to Himanen (2001, p. 140), the hacker work ethic consisted of "melding passion with freedom." For hackers, recognition within a community that shares their passion was more important and more deeply satisfying than money, just as it was for scholars in the academy. However, this recognition was no substitute for passion: it had to come as a result of passionate action, of the creation of something socially valuable to this creative community (Himanen, 2001). A "hacker" who lived according to the hacker ethic on all three of these levels – work, money, ethic – gained the highest respect in his/her community (Himanen, 2001, p. 140–141).

## What is Ethical Sensitivity?

Skills in moral judgment and especially in moral sensitivity are necessary in order to combine excellence with ethics (Tirri, 2011). High-ability students have been shown to be superior in moral judgment when compared to students of average ability. However, high academic ability does not always predict high moral judgment (Narvaez, 1993; Tirri, 2011). Morality includes other components as well, such as sensitivity, motivation, and character. In the research on the ethical sensitivity of gifted people in science, we have used the definition by Bebeau, Rest, and Narvaez (1999, p. 22), on moral sensitivity. According to them, moral sensitivity is about the awareness of how our actions affect other people. Thus, without possessing a moral sensitivity it would be difficult to see the kind of moral issues that are involved in science. To respond to a situation in a moral way, however, a scientist must be able to perceive and interpret events in a way that leads to ethical action. A morally-sensitive scientist notes various situational cues and is able to visualize several alternative actions in response to that situation. He or she draws on many aspects, skills, techniques and components of interpersonal sensitivity. These include taking the perspective of others (role-taking), cultivating empathy for others, and interpreting a situation based on imagining what might happen and who might be affected. Moral sensitivity is closely related to a new suggested intelligence type – social intelligence – which can be defined as the ability to get along well with others and get them to cooperate with you (Albrecht, 2006; Goleman, 2006).

Ethical sensitivity includes similar components to the hacker ethics. Hackers wanted to realize their passion together with others, and they wanted to create something valuable for the community and be recognized for that by their peers. In a similar way, ethical sensitivity builds on caring and communication together with the idea of finding new innovative solutions to ethical dilemmas in a community of ethically-sensitive people.

## Gifted Researchers in Science

In a study on adult gifted females, including Academic Olympians, it was established that beliefs and values are important in their lives (Tirri, & Koro-Ljungberg, 2002; Tirri, 2002). In another study including researchers, the beliefs and values of successful Finnish scientists (N=16) which guide their academic work were identified (Koro-Ljungberg, & Tirri, 2002). In both studies, interviews were conducted in which the professional and personal lives of these individuals were discussed, as well as themes related to their choices of career, job, spouse, life-style, friends, and hobbies. All the scientists in the study worked in academic research environments (Tirri, 2001). One of the aims was to reveal the contextual and situational nature of the academic work ethic. Before this study, other researchers had acknowledged the situational and contextual essence of Kohlberg (1969) and Gilligan's (1982) moral orientations. Strike (1999) has argued that justice and caring aim at different moral goods. According to Noddings (1999), the ethical orientations of justice and care might also apply to the different domains. In some contexts, justice and care might work together to produce a genuinely moral solution, and, on other occasions, they might conflict with one another.

When placing ethical orientations of justice and care in the context of scientific work, it is often assumed that scholars need to acknowledge both forms of ethics in order to produce good science and build a just and caring society through their work. In academia, some general rules in order to evaluate the research findings and accomplishments of members need to be established. Every scholar wants to be treated fairly and have equal opportunities to publish his/her work and compete for academic ranking. In addition to equal rights, a good scientific community must acknowledge individual differences and build a sense of belonging among its members (Koro-Ljungberg, & Tirri, 2002).

In the study by Koro-Ljungberg and Tirri (2002), it was argued that, in the context of academia, justice and care do not rule separate spheres, nor does one dominate over the other. Scientists' narratives revealed that various ethical orientations sometimes work together and sometimes conflict with one another, as suggested by Strike (1999). Furthermore, the authors found that the ethical orientations of care and justice were insufficient to explain the essence of moral orientations among the scientists studied. Therefore, they proposed that the conceptualizations and understandings of scientists' work ethics must go beyond justice and care-oriented reasoning. Instead, ethical analyses and moral perceptions should create new horizons and give inner meanings to both scientists themselves and to their communities. Based on ethical analyses, the concepts of ethics of justice, care, and empowerment as possible value systems guiding researchers' work ethics were introduced. After the discovery of the theoretical misfit between the data and Kolhberg and Gilligan's models, as well as following the lack of emphasis within empowering self as a source of moral arguments and actions, a concept of 'ethic of empowerment' to describe values and beliefs connected to the moral practices of enabled, situated selves was developed. Ethic of empowerment described values and beliefs related to academic motivation, self-image, and academic work culture. It was practised through multiple conflicting subjectivities, which allowed scientists to follow their internal voices, to change and reevaluate their ethical assumptions, values and beliefs related to their personal and professional lives (Koro-Ljungberg, & Tirri, 2002).

## Implications for Moral Education of High-Ability Students

According to ethical competence theory, morality can be taught. Ethical competence theory views moral character as a set of skills that can be honed towards expert levels of performance (Narváez & Endicott, 2009). In this article, a hacker ethic is introduced as a new approach to combining ethics with excellence. Ethical sensitivity is identified as a necessary skill for high-ability students so as to identify and solve ethical dilemmas in caring and communicative ways. Ethically sensitive and creative solutions to moral dilemmas should be encouraged and modelled in moral education. Socio-scientific issues could be integrated into the curriculum and moral questions in science, which might influence the future of humankind, should be discussed. High-ability students also need opportunities to study with likeminded friends and to be challenged both academically and socially. This would provide them with the peers that are needed in hacker ethics to inspire students to give their best and passionate effort in their studies. The ethical orientations of care and justice are insufficient orientations for high-ability students. Therefore, the conceptualization and understanding of scientists' work ethics must go beyond justice and care-oriented reasoning. Gifted, creative scientists need an ethics of empowerment that is built on their own inner drive to excel and create new things. The hacker work ethic includes many aspects that suit gifted and creative minds. The hacker ethics also has great potential to help high-ability students to combine excellence with ethics.

## References

Albrecht, K. (2006). *Social intelligence: The new science of success*. San Francisco, CA: Jossey-Bass.

Bebeau, M., Rest, J., & Narvaez, D. (1999). Beyond the promise: A perspective on research in moral education. *Educational Researcher, 28*(4), 18–26.

Gilligan, C. (1982). *In a different voice*. Cambridge: Harvard University Press.

Goleman, D. (2006). *Social intelligence*. New York: Bantam Books.

Himanen, P. (2001). *The hacker ethic and the spirit of the information age*. London: Vintage.

Kohlberg, L. (1969). Stage and sequence: The cognitive-developmental approach to socialization. In D. A. Goslin (Ed.), *Handbook of socialization theory and research* (pp. 347–480). Chicago: Rand McNally.

Koro-Ljungberg, M., & Tirri, K. (2002). Beliefs and values of successful scientists. *The Journal of Beliefs and Values, 23*(2), 141–155.

Narvaez, D. (1993). High achieving students and moral judgment. *Journal for the Education of the Gifted, 16*(3), 268–279.

Narváez, D. & Endicott, L. G. (2009). *Ethical Sensitivity, Nurturing Character in the Classroom*, Ethex Series Book 1, Alliance for Catholic Education Press.

Noddings, N. (1999). Introduction. In M. Katz, N. Noddings, & K. Strike (Eds.), *Justice and caring: The search for common ground in education* (pp. 21–37). New York: Teachers College Press.

Strike, K. (1999). Justice, caring, and universality: In defence of moral pluralism. In M. Katz, N. Noddings, & K. Strike (Eds.), *Justice and caring: The search for common ground in education* (pp. 21–37). New York: Teachers College Press.

Tirri, K. (2001). Finland Olympiad studies: What factors contribute to the development of academic talent in Finland? *Educating Able Children, 5*(2), 56–66.

Tirri, K. (2002). Developing females' talent: Case studies of Finnish Olympians. *Journal of Research in Education, 12*(1), 80–85.

Tirri, K. (2011). Combining excellence and ethics: Implications for moral education for the gifted. *Roeper Review 33*(1), 59–64.

Tirri, K., & Campbell, J. R. (2002). Actualizing mathematical giftedness in adulthood. *Educating Able Children, 6*(1), 14–20.

Tirri, K., & Koro-Ljungberg, M. (2002). Critical incidents in the lives of gifted female Finnish scientists. *The Journal of Secondary Gifted Education, 13*(4), 151–162.

# Evoking Excellence with Special Undergraduate Programmes

## A German – Dutch Comparison

*Lyndsay Drayer, Marca Wolfensberger and Julia Moeller*

### Abstract

This article compares the two main gifted education programmes for undergraduate students in the Netherlands and Germany, named the Sirius Programme and the Ideational Support programme respectively. It provides an overview of the two programmes, their commonalities and differences in terms of aims and ideologies as stated in programme documentation, the institutions involved and the nature of support provided to students. The programme comparison reveals that, due to the different ways in which the two programmes are organized, different effects on stimulating student excellence are to be expected.

### Introduction

Educational programmes specifically designed for talented and motivated students in higher education are currently being developed in a number of European countries. Research on high ability in higher education is a new field and reports on gifted education programmes in this education sector are rare (Rinn, & Plucker, 2004). The articles available on higher education programmes for the gifted mainly concern the presence (or absence) of specific programmes at universities (Long, 2002; England, 2010; Wolfensberger, De Jong, & Drayer, 2011; 2012) and report on evaluations of such elements as grades, time to graduation, retention, and grade point averages (Fenderson, Hojat, Damjanov, & Rubin, 1999; Cosgrove, 2004; Shushok, 2006; Slavin, Coladarci, & Pratt, 2008). Only one study describes the impact of honours programmes on student experiences in undergraduate education and on cognitive development (Seifert, Pascarella, Colangelo, & Assouline, 2007). Programme comparison, rather than evaluation of an individual programme, could provide insight into the relative value of different programme elements. We therefore set out to analyze the commonalities and differences in the government-initiated excellence programmes in Germany and the Netherlands (Bundesministerium für Bildung und Forschung, 2009; Subsidieregeling Sirius Programma, 2008). The central goals and activities of the Sirius Programme and Ideational Support programme were identified and compared, by analysis of the main documents published by both governments and participating universities and foundations (see www.siriusprogramma.nl and www.gifts-up.de).

The study in the Netherlands focuses on the Sirius Programme for which universities were invited to submit their ideas for the promotion of student excellence. In total, 37 universities applied for funding from the Programme, from which 19 plans were selected. Eight academic universities and 11 universities of applied sciences now participate in the Sirius Programme for undergraduate students. Research universities, universities of technology, teacher-training colleges, arts academies and broad-based professional universities are all represented.

The German programme is named 'Ideational Support'. It is an enrichment programme provided by twelve national foundations that is supported with money and guidelines from the German government. These institutions represent the most important political parties, the two main churches, the labour unions and the German economy, and there are also a Jewish foundation and a governmental foundation aiming at academic excellence.

## Governmental Policies

Both programmes are endowed with public funding and are thus shaped by political objectives. Both programmes are also conducted by non-governmental institutions: universities in the Netherlands, and political, religious and social foundations in Germany. The Ideational Support programme and the Sirius Programme were initiated by governments in order to stimulate high achievement. The programmes aim at above-average performance of students in terms of grades, increase in graduation rates and graduation within in the prescribed time. In addition, the Sirius Programme was set up within the universities to stimulate a 'culture of excellence' with the aim of also enhancing the achievement of regular students who do not participate in the programme.

A specific goal of the German Ideational Support is the stimulation of social commitment – as indicated, for example, by voluntary activities in politics, religion, or culture and positive personal traits (such as motivation). Both the German and Dutch government aim to increase the number of students participating in excellence programmes, highly-qualified graduates in various fields being required in today's knowledge-based economies.

## Objectives of the Involved Institutions

Giftedness as a label is only applied to persons who achieve highly in something that is valued by society at a large (Sternberg, 2005; Gardner, Csikszentmihalyi, & Damon, 2001). The product, but also the process of high achievement must meet the common good in order to be considered an aspect of giftedness. High achievement is the central objective of every educational programme to support gifted students (Gagné, 2005; Renzulli, 2005; Heller, Perleth, & Keng Lim, 2005). In higher education, different forms of high achievement exist. One important form of high achievement is academic excellence. Academic excellence is here defined as the scientific mastering of a chosen field, as traditionally indicated by grades, grade point average (GPA), time to graduation, post graduation, academic prizes, and scientific publications. Another form of high achievement which becomes important in higher education is professional excellence. Professional excellence is here defined as the successful mastering of a chosen vocational field including objective and subjective vocational success (as indicated by prompt engagement, income, leadership position, important contributions to the field or organization, work satisfaction, and so on). In general, the programmes in both countries aim at stimulating academic and professional excellence, social commitment and positive personal development.

Universities in the Netherlands invested money and time in the Sirius Programme as the excellence programmes are expected to be of benefit to the participating universities, besides their positive effect on students. A more ambitious study culture is expected to lead to an increase in graduation rates, which is of financial interest to universities. With these special programmes, universities additionally hope to attract high-achieving prospective students, which in turn is expected to stimulate the 'culture of excellence'. The excellence programmes are seen as a way of competing for high-achieving students, nationally and internationally, and also attracting the top lecturers wanting to work with high-achieving students (Long, 2002). Lecturers can use the programmes to develop new approaches to teaching; educational programmes can be developed and tested in a small community of students wanting to be challenged. The newly-developed programmes are seen as a way of increasing the interaction between university and the working field. High-achieving students work on real-life problems, including projects supported by the future working fields of the students. In addition, the universities of applied sciences anticipate that the programmes are a way of stimulating applied research at the university. Participating in research projects is a relatively new field for the universities of applied sciences in the Netherlands in that they traditionally focused on teaching.

In Germany, the institutions participating in the Ideational Support Programme had goals that varied widely between the involved foundations, depending on their convictions. Social commitment in students is stimulated according to the foundations' agenda in political, religious or social domains. High achievement is also stimulated according to the foundations' agenda; some aim at above-average achievement, some at entrepreneurial success, some explicitly aim at high academic performance.

## Selection and Promotion of the Participating Students

All institutions focus on motivation as a selection criteria; participation in an excellence programme requires a letter of motivation or an interview. For the Sirius Programme, the selection of participating students differs between the participating institutions; it can be by invitation or by self-selection. Most academic universities require high grades, while many universities of applied sciences require students to have passed all exams and not be behind in their study programme.

For the Ideational Support programme, the students are selected by the foundations offering the programmes. All foundations allow self-applica-tion, but aspects of the selection procedure vary between the foundations. Many foundations require recommendations by professors, some require assessment in an assessment center and, in some cases, entrance tests must be passed. Some institutions let the present scholarship recipients participate in the selection decisions whilst others do not. Usually, indicators of high achievement (such as grades), and of social commitment (such as documents of confirmation for religious foundations), are assessed.

Both programmes provide students with diversified learning opportu-nities: seminars, mentoring and self-organization (activities organized by the scholarship recipients themselves). In the German Ideational Support programme, students receive financial scholarships, dependent on family in-come, besides the enrichment programme. Most of the German foundations define their learning opportunities as "complementary" to the academic stud-ies, focusing on learning opportunities which are not provided during regular university studies, such as interdisciplinary exchange, studies and language courses abroad, and learning opportunities aiming at social commitment or personal growth. In the Sirius Programme, some universities focus on academic excellence and professional excellence, while others focus more on an interdisciplinary approach and personal development.

## Discussion

In this article, we have depicted commonalities of and differences between two programmes for gifted education in the tertiary sector, the Dutch Sirius Programme and the German Ideational Support programme. Both programmes differ in central aspects such as the involved institutions (universities in the Netherlands and foundations in Germany). By organizing the programmes in the universities, the Sirius Programme aims at stimulating a culture of excellence in the whole university community. Regular students not participating in the programmes could be positively affected by this culture and also aim higher. In both programmes, high-achieving students are grouped. In the Ideational Support programmes, however, students with similar views are often grouped because the foundations offer programmes which are for a specific population (e.g. the religious foundations), while, in the Sirius Programme, students with various views are mixed. This could have an impact in the way in which discussions are held. Furthermore, a difference is found in the way the funding is distributed: to the universities in the Sirius Programme and, in part, directly to the participating student's in the Ideational support programme. This could mean that in the German system students have more time to spend on the additional programme, whilst, in the Dutch system, many students have a job besides their studies and have to find the extra time for the additional programme.

   With this descriptive comparison we hope to stimulate future research on the commonalities of and differences between gifted education programmes in the tertiary sector. In order to find out how relevant criteria of excellence can be fostered among students of universities and universities of applied sciences, systematic comparisons of the aims, instruments, and outcomes of corresponding gifted education programmes are required. Future work will have to take account of differences in the tertiary education found in different countries, because some of the relevant gifted education programmes are organized at national level and can only be compared to comparable programmes in other countries. The identification of the best way to promote excellence in higher education requires the systematic comparison of the objectives, instruments, selection processes and outcomes of these programmes by using comparable evaluation methods.

## References

Bundesministerium für Bildung und Forschung (BMBF) (2009). *Mehr als ein Stipendium – Staatliche Begabtenförderung im Hochschulbereich.* [More than a scholarship: Governmental Gifted Education in Higher Education] Bonn: BMBF.

Cosgrove, J. (2004). The Impact of Honors Programs on Undergraduate Academic Performance, Retention, and Graduation. *Journal of the National Collegiate Honors Council Fall/Winter 2004,* 45–54.

England, R. (2010). Honors programs in four-year institutions in the Northeast: a preliminary survey towards a national inventory of honors. *Journal of the National Collegiate Honors Council Fall/Winter 2010,* 71–82.

Fenderson, B. A., Hojat, M., Damjanov, I., & Rubin, E. (1999). Characteristics of Medical Students Completing an Honors Program in Pathology. *Human Pathology, 30*(11), 1296–1301.

Gagné, F. (2005). From Gifts to Talents: The DMGT as a Developmental Model. In: R. J. Sternberg, & J. E. Davidson (Eds.), *Conceptions of Giftedness* (2nd ed., pp. 98–119). New York: Cambridge University Press.

Gardner, H., Csikszentmihalyi, M., & Damon, W. (2001). Good Work. *When Excellence and Ethics Meet.* New York: Basic books.

Heller, K. A., Perleth, C., & Keng Lim, T. (2005). The Munich Model of Giftedness Designed to Identify and Promote Gifted Students. In R. J. Sternberg, & J. E. Davidson (Eds.), *Conceptions of Giftedness* (2nd ed., pp. 147–170). New York: Cambridge University Press.

Long, B. (2002). Attracting the best: *The use of honors programs to compete for students.* Chicago, IL: Spencer Foundation. (ERIC Reproduction Service No. ED465355)

Renzulli, J. S. (2005). The Three-Ring Conception of Giftedness. A Developmental Model for Promoting Creative Productivity. In R. J. Sternberg, & J. E. Davidson (Eds.). *Conceptions of Giftedness* (2nd ed., pp. 246–279). New York: Cambridge University Press.

Rinn, A. N., & Plucker, J. A. (2004). We recruit them, but then what? The educational and psychological experiences of academically talented undergraduates. *Gifted Child Quarterly, 48*(1), 54–67.

Seifert, T. A., Pascarella, E. T., Colangelo, N., & Assouline, S. (2007). The Effects of Honors Program Participation on Experiences of Good Practices and Learning Outcomes. *Journal of College Student Development 48*(1), 57–74.

Shushok, F., Jr. (2006). Student Outcomes and Honors Programs: A Longitudinal Study of 172 Honors Students 2000–2004. *Journal of the National Collegiate Honors Council, Fall/Winter 2006*, 85–96.

Slavin, C., Coladarci, T., & Pratt, P. A. (2008). Is Student Participation in an Honors Program Related to Retention and Graduation Rates? *Journal of the National Collegiate Honors Council Fall/Winter 2008*, 59–69.

Sternberg, R. J. (2005). The WICS Model of Giftedness. In R. J. Sternberg, & J. E. Davidson (Eds.), *Conceptions of Giftedness* (2nd ed., pp. 327–342). New York: Cambridge University Press.

Subsidieregeling Sirius Programma (2008). Regeling van de Minister van Onderwijs, Cultuur en Wetenschap van 13 maart 2008, nr. HO/BS/2008/2196, houdende regels voor het verstrekken van subsidie voor projecten in het kader van het programma Rendement en Excellentie [Governmental guidelines for applications for the Sirius Program].

Wolfensberger, M., Jong, N. de, & Drayer, L. (2011). Excellentieprogramma's in het hoger onderwijs – Boden van een stille revolutie. *HO Management, juni 2011*, 18–21.

Wolfensberger, M., Jong, N. de, & Drayer, L. (2012). *Leren excelleren. Excellentieprogramma's in het HBO, een overzicht.* [Learning to excell: An analysis of honours programmes in Dutch Higher Education] Groningen, Netherlands: Hanzehogeschool Groningen.

# Promoting Talent for University Education
## Raising the Corner of the Veil

*Ellen Jansen*

## Abstract

In the Netherlands, there are many initiatives in schools for pre-university education as well as in universities anticipating students' talent development. Actually, talented students are already a selected group with above-average achievements. Still, it seems that there are too many students underachieving in high school and university. They feel themselves not really challenged and develop an attitude that does not comply with the demands of university education. This relates to metacognitive skills, critical thinking and a creative problem-solving. To promote excellence at universities, it is important to have insights in the mechanisms that are influencing prospective university students' attitudes and achievements. Is it possible to detect factors that relate to underachievement and that can be influenced by teachers and the learning environment? This research project on underachievement in pre-university education raises the corner of the veil.

## Introduction

In the Netherlands, selection in education starts after elementary school. Most students are about 12 years of age at that moment and they have to choose a school for their secondary education. Almost 85% of elementary schools participate in the national CITO-test; this is a test which to a large extent predetermines the type of secondary education which a student attends. The educational system is rather streamed: based on the CITO-score and the advice of primary school teacher, students are advised to go to a school for vocational training (4 years), general upper-secondary education (5 years) or pre-university education (6 years). In the latter category, we also have grammar schools, which are more selective than general pre-university schools.

All in all, schools for pre-university education do have a rather selected group of students who performed well at elementary school and belong to the top 20 % of the Dutch secondary school students. It is therefore alarming that we see a decreasing percentage of excellent students in the international ratings (OECD, 2010). The lack of competition and equality thinking in education could be a factor. According to teachers, many students are underachieving. To stimulate excellence in primary, secondary and tertiary education, special programmes for talented students have been developed. The question is whether this is the best way to prevent underachievement and to stimulate excellence. But, first we have to have more insight into the factors that are related to underachievement; in our case, at pre-university level.

## Theoretical Background

Preckel, Holling and Vock (2006) showed that fear of failure, a lack of interest and a lack of metacognitive and regulative skills are the most important factors related to the underachievement of high-ability students. Because talent and learning competence are not an inheritance but can be stimulated and developed, especially in adolescents (Feldhusen, 1998), it is important to look for learning environments (and the role of the teacher in those learning environments) that motivate students to perform at an excellent level. According to Renzulli (2000), talented students show a combination of intelligence, task commitment and creativity. Schools should, therefore, reinforce this combination of characteristics.

## Research Questions and Design

1. How can underachievement be measured?
2. Are teachers able to detect underachievers? What is the basis of their judgements?
3. What are the student characteristics of regular and underachieving students regarding study behaviour, need for cognition, and aiming for excellence?
4. What do students indicate as teacher characteristics that could move them forward towards excellent achievements?

A pilot project was started in October 2011 at a grammar school in the northern region of the Netherlands. In this project, we used a mixed-method design, including a survey, analysis of administrative data, and interviews. From March 2012 onwards, the project was extended to four other schools for pre-university education in the same region.

*Pilot Project*

Six teachers indicated underachievers in classes in grades 10–12, aged 16–18 years. All students (n= 154) from those classes filled out a questionnaire on study behaviour/metacognitive skills and took an analogical reasoning test. Previous achievement data and the grades from the last school term, as well as the CITO test scores, were obtained from the administrative system. 10 small-group interviews with students provided qualitative data on study behaviour and goal motivation.

*Extended Project*

In the extended project, four other schools for pre-university education participated. Students from grade 10 (age 15–16) filled out the analogical reasoning test and the survey about their study behaviour and metacognitive skills. Performance data were provided by the administration. A selection of students participated in small-group interviews.

*Instruments*

For an indication of ability, we used a analogical reasoning test. Study behaviour and metacognitive skills were measured by a survey. Both instruments were administered during a regular class. The survey consisted of several scales regarding:

- Need for cognition
- Achievement motivation
- Metacognitive skills: planning, monitoring, debugging, information-management strategies and evaluation.

## Results

*Identifying Underachievers*

To identify underachievers more objectively, we compared the standardized score on the analogical reasoning test with the standardized score on the gpa in the last school term. Students who had a score of minus 1 standard deviations between gpa and the test score were indicated as underachievers. The standardized scores were calculated at class level to avoid influences of age and maturation.

The teachers in the pilot project had specified 29 students as underachievers. The objective method indicated 18 students. Only three students were identified by both methods.

## Differences in Study Behaviour

Five scales from the Metacognitive Awareness Inventory (Schraw, & Denisson, 1994), the Need for Cognition Scale (Schouwenburg, 1996) and a scale indicating aiming at excellence were used in the comparison between underachievers, regular students and "over"achievers. There were significant differences between the three groups of students: the underachieving students scored lower than the regular students; the "over"achieving students scored significantly higher. This applied to the scales for debugging, monitoring and information management strategies, as well for achievement motivation and need for cognition.

## Relation with Prior Achievement

The pilot project indicated that underachieving seems to be a process that is visible across the years. Comparing the gpa at the end of the years prior to the year of investigation with the gpa at the last term school report, the underachievers were getting lower grades every year. This decrease was at a higher pace for the underachieving students than it was with the regular students (Table 1).

*Table 1:    gpa school reports during four years*

|                | Last term report | Year minus 1 | Year minus 2 | Year minus 3 |
|----------------|------------------|--------------|--------------|--------------|
| underachievers | 6.91             | 6.99         | 7.29         | 7.53         |
| regular        | 6.99             | 7.05         | 7.17         | 7.31         |

## Reasons for Possible Underachievement According to Students

The small-group interviews (three or four students) revealed that there were hardly any specific reasons mentioned only by underachieving students. Both groups of students reported that they did not experience any incentives from the school or the environment. Furthermore, most students sought a balance between time they invested in school and time for their own hobbies (music, sports, friends et cetera). Underachieving students spent less time on homework than regular students.

*Good Teacher Characteristics According to Students*

Both groups of students agreed on the characteristics of a good, stimulating teacher: a teacher has to be clear and consequently, has to be an expert in his/her domain; has to be a good planner and provide structure; and has to be enthusiastic and interactive.

There were no specific types of learning task that were mentioned as being motivating. Some students were in favour of projects or papers, whereas others were not.

## Conclusion and Discussion

When we define underachievement as a discrepancy between ability and performance, it is apparently difficult for teachers to identify underachievers. However, it is not only cognitive ability that leads to excellence, although it is a prerequisite especially for university. High-ability students, underachieving or not, have clear ideas about stimulating teacher characteristics. Promoting programmes for stimulating talent-development in pre-university education could benefit all students and could prepare them better for university. Furthermore, it is important to get more insight into possible selective underachievers – that is, those students that could be indicated as being an underachiever in a specific domain. Probably, students do not underachieve in general, but only in the domains that do not have their interest or that are less important for their future educational career.

## References

Feldhusen, J. F. (1998). Programs for the gifted few or talent development for the many? *Phi Delta Kappan, 79*, 735–738.

OECD (2010), *PISA 2009 at a Glance*. OECD Publishing. http://dx.doi.org/10.1787/9789264095298-en

Preckel, F., Holling, H., & Vock, M. (2006). Scholastic underachievement: Relationship with cognitive motivation, achievement motivation, and conscientiousness. *Psychology in the Schools, 43,* 401–411.

Renzulli, J. S. (2000). The identification and development of giftedness as a paradigm for school reform. *Journal of Science Education and Technology, 9,* 95–114.

Schouwenburg, H. C. (1996). *Handleiding bij INTEL'95: een test voor Intellectualisme*. Rijksuniversiteit Groningen, Studieondersteuning.

Schraw, G., & Dennison, R. S. (1994). Assessing metacognitive awareness. *Contemporary Educational Psychology, 19,* 460–475.

# Standards and Rubrics for Honours Evaluation, Certification and Benchmarking Criteria

*Gregory Lanier*

The question of how to effectively evaluate honours programmes and colleges has been a concern of many individuals in the honours community for many years. The first significant step taken towards developing methods for effective evaluation of honours educational activities was the creation and adoption of the "Basic Characteristics of a Fully-Developed Honors Program" by the National Collegiate Honors Council in 1994 (NCHC, 1994). Although the development of the "Basic Characteristics" was quite controversial at the time, nearly twenty years later they are now firmly interwoven into the fabric of honours teaching, and nearly every honours programme and college in the United States and elsewhere uses them to measure the scope and effectiveness of its honours efforts. The next milestone towards systematic and objective evaluation occurred in 2005 when Dr. Rosalie Otero of the University of New Mexico and Dr. Robert Spurrier of Oklahoma State University published "Assessing and Evaluating Honors Programs and Honors Colleges: A Practical Handbook" (Otero, & Spurrier, 2005). In 2008, Greg Lanier published the article "Towards Reliable Honors Assessment" in the journal of the National Collegiate Honors Council (Lanier, 2008). Much of that new material, focused primarily on the development of student learning outcomes and assessment plans tailored specifically for honours education, was incorporated into the 2010 NCHC Monograph "A Practical Handbook for the Review of Honors Programs and Honors Colleges", authored by Otero, Spurrier and Lanier (2010). In 2010, the Board of Directors of the National Collegiate Honors Council charged its Assessment and Evaluation Committee with the task of developing a methodology for the voluntary certification of honours programmes and colleges. As a member of the Assessment and Evaluation Committee, Dr. Lanier undertook the task of converting the at-times multivalent and unfocused language that appears in the "Basic Characteristics" into the single-focused declarative statements that are recommended by nationally recognized leaders in assessment best practices (Suskie, 2009; Halonen, & Lanier, 2009). The presentation of a sample those standards, as well as exemplary rubrics that can be utilized to evaluate an institution's accordance with them, compose the bulk of this article.

## A Proposed Philosophy of Honours Certification

Self-regulation through certification embodies a traditional U.S. philosophy that a free people can and ought to govern themselves through a representative, flexible, and responsive system. Accordingly, certification is best accomplished through a voluntary association of educational institutions.

Both a process and a product, honours certification relies on integrity, thoughtful and principled judgment, rigorous application of requirements, and a context of trust. The process provides an assessment of an honours programme or college's effectiveness in the fulfillment of its mission and its continuing efforts to enhance the quality of student learning and its programmes and services. Based upon reasoned judgment, the process stimulates evaluation and improvement, while providing a means of continuing accountability to constituents and the public.

The product of certification is a public statement of an honours programme or college's continuing capacity to provide effective programmes and services that significantly enhance the education of high-achieving students. The statement of an honours programme or college's certification status is an affirmation of an honours programme or college's continuing commitment to ensure that the honours students at that institution reach accepted and agreed-upon levels of achievement.

Those institutions that achieve certification would be expected to dedicate themselves to enhancing the quality of their programmes and services within the context of their resources and capacities and to creating an environment in which high-achieving levels of teaching, public service, research, and learning occur.

## Fundamental Characteristics of Honours Certification

- Participation in the certification process is voluntary and is an earned and renewable status.
- Involved institutions would develop, amend, and approve Honours certification requirements.
- The process of certification is representative, responsive, and appropriately modified when necessary to the types of institutions accredited.
- Honours certification is based upon a peer-review process.
- Honours certification requires an overall institutional commitment to honours student learning and achievement.

- Honours certification acknowledges an honours programme or college's prerogative to articulate its mission within the recognized context of higher education and its responsibility to show that it is accomplishing its mission.
- Honours certification expects an institution to ensure that its honours programme or college is complemented by support structures and resources that allow for the total growth and development of its honours students.

## The Organization of the Standards

Although the "Basic Characteristics" cover many, if not all, of the facets of honours education, there was never any overarching conception that governed their presentation. The order of the standards is clearly random, and, as in the readily apparent in the case of programme characteristic #2, sometimes an uneasy conglomeration of a number of differently focused concepts. In contrast, the proposed paradigm contains eight focused sections:

Section 1: Honours Mission and Vision
Section 2: Admission, Retention, and Advising
Section 3: Administrative Structures
Section 4: Curriculum
Section 5: Infrastructure
Section 6: Faculty Governance
Section 7: Student Governance and Student Life
Section 8: Excellence, Innovation, and Assessment

Each section contains a number of specific standards related to that topic and, as can be seen below, the basic characteristic that "fathered" each standard is clearly referenced. What follows is the presentation of the proposed standards for two of the eight sections: 1) Honours Mission and Vision and 2) Curriculum. There are some standards that are applicable only to those institutions that have developed honours colleges and, accordingly, those standards are clearly prefaced by the phrase "honours college" in italics and they reference the "basic characteristics of a fully developed honours college."

## Section 1: Honours Mission and Vision

1.1     The programme has a clear mandate from the institution's administration in the form of a mission statement or charter document that includes the objectives and responsibilities of honours. (*ref. Programme Characteristics #2*)

1.2   The institution allocates adequate infrastructure resources that ensure the permanence and stability of honours. (*ref. Programme Characteristics #2*)

1.3   The honours programme is self-reliant and does not rely on support from other units to deliver its mission and curriculum. (*ref. Programme Characteristics #2*)

## Section 4: Curriculum (a Selection of the 14 Standards)

4.1   The honours curriculum purposefully aligns with and enhances the mission of the institution. (*ref. Programme Characteristics #4*)

4.6   The programme requirements constitute a substantial portion of the participants' undergraduate work, typically 20% to 25% of the total course work but no less than 15%. (*ref. Programme Characteristics #5*)

4.7   The curriculum is designed so that honours requirements can, when appropriate, also satisfy general education requirements, major or disciplinary requirements, and preprofessional or professional training requirements. (*ref. Programme Characteristics #6*)

4.8   The programme emphasizes participation in regional and national conferences, honours semesters, international programmes, community service, internships, undergraduate research, and other types of extra-mural and experiential education. (*ref. Programme Characteristics #15*)

4.9   The curricular design leads to a mastery of identified learning outcomes. (*ref. Programme Characteristics #15*)

4.13  Honours college: The curriculum of the honours college constitutes at least 20% of a student's degree programme. (*ref. College Characteristics #9*)

4.14  Honours college: The honours college requires an honours thesis or honours capstone project. (*ref. College Characteristics #9*)

## On Rubrics and Benchmarks

In addition to the single-focus standards, rubrics that would allow both internal and external reviewers to judge in a straightforward and objective fashion how well the institution's performance accords with the objective of the standard were developed. Following a best practice that has been championed by the Association of American Colleges and Universities' (AAC&U) widely influential VALUES rubrics, a 4-part rubric scale has been employed, with the descriptors of "Mature," "Proficient," "Developing," and "Undeveloped" establishing the benchmarks. What follows are samples of the certification standards accompanied by the appropriate scoring rubric.

1.1    The programme has a clear mandate from the institution's administration in the form of a mission statement or charter document that includes the objectives and responsibilities of honours. (*ref. Programme Characteristics #2*)

| Mature | Proficient | Developing | Undeveloped |
|---|---|---|---|
| Mission statement/ charter documents clearly and specifically define the objectives, responsibilities, and unique curricular focus of honours. | Mission statement/ charter documents define one or two of the objectives, responsibilities, and focus of honours but not all. | Mission statement/charter documents clearly are fairly generic and don't reflect specific objectives, responsibilities, or focus of honours. | Mission statement/ charter documents are missing or are unworkably broad and vague. |

2.1    A clearly articulated set of admission criteria (e.g., GPA[1], SAT[2] score, a written essay, satisfactory progress) identifies the targeted student population served by the honours programme. (*ref. Programme Characteristics #1*)

| Mature | Proficient | Developing | Undeveloped |
|---|---|---|---|
| Admissions criteria are clear, widely available, and mission appropriate. | Admissions criteria somewhat unclear or contradictory, not readily available, fit with mission not readily apparent. | Admissions criteria unclear or contradictory or arbitrary, are not readily available, fit with mission not readily apparent. | Admissions criteria are absent, arbitrarily applied, or ignored. Admissions criteria have no relation to mission. |

---

1    Grade point average
2    Standardized test used for college admissions in the United States.

4.1   The honours curriculum purposefully aligns with and enhances the mission of the institution. (*ref. Programme Characteristics #4*)

| Mature | Proficient | Developing | Undeveloped |
|---|---|---|---|
| Design of programme is clearly focused and reflects a purposeful alignment with and enhancement of the institutional mission. | Design of programme is somewhat clear but lacks unity or focus; the purposeful alignment with and enhancement of the institutional mission is mostly but not always apparent | Overall design that governs programme is incomplete or clearly lacking in focus and/or purpose; alignment with and enhancement of the institutional mission is sometimes apparent. | Overall design that governs programme is missing; little or no alignment with or enhancement of the institutional mission apparent. |

5.1   The programme is allocated an annual budget that adequately supports the mission of the programme. (*ref. Programme Characteristics #2*)

| Mature | Proficient | Developing | Undeveloped |
|---|---|---|---|
| The budget allocated to honours adequately supports the teaching, operational, and extracurricular facets of the programme, and is derived from the institution's permanent and recurrent budget. | The budget allocated to honours supports the teaching, operational, and extracurricular obligations of the programme to some extent, but clear budgetary needs are apparent (most often in teaching support). The funding is derived from the institution's permanent and recurrent budget. | The budget allocated to honours is clearly inadequate or support for one or more of the teaching, operational, and extracurricular obligations of the programme are missing. Extensive budgetary needs are apparent (most often in teaching support). The funding is not derived from the institution's permanent and recurrent budget. | The budget allocated to honours does not support the teaching, operational, and extracurricular obligations of the programme, and extensive budgetary needs are apparent. (i.e. a programme with a $5,000 budget and a director who receives only a 1 course release). |

8.1   The programme provides a locus of visible and highly reputed activity across the campus. (*ref. Programme Characteristics #7*)

| Mature | Proficient | Developing | Undeveloped |
|---|---|---|---|
| Honours activity is prominent on the campus and is highly visible to faculty, students, and visitors. | Honours activity is somewhat prominent on the campus and is mostly visible to faculty, students, and visitors, but is not readily recognized by all. | Honours activity has a presence on the campus but is not prominent, highly visible, or easily found by faculty, students, and visitors. | Honours activity is mostly invisible to faculty, students, and visitors. |

## Curricular Specifics

Although there are no "Basic Characteristics" that speak to the design or content of an honours curriculum, there are a number of individuals who feel that the honours community would be well severed by guidance in this area. Accordingly, the paradigm also offers standards and rubrics in the four most common areas of foci widely found in honours programmes: Critical Thinking, Interdisciplinary Learning, Independent Research, and Leadership. Examples of the standards and rubrics for the second, Interdisciplinary Learning, are offered below.

## Section B: Curricular Focus: Interdisciplinary Learning

B.1.1 Programme level outcome: The programme's curricular design demonstrates an intentional structure that integrates diverse knowledge, methods, perspectives, and/or skills.

| Mature | Proficient | Developing | Undeveloped |
|---|---|---|---|
| Multiple opportunities for students to engage in interdisciplinary learning appear across the honours curriculum. The sequence of course offerings reflects a careful sequencing and correspondent scaffolding of knowledge, methods, and skills. | Some opportunities for students to engage in interdisciplinary learning appear across the honours curriculum. The sequence of course offerings may reflect some sequencing and scaffolding of knowledge, methods, and skills. | A limited number of opportunities for students to engage in interdisciplinary learning appear across the honours curriculum. There is little sequencing of course offerings or students can select courses in any order. | Few or no opportunities for students to engage in interdisciplinary learning across the curriculum. No intentional sequencing of courses is apparent in the curricular design. |

B.2.2 Course level outcome: Student designs and produces a research and/or creative project in the appropriate interdisciplinary or multidisciplinary context.

| Mature | Proficient | Developing | Undeveloped |
|---|---|---|---|
| Independently transfers skills, abilities, theories, and/or methodologies acquired in an interdisciplinary or multidisciplinary instructional situation to new situations to solve complex research and/or creative problems in a project of one's own design. Expresses insight and originality in projects, e.g., by synthesizing primary resources accurately with secondary sources. | Synthesizes skills, abilities, theories, and/or methodologies attained in disciplinary or multidisciplinary instruction to frame research and/or creative problems. Analyzes ideas in a thorough way, organizes materials and research data or creative techniques to produce detailed projects. | When prompted, analyzes skills, abilities, theories, and/or methodologies learned in disciplinary or multidisciplinary instruction to demonstrate detailed understanding of research and/or creative problems. | When prompted, identifies and applies in a basic way skills, abilities, theories, and/or methodologies discovered in disciplinary or multidisciplinary instruction to describe research and/or creative problems. |

## Next Steps

The Assessment and Evaluation Committee of the National Collegiate Honors Council met in the middle of June, 2013 to review the paradigm and sent forward to the NCHC Board of Directors its recommendation regarding the certification process.

## References

Halonen, J., & Lanier, G. (2009). Benchmarking Quality in Challenging Contexts: The Arts, Humanities, and Everything In-Between. In D. S. Dunn, M. A. Mc-

Carthy, S. Baker, & J. Halonen (Eds.), *Using Quality Benchmarks for Assessing and Developing Undergraduate Programmes*. San Francisco, CA: Jossey-Bass.

Lanier, G. (2008). Towards Reliable Honors Assessment. *Journal of the National Collegiate Honors Council, 9* (1), 81–149.

National Collegiate Honors Council (1994). *Basic Characteristics of a Fully Developed Honors Programme*. Retrieved from http://nchcHonors.org/faculty-directors/basic-characteristics-of-a-fully-developed-Honors-program/.

National Collegiate Honors Council (2005). *Basic Characteristics of a Fully Developed Honors College*. Retrieved from http://nchcHonors.org/faculty-directors/basic-characteristics-of-a-fully-developed-Honors-college/.

Otero, R., & Spurrier, R. (2005). *Assessing and Evaluating Honors Programs and Honors Colleges: A Practical Handbook*. Lincoln, NE: National Collegiate Honors Council.

Otero, R., Spurrier, R., & Lanier, G. (2010). *A Practical Handbook for the Review of Honors Programs and Honors Colleges*. Lincoln, NE: National Collegiate Honors Council.

Suskie, L. (2009). *Assessing Student Learning: A Common Sense Guide* (2nd ed.). San Francisco, CA: Jossey-Bass.

# Giftedness and Education at Upper Secondary Level

## Cooperative Fostering by Teachers and University Lecturers

*Jutta Moehringer*

### Abstract

Since 2009, the Technical University of Munich (TUM) has been running a pilot project on special tuition for students interested and talented in mathematics, IT, sciences and technology (STEM). The programme itself differs from others in that it enhances the interconnection between school and university by taking into account whatever the institutions may require in terms of organisation, personnel and contents.

This study aims at the evaluation of the special tuition in terms of its processes and effects upon students, teachers, and university lecturers.

The design uses qualitative methods, including case studies. At the same time and despite small samples only, quantitative methods are applied and set against data derived from large-scale studies. The study is based on several year groups the data of which are compared to control groups.

First findings show that the TUMKolleg students are capable of handling scientific methods and that neither their performance motivation nor their extra-curricular activities are affected by the heavy workload they are facing. Teachers and university lecturers also profit from this interexchange.

### Background

The shortage of qualified young people talented in mathematics, IT, sciences and technology (STEM), not only in Germany but all over Europe, has given rise to frequent initiatives aimed at sparking young students' interest in the sciences (Ley, 2001).

This is why TUM started a pilot project, together with a grammar school, focusing on STEM and directed at highly-gifted students. At the beginning of the school year 2009/2010, the Otto-von-Taube-Gymnasium (OvTG), an ordinary state grammar school not far from Munich, started introducing a distinct upper secondary-level track. 30 students at TUMKolleg were given the chance to take part in a special tuition programme developed exclusively for their purposes. The tuition programme itself is based on the principles of both enrichment and acceleration. Enrichment implies widening the curriculum by adding learning facilities whilst acceleration means providing measures to achieve utmost efficiency by shortening the learning process (Southern, Jones, & Stanley, 1993).

In TUMKolleg, enrichment comprises both school and university. The school provides curricular contents in an all-encompassing and more profound manner and offers a way of teaching that leaves enough flexibility for inductive and independent acquisition.

At the university, the students are acquainted with scientific work and given the opportunity to specialise in individual small research projects. Acceleration in this case implies that the students are given some credits for their future studies, provided that they have succeeded in working on their tasks. They are equally enabled to minimise their phase of orientation, once they are matriculated. The independence of TUMKolleg in terms of structure and organisation allows students to be guaranteed each week a whole day reserved for getting used to doing their research on campus.

Unlike other initiatives aiming at the tuition given to the students in the field of STEM, the TUMKolleg pilot project has the advantage of resting upon two institutions, the grammar school on the one hand and the university on the other. This helps to smooth out the processes at school and university as well as alleviating the interconnection between lessons at school and research at university.

## Aims

This study aims at the evaluation of the special tuition in terms of its processes and effects upon students, teacher and university lecturers. The evaluation concept is based on the CIPP model as developed by Stufflebeam and Shinkfield (2007) with its focus on context, input, process, and product. The leading questions are:

1.  To what extent can students acquire scientific methods?
2.  Which development concerning non-cognitive personal attributes (achievement motivation, coping with stress and interests) can be recognised?
3.  What effect does the interexchange between teachers and university lecturers have upon teachers' professional development and upon lecturers' awareness and accessibility to school students.

## Methodology

The design uses qualitative methods including case studies. At the same time and despite small samples only, quantitative methods are applied and set against data derived from large-scale studies. The study is based on several year groups the data of which are compared to control groups.

As the CIPP-model demands, the elements of evaluation are as follows: The context is represented by the regular state grammar school OvTG and the particular target group of gifted students. The key elements regarding the particular target group were the following: a questionnaire with questions regarding the respective students' biographical background, motivation and interest, together with a written pre-test assessing competence in mathematics, natural sciences and problem solving (Prenzel, Baumert, Blum, Lehmann, Leutner, Neubrand, Pekrun, Rost, & Schiefele, 2004).

The input implies the special tuition programme with its particular offers at both grammar school and university.

For the evaluation of the process, the students were asked to keep structured diaries in which questions on achievement motivation, interest, and coping with stress must be answered. Apart from that, standardised questionnaires help to make explicit how lesson plans and teaching are experienced by teachers and lecturers and how students perceive their lessons (Seidel, Prenzel, & Rimmele, 2006; in Prenzel, 2006).

The product evaluation at the end of the TUMKolleg is done by means of semi-structured interviews involving lecturers, students, teachers, parents and student mentors. The results achieved through individual research projects reflect how well scientific methods have been learned and applied.

## Findings

The findings show that the selection procedure is reliable in that the most interested and intellectually capable students of grade 10 are entering the programme. The first three year groups (n=57) had 56% female students and 44% male students.

The students of the TUMKolleg acquired scientific methods at university level. All of the students received certificates proving the high quality of their research projects. Two of the research projects were accepted as bachelor theses.

Neither students' performance motivation nor their extra-curricular activities were affected by the heavy workload they were facing. Teachers and university lecturers also profited from this interexchange. All graduates of the first year group started to study in the field of STEM.

## Significance for Theory, Policy, and Practice

Research on highly-gifted students has shown that only a minor part of tuition programmes offered to them has been evaluated (Vock, Preckel, & Holling, 2007). At this stage, the TUMKolleg is the only STEM-related tuition project in Germany and, therefore, the only one which involves the institutionalisation of co-operation between school and university. Given the unique significance of this project, then, there is unquestionable value in the evaluation results for theory and education, the more so when it comes to applying the model of TUMKolleg to other schools.

## References

Ley, M. (2001). Übergang Schule-Hochschule: Klassifikation von Initiativen zur Förderung des naturwissenschaftlichen Nachwuchses. Bonn.

Prenzel, M., Baumert, J., Blum, W., Lehmann, R., Leutner, D., Neubrand, M., Pekrun, R., Rost, J., & Schiefele, U. (Eds.). (2004). *PISA 2003: Der Bildungsstand der Jugendlichen in Deutschland: Ergebnisse des zweiten internationalen Vergleichs.* Münster: Waxmann.

Seidel, T., Prenzel, M., & Rimmele, R. (2006). Unterrichtsmuster und ihre Wirkungen: Eine Videostudie im Physikunterricht. In M. Prenzel (Ed.), *Untersuchungen zur Bildungsqualität von Schule. Abschlussbericht des DFG-Schwerpunktprogramms: [BIQUA]* (pp. 99–123). Münster: Waxmann.

Southern, W. T., Jones, E. D., & Stanley, J. C. (1993). Acceleration and enrichment: The context and development of program options. In K. Heller, F. J. Mönks, & A. H. Passow (Eds.), *International handbook of research and development of giftedness and talent* (1st ed., pp. 387–410). Oxford, New York: Pergamon Press.

Stufflebeam, D. L., & Shinkfield, A. J. (2007). *Evaluation theory, models, and applications* (1st ed.). San Francisco: Jossey-Bass.

Vock, M., Preckel, F., & Holling, H. (2007). *Förderung Hochbegabter in der Schule: Evaluationsbefunde und Wirksamkeit von Maßnahmen.* Göttingen [u.a.]: Hogrefe.

# Connecting Excellence in Secondary and Higher Education

## Lessons from Junior College Utrecht

*Ton van der Valk*

## Introduction

Many talented secondary school students do not need to work hard at school and get bored in classroom as they understand subject matter quickly and need few explanations and little drill-and-practice (Betts, & Neihart, 1988). They have plenty time for going deeper into subject matter but are not challenged to do so. As a consequence, they are likely to develop bad study habits. So, when they enter higher education, they risk failing (Winstantley, 2007). Therefore, secondary education should challenge talented students and promote excellence. In upper secondary education, a thorough orientation towards higher education studies can provide plenty of opportunities for this. In science particularly, there is a need for challenging the most capable students (Taber, 2007).

## JCU

Junior College Utrecht (JCU), a science education partnership between Utrecht University (UU) and 28 schools, founded in 2004, aims to be a working place for improving science education by teaching students as well by providing a teacher programme. Its main focus is promoting excellence in upper secondary science teaching and learning. JCU has adopted the view that, for this, the teacher is the main actor in the classroom. In his/her development, (s)he has to be supported by other stakeholders within the JCU context:

- Talented students and their parents
- Secondary schools principals
- Utrecht University (UU), in particular its Faculty of Science (FoS).
- National policy makers, in particular the National Platform Science and Technology (Dutch acronym PBT) which promotes science and technology as well as excellence in all levels of education.

JCU is presented here as exemplifying 'good practice'. *What are its success factors and challenges in connecting excellence in secondary and university education?* We describe developments in the student and teacher programmes in three main stages: 1.0 (2003–2008), 2.0 (2008–2011) and 3.0 (2011 onwards), related to developments in national policy and in university.

## JCU 1.0 (2003–2008)

Since the late '90s, UU has been a leader in introducing honours (Wolfensberger, Van Eijl, & Pilot, 2004). In 2003, successful experience with honours and the need for more science students were reasons for suggesting the founding of JCU. This idea received support from the UU Executive Board. Network schools were consulted about participating in JCU. Principals were enthusiastic, but some teachers were reluctant in that they would miss having talented students in their lessons.

Figure 1 shows the design of the student programme, teaching the sciences to selected upper secondary students over two years for two days a week. In grade 11, the emphasis was on teaching the national science syllabuses at an accelerated pace, in grade 12 on enrichment topics orientated towards university studies.

| JCU students' lessons | At JCU | | At home schools | | |
|---|---|---|---|---|---|
| When? | Monday | Tuesday | Wednesday | Thursday | Friday |
| Subjects | Biology | Physics | Non-science subjects | | |
| | Chemistry | Mathematics | | | |
| | Enrichment topics | | | | |
| Taught by | Selected partner school teachers UU teachers/researchers | | Regular school teachers | | |

JCU was housed in University College Utrecht-buildings and financed by UU and the partner schools. PBT allocated a starting grant. The JCU Board had representatives from UU and partner schools. JCU staff consisted of a director and a curriculum coordinator.

*Developments in the Student Programme 1.0*

In September 2004, the student programme started. In 2006, the maximum number of students was reached: 50 grade 11, 50 grade 12, from 26 schools. JCU teachers developed comprehensive curricula and taught the syllabi at an accelerated pace. The students enjoyed learning in a community of talented peers and in an academic environment. But they expressed a dislike for acceleration first, with enrichment following later: they wanted *enrichment now*. So, JCU asked UU teachers to develop and teach enrichment modules about developments in modern scientific research. In spite of promises, however, getting UU teacher time for JCU tasks was hard. Nevertheless, some UU teachers, although experiencing extra teaching load, accepted the challenge and, as they really enjoyed teaching the JCU students, they motivated their colleagues to join.

The first three months in JCU appeared to be crucial for students. During this period, they had to change their working habits and develop academic competencies. Some students (average 10%) did not succeed in this and left JCU.

Students were very happy with JCU. At the end of grade 12, all remaining students passed their examinations. However, the marks were lower than expected. Research (Van der Valk, Grunefeld, & Pilot, 2011) revealed an underlying problem: offering all JCU students the same curriculum in the same pace. In spite of selection, talents and abilities were diverse. JCU therefore faced the challenge of providing more opportunities for choice and student contribution (Van Tassel-Baska, 2002).

*Developing the Teacher Programme 1.0*

The teacher programme 1.0 had a slow start. Twice a year, partner school teachers were invited to come to JCU to become informed about the JCU curriculum and teaching. Teachers discovered that JCU gave students challenges they could not offer. Their initial resistance against JCU decreased. Some teachers were involved in developing enrichment modules. In 2007, the first annual JCU conference took place, aiming at involving partner schools in developing and testing JCU materials on a regular basis.

*Developments in National Education Policy 1.0*

In 2007, a new optional interdisciplinary subject, Nature, Life and Technology (NLT), was introduced in upper secondary education. This was guided by the NLT Steering Committee. Inspired by the JCU enrichment modules, it set aims such as orientation towards modern scientific research. JCU met the challenge of developing its modules for a full curriculum for NLT.

## JCU 2.0 (2008–2011)

JCU accepted the challenge of transforming its set of enrichment modules into a NLT curriculum that could be an example for the emerging national NLT curriculum. For this, JCU developed a three-step implementation and dissemination model: (1) a module was developed, taught in the JCU student programme and evaluated. (2) the module was revised and tested in JCU partner schools, results and experiences being documented. (3) After a second revision, the module was disseminated nationwide. This model fitted in the certification procedure for NLT modules of the NLT Steering Committee.

*Developments in the Student Programme 2.0*

The introduction of NLT in the JCU curriculum resulted in a better balance, distributing enrichment between grades 11 and 12. It showed the variety of scientific topics that are investigated in Utrecht. JCU was successful in disseminating its NLT modules over the country. More UU science research groups wanted to develop NLT modules and contacted JCU for cooperation. In addition, parents brought JCU into contact with external institutions. Thus, for example, the module 'Heart and Veins' was developed for the Netherlands Heart Foundation.

The number of modules that became available made it possible to meet the differences of interest of JCU students. Students had to choose between two modules that were scheduled at the same time. Moreover, aiming at a more differentiated curriculum, JCU allotted time for differentiation assignments (JCU, 2011). JCU teachers developed assignments at different levels. It elaborated a pedagogy for differentiation, including presenting results to the class as a 'research community' and students giving feedback to each other.

As a result of the improved curriculum, the mean examination marks increased to the level that had been aimed for. The JCU testimonial that alumni received also appeared to be valuable for getting into honours programmes and other special tracks in Dutch universities and abroad.

## Developments in the Teacher Programme 2.0

The 2.0 teacher programme aimed at contributing to teachers' professional development by having them test NLT modules in their classes and reporting on experiences. In 'experimentation groups', partner school teachers discussed a module, prepared for teaching and reported on experiences. JCU gathered data to meet the *certification procedure* for NLT modules. Thus, by 2012, 14 JCU NLT modules had been awarded a certificate.

Moreover, partner school teachers tested the optional assignments developed by JCU. By doing so, they prepared for including differentiation in their classrooms.

The JCU Board felt that, for being a partner school, participation in the teacher programme was required. It had interviews with schools that did not participate sufficiently. As a result, some schools became more involved, whilst some others withdrew from the partnership. New partner schools were selected and the number increased to 29.

Through these developments, being a JCU partner made a real impact on schools. At the annual JCU conferences, schools exchanged experiences with JCU materials in their classes and with other relevant topics, such as emerging talent programmes. Thus, the partnership approach developed from being mainly top-down towards networking.

## Developments in National and University Education Policy 2.0

By starting the Sirius project, the Ministry of Education promoted excellence in Dutch Higher Education. UU received a Sirius grant and started honours courses in all faculties. As JCU alumni were candidates for joining honours courses, the importance of JCU for the Faculty of Science increased. As JCU was on track, the UU Executive Board wanted to bring JCU under the wing of the FoS and to house it in a FoS building. FoS agreed and planned to evaluate JCU performances. The Evaluation Commission was very positive, in particular about the benefits of the JCU school network and its effect on school development. So, it advised FoS to continue JCU (Van Weert, 2010) which FoS did, in spite of severe spending cuts at that time.

The Ministry of Education started a new programme aiming at promoting excellence in secondary education. This was motivated by the Dutch PISA results, which showed that the low ranges performed well, but the more able students performed at a lower level than comparable countries. This presented JCU with a new challenge: how to involve more students.

## JCU 3.0 (2011 onwards)

JCU stimulated its partner schools to join the national *Excellence* programme. Most of them did so and started experimental 'excellence' programmes in some classes. The JCU differentiation assignments worked well as exemplars of concrete student tasks. As a consequence, new views on promoting talent development arose in the schools. Promoting excellence is a primary task for schools which can be supported by JCU. As a consequence, at the present time (2013) big changes are taking place in the JCU student and teacher programmes.

### Developments in the Student Programme 3.0

To support the emerging 'excellence' programmes in partner schools, JCU successfully organised two-day 'U-Talent' programmes for talented lower secondary students. 450 students participated in 2012, 600 in 2013. Through experience, partner schools saw that this group also needs – and enjoys – enrichment in lessons. U-Talent gave a new 'flow' to teachers and generated a need for differentiated lessons and for more places in the JCU grade 11/12 student programme. Thus, time was ripe for changing the JCU student programme into the *U-Talent Academy*. In it, teaching the science syllabuses to talented grade 11 and 12 students in a compacted and comprehensive way became part of the school programme. In the additional campus programme, selected students go to JCU for enrichment once a month. As the programme at JCU is shorter, the number of students could increase from 100 to more than 400 in 2016 without additional costs.

In the fall of 2012, the JCU Board communicated the U-Talent Academy proposal to partner school principals and science departments, expecting a sceptical reception. Surprisingly, the schools were enthusiastic. They felt challenged to develop their 'excellence' programmes this way and teachers were glad to get their talented students back in their classes. However, JCU teachers and students regretted the 'abolition' of the cherished JCU programme. Now, in June 2013, 100 students from 23 schools have been selected and are eager to participate in the U-Talent Academy from September on. In 2014, four more schools will join. Then, the old student programme will stop and the number of *Academy* students will grow to 250.

## Developments in the Teacher Programme 3.0

The aim of the JCU teacher programme has been changed towards preparing and supporting teachers in starting 'excellence' programmes in their schools and classes. For this, *teacher development teams* were created. 80 teachers participated, developing and discussing suitable teaching materials. Alongside this, a *principal development team* was started. 22 participants discussed how to organise excellence programmes in school and how to support teachers in realising the programme in their classes. Moreover, an intensive teacher professionalization course (a load of 180 hours of study) on 'promoting excellence in science classes' was developed and tested, with 25 participatory teachers.

In 2013, JCU prepared all school teams by giving a three-hour workshop on implementing U-Talent Academy.

## Developments in National and University Policy 3.0

From 2012, the Ministry of Education gave all Dutch school additional funding for, among other things, promoting excellence in the schools. JCU partner schools use this for financing U-Talent student and teacher activities.

At Utrecht University, the Sirius project ended in December 2012. UU continues teaching honours programmes and plans to extend them to the first year of study. The FoS has decided that students entering with the *U-Talent Academy certificate* will be admitted to the Faculty's honours course. Through this, it can be seen that the U-Talent Academy leads to a clear benefit, thus motivating more students to participate.

## JCU Success Factors and Challenges

JCU has been successful in its student and teacher programme by meeting needs and challenges from all its stakeholders. The main success factors have been:

- For students and parents:
  - carefully selecting students and involving them in a community
  - the JCU student programme connects secondary and university education
  - monitoring students' experiences and adapting the JCU curriculum accordingly
  - involving parents, e.g. by inviting them to student presentation meetings

- For teachers and school principals:
  - giving them opportunities for cooperation within and between schools and with the university
  - developing a teacher programme aiming at a progression towards school development
  - providing examples of challenging education and pedagogy way of concrete lesson materials

- For Utrecht University:
  - connecting with developments in honours education
  - meeting the needs of the Faculty of Science: more talented students; making UU research visible in secondary science lessons by way of NLT modules

- For national education policy:
  - connecting with new programmes and making them concrete for schools
  - providing new ideas and opportunities for policy development.

Now, the great challenge for the partners of the JCU partnership is to make U-Talent programmes in the lower grades and the U-Talent Academy a success. In particular, teachers have to be supported in their classes in order to meet the increasing differences between the students. Let 'excellence' in secondary and higher education not be a temporary hype, but a solid base for the continuation of these promising developments.

## References

Betts, G. T., & Neihart, M. (1988). Profiles of the gifted and talented. *Gifted Child Quarterly, 32*, 248–253.

JCU (2011). *Differentiation Assignments for Mathematics, Physics, Chemistry and Biology*. Utrecht: JCU/Utrecht University. Retrieved from www.beta differentiatie.nl (in Dutch).

Taber, K. S. (2007). *Science Education for gifted learners*. London and New York: Routledge.

Valk, T. van der, Grunefeld, H., & Pilot, A. (2011). Empowerment en leerresultaten bij getalenteerde bètaleerlingen in een verrijkte onderwijsleeromgeving. (Empowerment and learning results with talented science students in an enriched learning environment) *Pedagogische Studiën, 88,* 73–89.

Van Tassel-Baska, J. (2002). Theory and research on curriculum development for the gifted. In K. A. Heller, F. J. Mönks, R. J. Sternberg, & R. F. Subotnik (Eds.), *International Handbook of Giftedness and Talent –second edition (revised reprint)* (pp. 345–365). Oxford: Pergamon.

Weert, C. van (2010). *Eindrapport van de Evaluatiecommissie Junior College Utrecht* (Final report of the Evaluation Commission Junior College Utrecht). Utrecht: Utrecht University (internal report).

Winstantley, C., 2007. Gifted science learner with special educational needs. In Taber, K.S. (Ed.), *Science Education for gifted learners*. London and New York: Routledge.

Wolfensberger, M. V. C., Eijl, P. van, & Pilot, A. (2004). Honours programmes as laboratories of innovation: A perspective from the Netherlands. *Journal of the NCHC, 5*(1), 115–142.

**Websites**

JCU: www.uu.nl/faculty/science/EN/vwo/juniorcollege/Pages/default.aspx
www.betadifferentiatie.nl
PBT: www.platformbetatechniek.nl
Sirius: www.siriusprogramma.nl
Steering Committee NLT (2013): http://betavak-nlt.nl/English/

# Characteristics of a Challenging Learning Environment Affecting Students' Learning Processes and Achievements

*Suzanne Vrancken and Sanne Tromp*

## Introduction

Talented students can do more than is offered to them in the regular curriculum. These students need more challenging education to fully use their capabilities and achieve optimal talent development. Education for talented students should be adapted to their needs and capacities (Heller, 1999; Tomlinson, 2005; VanTassel-Baska, 2003). The national Inspection of Education concluded that Dutch secondary education is insufficiently adapted to talented students' needs and that teachers do not challenge their most talented students appropriately (Inspectie van het Onderwijs, 2012).

In 2011, the Dutch government issued a policy aiming, amongst other things, at schools offering a motivating and challenging learning environment appropriate for talented students (OCW, 2011). Schools are encouraged to develop 'excellence programmes'. Schools that already offer excellence programmes can serve as sources of knowledge and inspiration for schools that want to develop such a programme.

Junior College Utrecht (JCU) is an example of such an excellence programme, focused on science and mathematics. Since 2004, JCU offers a challenging learning environment to a selected group of 100 talented students who are in grade 11 and 12 of their pre-university education. Participating students are selected based on previous achievements and motivation. Over two years, the students attend their biology, chemistry, physics and mathematics courses at JCU based at Utrecht University. The lessons in non-science subjects are attended at students' home schools during the remaining three days.

JCU offers an accelerated and enriched science curriculum to students. The regular curriculum is addressed in 60% of the teaching time; the remaining time is spent on enrichment activities, like interdisciplinary modules and research activities (Van der Valk, Van den Berg & Eijkelhof, 2007). Despite this challenging curriculum, JCU students score well above average in the national exams, research by Van der Valk, Grunefeld and Pilot (2010) showing that the adapted learning environment has a positive influence on student empowerment. Therefore, JCU is considered an example of a challenging learning environment for talented students.

## Research Aim and Questions

The aim of the research outlined in this study is to identify characteristics of a challenging learning environment that affect the learning processes and achievements of 11th and 12th grade pre-university students. Three research questions are addressed:

1) What, according to students, are the characteristics of the JCU learning environment?
2) What do students perceive to be the effects of the JCU learning environment on their learning processes and achievements?
3) How do students relate perceived effects to the characteristics of the JCU learning environment?

## Theoretical Framework

To empirically identify the characteristics of a learning environment that influence students learning processes achievements, the concepts 'learning process' and 'learning achievement' are defined. A learning process refers to students' growth and development concerning knowledge, skills, perseverance and self-regulation (Dembo & Eaton, 1997). Learning achievements indicate students' results and accomplishments (Solaiman Ali, 2007). Students' learning processes and achievements are interrelated: changes in a student's learning process will affect achievements, and vice versa.

Literature describes a wide variety of factors that influence the learning processes and achievements of talented students. Theoretical models, like the Differentiated Model of Giftedness and Talent (Gagné, 2002) or Pudue Pyramid Model of Talent Development (Feldhusen, 2003), describe coherency between influential factors and development of talented students. However, given the nature of the research questions and the selected research approach, these comprehensive models will not be utilized in this study. An open model is developed which allows for inductive data collection and analysis (figure 1). This study focuses on the learning environment within a school, individual capacities and previous experiences, and the learning environment outside the school are disregarded in this study even though it is known that these factors influence students' learning processes and achievements.

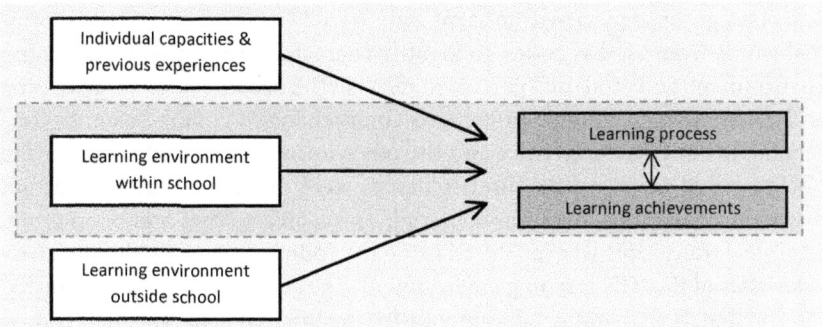

*Figure 1:* *Applied model of factors influencing students' learning processes and achievements*

## Method

The study is based on a grounded theory approach (Creswell, 2009) where students' experiences with the JCU learning environment serve as the starting point. This inductive research method ensures that results are directly derived from students' experiences without intermediate theoretical interpretations. JCU is selected as the site for data collection based on critical case sampling (Patton, 2001).

### Data Collection

Data on characteristics of the JCU learning environment are collected from graduation speeches of 240 JCU students from 2006 to 2012 (except 2010) and four open group interviews with three students in 2012. Semi-structured interviews with nine students are used to discuss the identified characteristics and to gain insight into effects students relate to specific characteristics of the JCU learning environment. All data are transcribed verbatim. Summaries of the most important interview outcomes were sent to the respondents for member checks.

*Data Analysis*

Qualitative data analysis was performed in five steps. First, all speeches and one open group interview transcript were coded "in vivo" i.e. students' original words were used as codes, to identify characteristics of the JCU learning environment and students' perceived effects. The second step was grouping and categorizing all codes to get two comprehensive coding schemes: one scheme to code characteristics and the other to code perceived effects of the JCU learning environment. Both schemes were discussed with the second researcher until consensus was achieved. Third, all speeches and open group interview transcripts were analyzed using the coding scheme to identify characteristics of the JCU learning environment. The coding scheme was adjusted intermediately to maintain alignment with the original data. The final coding scheme presented an overview of the characteristics of the JCU learning environment according to students (research question 1). This overview was presented to nine students in semi-structured interviews where they were asked about perceived effects of the identified characteristics.

Fourth, all semi-structured interview transcripts were coded using the coding scheme of perceived effects generated in the second data analysis step. Since the speeches and open group interviews also contained valuable information on students' perceived effects of the JCU learning environment, 50% of the speeches and all open interview transcripts were coded using the coding scheme of perceived effects. The coding scheme was adjusted during data analysis to ensure alignment with the original data. The final coding scheme presented an overview of students' perceived effects of the JCU learning environment (research question 2).

Fifth, an overview of quotations encoded with at least one characteristic and one effect was produced to gain insight into what effects students relate to specific characteristics of the JCU learning environment (research question 3). The second researcher validated 40% of all encodings which resulted in an intercoder agreement of 95%.

## Results

*(1) What, according to students, are the characteristics of the JCU learning environment?*

Data analysis resulted in eleven characteristics of the JCU learning environment (figure 2). Students describe science education at JCU as challenging due to the accelerated curriculum and enrichment activities. The shared culture of excellence among participants in the JCU learning community is also put forward by students as an important characteristic. Students appreciate being grouped with other motivated students who are willing to work hard in order to get good results. Teachers' teaching skills are also mentioned. Students value their teachers' content knowledge and the way they enthuse them in their subjects.

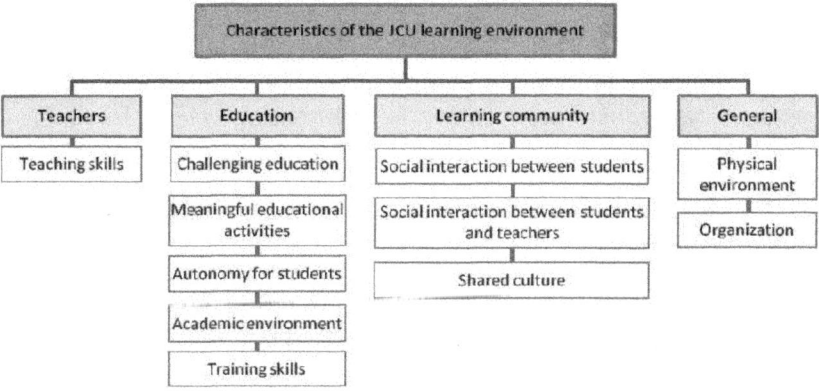

*Figure 2:  Overview of characteristics of the JCU learning environment*

*(2) What do students perceive to be the effects of the JCU learning environment on their learning processes and achievements?*

Students perceive twelve kinds of effects of the characteristics of the JCU learning environment (figure 3). An effect students frequently refer to is acquisition of knowledge. Students also become more enthusiastic about science courses which lead to an increasing urge to learn and work attitude. Students indicate that their active participation in the classroom increases and they feel more responsible for their own learning process. Changing results are also attributed to characteristics of the JCU learning environment, whether these changes are positive or negative.

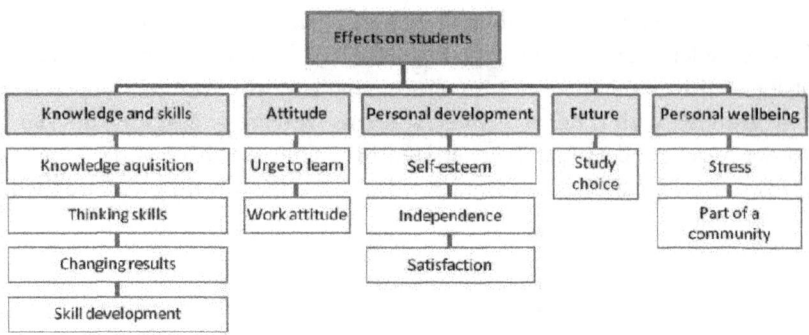

*Figure 3:*    *Effects students attribute to the characteristics of the JCU learning environment*

*(3) How do students relate perceived effects to the characteristics of the JCU learning environment?*

Students draw various relationships between perceived effects and the characteristics of the JCU learning environment. Table 1 provides an overview of what characteristic of the JCU learning environment students relate to a perceived effect. The numbers in the table indicate how often a characteristic and an effect are attached to the same quotations during data analysis. How students relate characteristics of the JCU learning environment to perceived effects will be described on the bases of students' reported experiences.

Students perceive that they gain much new knowledge at JCU. This effect is most often related to meaningful educational activities, like doing independent research or working on interdisciplinary modules.

> *"I really learned a lot from my thesis research at the university research group. You work together with scientists and share your knowledge with each other. That was a very valuable experience."*

Some students perceive negative effects on their knowledge acquisition due to the challenging education at JCU. These students feel that, due to the accelerated curriculum, there is not enough time to learn all the content knowledge thoroughly.

> *"Because of the high pace you don't always have time to practise everything and take time to learn. I feel that I know the things I learn less thoroughly."*

Engagement in enrichment and research activities is known to have a positive effect on students' knowledge acquisition and talent development in science subjects (Pyryt, 2002; Rogers, 2007; Reis, & Renzulli, 2010). However, it is important to consider differences between talented students; all students learn at their own pace (Tomlinson, 2005; Subban, 2006; Rogers, 2007). An accelerated curriculum can lead to negative effects on students' learning processes and achievements and result in stress among students.

It is noteworthy that only a few students relate their knowledge gains to teachers' teaching skills, because in literature teachers are considered the most important factor in students' education (Hattie, 2009). However, students do relate growth in their urge to learn to teachers' teaching skills. Teachers are enthusiastic about their subject and ask students challenging questions and this stimulates students' curiosity and enthusiasm for science. These findings are consistent with literature (Pyryt, 2002; Croft, 2003; Hattie, 2009).

> *"The teachers at JCU ask more challenging questions. I like that and it stimulates me to ask more challenging questions too."*

The shared culture of excellence among participants of the JCU learning community is also related to students' urge to learn and their work attitude. Students appreciate being grouped with other talented students who are interested in science. Most JCU students have a competitive spirit and like being challenged by other students. However, some students experience negative effects of being grouped with high-ability peers.

> *"I never want to be the worst at anything. I always want to be the best, but the bar is set much higher at JCU than at my own school."*

> *"I'm used to always being the best of my class, but at JCU I'm not. I feel really stupid sometimes."*

Literature shows that peers can stimulate and challenge each other (Gallagher, 2003; OECD, 2010), especially in homogeneous classrooms (Lens, & Rand, 2002). Kulik (2003) and Subotnik, Olszewski-Kubilius and Worrel (2011) found that talented students may experience a slight drop in self-esteem when grouped with other high achievers.

*Table 1:*   Overview of how often students relate a characteristic of the learning environment to a perceived effect

| | Teachers | Education | | | | | Learning community | | | General | |
|---|---|---|---|---|---|---|---|---|---|---|---|
| | Teaching skills | Challenging education | Academic environment | Autonomy for students | Meaningful educational activities | Training skills | Social interactions between students and teachers | Social interaction between students | Share culture | Physical environment | Organisation |
| **Knowledge and skills** | | | | | | | | | | | |
| Thinking skills | 2 | 5 | 3 | | 8 | | | | 4 | | |
| Knowledge acquisition | 2 | 16 | 6 | 5 | 29 | 2 | 1 | 3 | 2 | | |
| Skill development | 1 | 2 | 1 | 1 | 5 | 10 | | | 3 | | |
| Changing results | 4 | 8 | | 7 | 2 | 1 | 1 | 1 | 3 | | 1 |
| **Attitude** | | | | | | | | | | | |
| Urge to learn | 16 | 11 | 3 | 8 | 11 | 2 | 2 | 6 | 16 | | |
| Work attitude | 5 | 9 | 1 | 7 | 4 | | 5 | 5 | 17 | 2 | |
| **Personal development** | | | | | | | | | | | |
| Satisfaction | | 10 | | | 1 | | | | 1 | | |
| Independence | | 4 | 1 | 11 | 1 | | 1 | 1 | | 3 | 1 |
| Self-esteem | | 5 | 2 | 2 | 2 | 3 | 5 | 7 | 2 | 1 | |
| **Future** | | | | | | | | | | | |
| Study choice | 1 | 12 | 11 | 4 | 41 | 1 | | | | | |
| **Personal well-being** | | | | | | | | | | | |
| Stress | | 9 | | 2 | 2 | | | | | 5 | 2 |
| Part of a community | | 1 | 1 | 1 | 4 | 1 | 3 | 30 | 10 | 1 | |

Students also experience increasing self-esteem and satisfaction with their achievements. In the regular curriculum, they never had to work hard to get good grades, but at JCU they do.

> *"I rather work hard and get a 6 (B-), than do nothing and get an 8 (A). The results I get at JCU are much more satisfying and I can really be proud of my grades."*

Lens and Rand (2002) found that talented students often attribute good grades to the low level of a test instead of to their own competence. Students feel more competent when they are challenged.

## Conclusion

The aim of this study was to identify characteristics of a learning environment that affect the learning processes and achievements of 11th and 12th grade pre-university students. This study identified eleven characteristics that contribute to creating a motivating and challenging learning environment for talented students. Analysis of the effects perceived by students shows that changing results are only a small part of the effects; changes in students' learning process are more common.

The results also show that, for students, effects of the learning environment can be positive or negative. When designing a learning environment for motivated and talented students, it is important to consider differences between the members of a group. The results of this qualitative research project could be used as a basis for the development of a quantitative instrument that aims to measure the characteristics of a challenging learning environment and their effects on students' learning.

## References

Creswell, J. W. (2009). *Research design: qualitative, quantitative and mixed methods approaches.* Thousand Oaks, CA: Sage.

Croft, L. J. (2003). Teachers of the gifted: gifted teachers. In N. Colangelo, & G.A. Davis (red.), *Handbook of gifted education (3rd ed.)* (pp.558–571). Boston, MA: Allyn and Bacon.

Dembo, M. H., & Eaton, M.J. (1997). School learning and motivation. In: G. D. Phye (Ed.), *Handbook of academic learning: construction of knowledge.* San Diego, CA: Academic Press, Inc.

Feldhusen, J. F. (2003). Talented youth at the secondary level. In: N. Colangelo, & G. A. Davis (red.), *Handbook of gifted education (3rd ed.)* Boston, MA: Allyn and Bacon.

Gagné, F. (2002). Understanding the complex choreography of talent development through DMGT-bases analyses. In: K. Heller, F. Mönks, R. Sternberg, & R. Subotnik (Eds.), *International Handbook of giftedness and talent (2nd ed.).* Oxford, UK: Pergamon.

Gallagher, J. J. (2003). Issues and challenges in the education of gifted students. In N. Colangelo, & G. A. Davis (red.), *Handbook of gifted education (3rd ed.)* (pp. 11–23). Boston, MA: Allyn and Bacon.

Hattie, J. (2009). *Visible learning: a synthesis of over 800 meta-analyses relating to achievement.* London, UK: Routledge.

Heller, K. A. (1999). Individual (learning and motivational) needs versus instructional conditions of gifted education. *High Ability Studies, 10*(9), 9–21.

Inspectie van het Onderwijs. (2012). De staat van het onderwijs – onderwijsverslag 2010–2011 [The status of education – education report 2010–2011]. Utrecht: Inspectie van het Onderwijs.

Kulik, J. A. (2003). Grouping and tracking. In N. Colangelo, & G. A. Davis (red.), *Handbook of gifted education (3rd ed.)* (pp.268–281). Boston, MA: Allyn and Bacon.

Lens, W., & Rand, P. (2002). Motivation and cognition: their role in the development of giftedness. In K. Heller, F. Mönks, R. Sternberg, & R. Subotnik (Eds.), *International Handbook of giftedness and talent (2nd ed.)* (pp. 193–202). Oxford, UK: Pergamon.

OCW (2011). *Actieplan Beter Presteren: opbrengstgericht en ambitieus [Action plan Better Performance: result-oriented and ambitious].* Den Haag: Ministerie voor Onderwijs, Cultuur en Wetenschap.

OECD (2010). PISA 2009 results: what makes a school successful? (volume IV). Paris: OECD.

Patton, M. Q. (2001). *Qualitative research and evaluation methods.* Thousand Oaks, CA: Sage.

Pyryt, M. C. (2002). Talent development in science and technology. In: K. Heller, F. Mönks, R. Sternberg, & R. Subotnik (Eds.), *International Handbook of giftedness and talent (2nd ed.).* (pp. 427–438). Oxford, UK: Pergamon.

Reis, S. M., & Renzulli, J. S. (2010). Is there still a need for gifted education? An examination of current research. *Learning and individual differences, 20*, 308–317.

Rogers, K. B. (2007). Lessons learned about educating the gifted and talented: a synthesis of the research on educational practice. *Gifted child quarterly, 51*, 382–396.

Solaiman Ali, M. (2007). *Dictionary of education: language of teaching and learning.* Bloomington, IN: AuthorHouse.

Subban, P. (2006). Differentiated instruction: a research basis. *International education journal, 7*(7), 935–947.

Subotnik, R. F., Olszewski-Kubilius, P., & Worrell, F. C. (2011). Rethinking giftedness and gifted education: a proposed direction forward based on psychological science. *Psychological science in the public interest, 12*(1), 3–54.

Tomlinson, C. A. (2005). Quality curriculum and instruction for highly able students. *Theory into practice, 44*(2), 160–166.

Valk, A. E. van der, Berg, E. van den, & Eijkelhof, H. (2007). Junior College Utrecht: Challenging talented secondary school students to study science. *School science review, 88*(25), 63–71.

Valk, A. E. van der, Grunefeld, H., & Pilot, A. (2011). Empowerment en leerresultaten bij getalenteerde bètaleerlingen in een verrijkte onderwijsleeromgeving [Empowerment and learning results of talented science students in an enriched learning environment]. *Pedagogische studiën, 88*(2).

Van Tassel-Baska, J. (2003). What matters in curriculum for gifted learners: reflections on theory, research and practice. In N. Colangelo, & G. A. Davis (red.), *Handbook of gifted education (3rd ed.)* (pp. 174–183). Boston, MA: Allyn and Bacon.

# About the Authors

**Tamara van Batenburg-Eddes**, PhD, works as an epidemiologist at the Municipal Health Service of South Netherlands in Dordrecht, the Netherlands. Her research interests include monitoring local public health as well as monitoring and evaluating the (upcoming) changes in the health care system in the Netherlands i.e. transition and transformation. T.van.Batenburg@dienst-gezondheidjeugd.nl

**Johannes Boonstra**, PhD, is Professor of Cell Biology at Utrecht University and head of the Science Department of University College, Utrecht. Currently, he is also director of education of the Biology Department at Utrecht University, the Netherlands. j.boonstra@uu.nl

**Karen Bruhn**, PhD, is Principal Lecturer and Dean's Fellow at Barrett, The Honors College at Arizona State University, United States. Her research interests include pedagogy in honours education, as well as how the religious controversies of sixteenth-century England figured in the plays of William Shakespeare. kbruhn@asu.edu

**Simone van der Donk**, MSc, researcher at the Research Centre for Educational Innovation and Effectiveness at Saxion University of Applied Sciences in Enschede/Deventer, the Netherlands. Her research interests include the characteristics of honours programmes, technology-enhanced learning and the quality of career counselling. s.e.vanderdonk@saxion.nl

**Lyndsay Drayer**, PhD, is a lecturer in biochemistry and a member of the research centre Talent Development in Higher Education and Society at Hanze University of Applied Sciences in Groningen, the Netherlands. She is involved in teaching the interdisciplinary honours course 'Catchy Claims', and her research interests include the policies, content and organization of honours programmes in higher education. a.l.drayer@pl.hanze.nl

**Pierre van Eijl**, MSc, is an honorary researcher at the Centre for Teaching and Learning of Utrecht University, the Netherlands, and an independent senior educational consultant. He is involved in a number of research projects about talent development and excellence in higher education. In collaboration with other authors, he wrote and edited several books on talent development. p.j.vaneijl@uu.nl

**Linda Frost**, PhD, is Dean of the Honours College of the University of Tennessee at Chattanooga, United States. She is a member of the National Collegiate Honors Council Publications Board and the immediate past President of the Southern Regional Honors Council Executive Committee. Linda-Frost@utc.edu

**Mark Gellevij**, PhD, heads the Research Centre for Educational Innovation and Effectiveness at Saxion University of Applied Sciences in Enschede/Deventer, the Netherlands. He is also academic director of the Talent Development in Higher Education and Society programme Learning & Innovation and the masters programme Educational Leadership. His research interests include design-based research, learning, instruction, motivation, and appreciative inquiry. m.r.m.gellevij@saxion.nl

**Stan van Ginkel**, MSc, is a PhD student at Wageningen University, the Netherlands. His research project 'Academic Skills Training' started in 2012 at the chair group Education and Competence Studies. He worked as a teacher of human geography, provided academic skills courses, and was active as a consultant with special interest in honours programmes within the field of higher education.

**Lynne Goodstein**, PhD, is Professor of Sociology at the University of Connecticut, United States. Until recently, she served that university as Associate Vice-Provost and Director of the Honours Programme. Dr Goodstein's recent research pertains to honours programme effectiveness and retention and graduation among honours programme students. She is currently also working on a book on women and crime. lynne.goodstein@uconn.edu

**Bouke van Gorp**, PhD, is an assistant professor in the Department of Human Geography & Planning of the Faculty of Geosciences, Utrecht University, the Netherlands. From 2005 onwards, she has been involved in honours teaching at the department. b.vangorp@uu.nl

**Thom de Graaf** is a Dutch jurist and politician. He is a member of the social liberal party, Democrats 66 (D66). Since June 2011, he has been a member of the Senate, and since February 2012 he has been President of the Netherlands Association of Universities of Applied Sciences (Vereniging Hogescholen). He was previously Deputy Prime Minister of the Netherlands, Minister for Government Reform and Kingdom Relations, and mayor of the city of Nijmegen.

**Marieke van Haaren**, MA, is co-ordinator of the Honours College and staff member of the Honours Academy at Leiden University, the Netherlands. She has been teaching in an honours class on Academic Entrepreneurship, and she was involved in research on metacognition and gifted students as well as in research on honours pedagogy. mhaaren@ha.leidenuniv.nl

**Kristen Joy Hermann**, EdD, is the Associate Dean for Student Services in Barrett, The Honours College at Arizona State University, United States. Her research interests and presentations focus on the history, development, and organization of honours colleges, honours communities, and honours academic, student, and residential engagement. knielsen@asu.edu

**Djoerd Hiemstra**, MSc, is an occupational and organizational psychologist, affiliated to NHL University of Applied Sciences and the University of Groningen, the Netherlands. His applied work entails the development, implementation and application of research-based methods to motivate students and professionals to learn. His research interests include achievement motivation, talent development, and self-regulated learning. d.hiemstra@nhl.nl.

**Barbara Hussey**, PhD, is Professor of English at Eastern Kentucky University, United States, and teacher in the Honours Programme. barbara.hussey@eku.edu

**Ellen Jansen**, PhD, is Associate Professor at the University of Groningen, the Netherlands, Department of Teacher Education. Her research focuses on the transition from secondary to higher education, with a special interest in talent development, and on factors relating to study success in higher education. e.p.w.a.jansen@rug.nl

**Jelle Jolles**, PhD, is Professor in Educational Neuropsychology at VU University Amsterdam, the Netherlands, and heads the Centre for Brain and Learning at VU. His activities centre around learning, 'talent' and neuropsychological development in children, adolescents and adults and Lifelong learning in teachers. A focus lies upon educational innovations from the perspective of a bio-psycho-social model. J.jolles@vu.nl

**Nelleke de Jong**, MSc, works as a junior lecturer in the department of Human Geography & Planning at Utrecht University, the Netherlands. She teaches an Honours class for first-year students and participated in research on Honours

Programmes in the Netherlands. She is also interested in implementation of educational policy regarding excellence education. n.a.dejong@uu.nl

**Diviyia Kanagalingam** is an engineering student at Fontys University of Applied Sciences, Eindhoven/Tilburg/Venlo, the Netherlands. Her research interests are in the areas of experiential and experience-based learning, product development, automotive and honours programmes. She was a participant in the PRogram OUtstanding Development (PROUD) honours programme, an excellence programme for students collaborating with industry at Fontys University. kdiviyia@gmail.com

**Peter van Kollenburg**, MSc, is lecturer at the department of Electrical Engineering of Fontys University of Applied Sciences, Eindhoven/Tilburg/Venlo, the Netherlands. His research interests are in the areas of integrated product development, competence-driven education, and honours programmes. He introduced the honours programme, PRogram for Outstanding Development (PROUD), an excellence programme for students collaborating with industry. For this, he was nominated for the FontysOnderwijsprijs 2011. p.vankollenburg@fontys.nl

**Bjorn de Koning**, PhD, works as an assistant professor at the Department of Educational Neuroscience and LEARN! Research institute for learning and education, Faculty of Psychology and Education, VU University Amsterdam, the Netherlands. His research interests include reading comprehension (instruction); instructional design and educational interventions; multimedia learning; and the student characteristics and institutional factors associated with (excellent) achievement in higher education. b.b.de.koning@vu.nl

**Hanke Korpershoek**, PhD, is assistant professor at the Groningen Institute for Educational Research (GION), University of Groningen, the Netherlands. Her research focuses on gender differences in career choices among adolescents and the impact of student motivation and school commitment on educational outcomes. h.korpershoek@rug.nl

**Andries Koster**, PhD, is associate professor of Pharmacology and Vice-Dean for Education in the department of Pharmaceutical Sciences, Utrecht University, the Netherlands. He teaches pharmacology in the College of Pharmaceutical Sciences and the University Colleges in Utrecht and Middelburg. His research concentrates on the role of motivational and other non-cognitive factors in the study success of undergraduate and postgraduate students. A.S.Koster@uu.nl

**Michael Kruger** is an electrical engineering graduate of Fontys University of Applied Sciences, Eindhoven/Tilburg/Venlo, the Netherlands. He is a member of the Fontys PRogramme for OUtstanding Development (PROUD) honours programme. As a member of PROUD, he researched and evaluated the programme's effectiveness and benefits. m.kruger@student.fontys.nl

**Anna Kushnareva** is an English teacher at Novosibirsk State University, Russia, and a postgraduate student at Novosibirsk State Pedagogical University. Her research interests include comparative pedagogy, education of migrant-students and working with gifted and talented youth. akush73@mail.ru

**Gregory Lanier**, PhD, is Dean of the University College and the Director of the Kugelman Honours Programme at the University of West Florida, United States. His research interests include honours assessment and evaluation techniques, and he has been a long-time leader in the field of education, having served for seven years on the Board of Directors of the National Collegiate Honours Council, including service as the President of that organization. glanier@uwf.edu

**Joseph Lewandowski** is Dean of The Honours College and International Affairs at the University of Central Missouri, United States. The author of *Interpreting Culture* and co-editor of two volumes on social capital theory, he has published widely in the areas of social and political theory, urban culture, and sport studies. His most recent work appears in German in *Berliner Debatte Initial.* lewandowski@ucmo.edu

**Catherine Little**, PhD, is an Associate Professor in Educational Psychology at the University of Connecticut, United States. She teaches courses in gifted and talented education and in the undergraduate honours programme, and she serves on the University's Honors Board of Associate Directors. Her research interests include professional development, differentiation of curriculum and instruction for advanced learners, and classroom questioning practices. catherine.little@uconn.edu

**Irma Meijerman**, PhD, is the programme coordinator of the College of Pharmaceutical Sciences, an honours bachelor programme at the Faculty of Science, University of Utrecht, the Netherlands. She is also a teaching fellow at the University of Utrecht and involved in the professional development of teachers. Her research interests include curriculum and course development, learning communities and the scholarship of university teaching. I.Meijerman@uu.nl

**Jutta Moehringer**, PhD, is a Postdoctoral Research Fellow at the TUM School of Education, Department of Empirical Educational Research, Germany. Her research interests include gifted education, pre-high school students at university, and research-based learning. jutta.moehringer@tum.de

**Julia Moeller**, PhD, is post-doctoral researcher at the University of Helsinki, Finland. She studies concepts of long-term persistent and affect-intense motivation (e.g. passion, commitment, engagement), particularly the interplay of state and trait components. Her research bridges topics of the psychology of motivation, development, and personality, using intensive longitudinal data (Experience Sampling Method) and person-oriented approaches. julia.moeller@helsinki.fi

**Marije Nije Bijvank**, MSc, is project leader of The Learning Brain (in collaboration with VU University) and is Policy Researcher at Saxion University of Applied Sciences, Enschede/Deventer, the Netherlands. She is also a thesis supervisor in the Bachelor Programme Applied Psychology. Her research interests include the evaluation of policy measures and (neuro-psychological) student determinants on students' study progress. m.nijebijvank@saxion.nl

**Johan Offringa**, MSc, is a senior lecturer at the Hanze University of Applied Sciences Groningen, the Netherlands. He developed and coordinates the honours programme of the School of Facility Management and is a member of the research centre Talent Development in Higher Education and Society. g.j.offringa@pl.hanze.nl

**Berend Olivier**, PhD, is Professor of Pharmacology of the Central Nervous System at the department of Pharmacology of Utrecht University, the Netherlands, and adjunct professor at Yale School of medicine in New Haven, United States. He has performed research on the mechanisms of psychoactive drugs and the brain. He teaches the pharmacology of the central nervous system. He retired from Utrecht University on April 1, 2014. b.olivier@uu.nl

**Tatiana Pavlova**, PhD, is a professor and heads the Department of Pedagogics at Novosibirsk State Pedagogical University, Russia. She is involved in teaching The history of Pedagogics course and also supervises a number of post-graduate students. Her research interests include comparative pedagogy, pedagogy of giftedness, challenges of twice exceptional, education of migrant-students, and how to evoke excellence in higher education. pavlova.tatjana.leo@gmail.com

**Anton Peeters**, PhD, is assistant professor and programme director of Undergraduate Biology at the Department of Biology, Faculty of Science, Utrecht University, the Netherlands. Over the past five years, he has been involved in honours teaching at department, faculty and university level. A.J.M.Peeters@uu.nl

**Albert Pilot**, PhD, is Emeritus Professor of Curriculum Development and Chemistry Education at Utrecht University, the Netherlands. His research focuses on curriculum development, design of learning and instruction, talent development, honours programmes, professional development of teachers and context-based science education. a.pilot@uu.nl

**Joseph Renzulli**, EEd, is a Distinguished Professor and Director of the National Research Center On The Gifted and Talented at the University of Connecticut, United States. His work has focused on applying personalized education strategies to K-12 and post-secondary education; and his most recent work is a technology-based programme that analyzes student strengths and uses the Internet to match resources that capitalize on student interests, learning styles, and preferred modes of expression with individual student profiles [www.renzullilearning.com]. joseph.renzulli@uconn.edu

**Roeland van der Rijst**, PhD, is assistant professor at Leiden University's Graduate School of Teaching, ICLON, the Netherlands. He is a member of the teaching staff at the teacher education programme and at the masters degree programme, teaching and learning in higher education. His research interests include the professional development of teachers and higher education pedagogy with a specific focus on inquiry-based teaching and the research-teaching nexus. rrijst@iclon.leidenuniv.nl

**Karin Scager**, PhD, is an educational consultant and teacher trainer at the Centre of Teaching and Learning at Utrecht University, the Netherlands. In her research, she focuses on creating challenging learning environments for honours students. K.Scager@uu.nl

**Ingrid Schutte**, PhD candidate, is educational advisor and member of the research centre Talent Development in Higher Education and Society at the Hanze University of Applied Sciences in Groningen, the Netherlands. Her research is about the ethical sensitivity of undergraduate honours students and how these students could also be prepared for social commitment in the globalized world. i.w.schutte@pl.hanze.nl

**Geert Speltincx** is head of Educational and Student Policy at Karel de Grote University College in Antwerp, Belgium. He is responsible for the policy and development of technology-enhanced learning and educational research. Geert.speltincx@kdg.be

**Patricia Szarek** is the associate director of the honours programme at the University of Connecticut, United States, in which position she has worked in a variety of capacities. Her responsibilities have included admissions, advising, orientation, curriculum planning, event planning, and oversight of honours records. Currently focusing on enrollment management, she is interested in the retention and graduation of honours students. patricia.szarek@uconn.edu

**Lammert Tiesinga**, MSc, is an educational specialist and policy advisor at Hanze University of Applied Sciences in Groningen, the Netherlands, and a member of the research centre Talent Development in Higher Education and Society. As a staff member of Hanze Honours College, he is involved in the development and improvement of honours programmes. As a researcher, his focus is on the culture of honours students and on school culture within institutions of higher education. l.tiesinga@pl.hanze.nl

**Kirsi Tirri**, PhD, is Professor of Education and Research Director at the Department of Teacher Education at the University of Helsinki, Finland. She is the Chair of the Doctoral Programme 'School, Education, Culture and Society' (SEDUCE). Her research interests include school pedagogy, moral and religious education, gifted education, teacher education and cross-cultural studies. kirsi.tirri@helsinki.fi

**Geertje Tonnaer**, MSc, is lecturer in research methodology for undergraduate students at the Hospitality Business School at Saxion University of Applied Sciences, Enschede/Deventer, the Netherlands. She coaches students during their bachelor's thesis with both the execution of research and the formulation of advice. Additionally, she coordinates the study career counselling programme. Lastly, Geertje studies the influence of neuro-psychological development of bachelor students on their study progress. g.h.tonnaer@saxion.nl

**Sanne Tromp,** MSc, is the director of Junior College Utrecht, a science excellence programme for grade 11 and 12 secondary school students at the Freudenthal Institute for Science and Mathematics Education (FIsme) at Utrecht University, the Netherlands. s.tromp@uu.nl

**Ton van der Valk,** PhD, is the curriculum coordinator of Junior College Utrecht, a science excellence programme for grade 11 and 12 secondary school students at the Freudenthal Institute for Science and Mathematics Education (FIsme) at Utrecht University, the Netherlands. His research and development interests are in how to involve secondary schools in university honours teaching in such a way that they get inspired to organise an excellence programme for their students. a.e.vandervalk@uu.nl

**Dries Vervecken,** PhD, is a higher educational policy officer at Karel de Grote University College in Antwerp, Belgium. His research interests include educational quality, academic achievement and the vocational development of individuals. Dries.vervecken@kdg.be

**Carien Verweij,** MSc, is a lecturer in research methodology and diagnostics at Saxion University of Applied Sciences, Enschede/Deventer, the Netherlands. She is a supervisor on students' theses in the Bachelor Programme Applied Psychology. She participates in various research projects e.g. the influence of neuro-psychological development of students on their study progress. cf.verweij@saxion.nl

**Judith Volker,** MSc, is an educational advisor at Hanze University of Applied Sciences in Groningen, the Netherlands, and a member of the research centre Talent Development in Higher Education and Society. Her research focuses on the culture of honours students and on school culture in general within institutions of higher education. j.j.m.volker@pl.hanze.nl

**Brenda Vos** coaches professionals and organisations. Her focus in coaching is on ethics, leadership, and talent development. She leads the reflective workshops for honours students from the Faculty of Geosciences at the University of Utrecht, the Netherlands. info@brendavos.nl

**Suzanne Vrancken**, MSc, is a researcher at the Freudenthal Institute for Science and Mathematics Education at Utrecht University, the Netherlands. Her research interests mainly focus on teacher professional development in professional learning communities and school-university networks. s.e.a.vrancken@uu.nl

**Fred Wiegant**, PhD, is Associate Professor at the Institute of Education, Department of Biology, Faculty of Science at Utrecht University, the Netherlands, with a special interest in honours education. He is also Fellow of Life Sciences at the University College Utrecht, the Honours College of Utrecht University. f.a.c.wiegant@uu.nl

**Lieke Woelders**, MSc, is an education advisor and policy officer at the central department of Hague University of Applied Sciences, the Netherlands. She is involved in developing and executing research activities to contribute to evidence-informed education and policy. Her research interests include intervention-based research in higher education, (neuropsychological) determinants of individual differences in study progress, and the evaluation of policy measures. c.s.woelders@hhs.nl

**Marca Wolfensberger**, PhD, heads the research centre Talent Development in Higher Education and Society at Hanze University of Applied Sciences in Groningen, the Netherlands, and is Honours Director of the Department of Geography and Planning of Utrecht University. Her research interests include honours faculty and honours pedagogies, honours communities and global citizenship, and how to evoke excellence. She is an appointed fellow of the National Collegiate Honors Council. m.v.c.wolfensberger@pl.hanze.nl

**Frank Wunschel**, MA, is a Senior Database Administrator Institutional Research at the University of Connecticut, United States. frank.wunschel@ uconn.edu

**John Zubizarreta**, PhD, is Professor of English, Director of Honors and Faculty Development, and former Dean of Undergraduate Studies at Columbia College, South Carolina, United States. He is a Carnegie Foundation/CASE U.S. Professor of the Year, a recipient of the South Carolina Independent Colleges and Universities Award for Excellence in Teaching, and the 1994 CASE Professor for South Carolina. He is also a past president of the National Collegiate Honors Council and the Southern Regional Honors Council. jzubizarreta@columbiasc.edu